To Judith
April 29, 2018
Nice meeting you. Hope you enjoy these true stories.

It Was Evening, It Was Morning

Scandinavia in the Aftermath of World War II

Best Wishes,
Chana Sharfstein

by Chana Sharfstein

with Sterna Maline

DEVORA
PUBLISHING
NEW YORK♦JERUSALEM♦LONDON

It Was Evening, It Was Morning:
Scandinavia in the Aftermath of World War II
Published by Devora Publishing Company
Text Copyright © 2012 Chana Sharfstein

COVER DESIGN: Shani Schmell
EDITORIAL AND PRODUCTION DIRECTOR: Daniella Barak
EDITOR: Sara Rosenbaum

Cover image: Israelplads, a small square in central Copenhagen, is the location of a large memorial stone, a gift from Eilat, Israel. The Hebrew inscription expresses gratitude to the Danes for the incredible rescue of their Jewish population. The phrase "And it was evening and it was morning," carved in Hebrew and Danish, is a reference to the display of humanity in the midst of beastly brutality.

Some names of individuals have been changed to protect privacy.

Soft Cover ISBN: 978-1-936068-30-2

First edition. Printed in Israel

Distributed by:
Urim Publications
POB 52287
Jerusalem 91521, Israel
Tel: 02.679.7633
Fax: 02.679.7634
urim_pub@netvision.net.il

Lambda Publishers, Inc.
527 Empire Blvd.
Brooklyn, NY 11225, USA
Tel: 718.972.5449
Fax: 718.972.6307
mh@ejudaica.com

www.UrimPublications.com

Dedication

To my husband, Mottel, and our children
Sterna, Sruli, Zlata, Seema and Raizel
for your encouragement and
interest in all my activities.

附

To my wonderful Maline, Sharfstein,
Gersten and Feder grandchildren
and my Maline, Goldberg and Penzias
great-grandchildren, you are my future –
you bring light and hope into my existence.

৻৽

The individuals who perished in the Holocaust must never be forgotten – neither the millions who were murdered nor the survivors. The tragedy of their horrifying fate must forever find a permanent place in our hearts. Their voices must never be extinguished, and every one of us must bear responsibility for transmitting their testimonials.

Chana Sharfstein is a messenger for these witnesses in her writings. Her gripping stories, told with unparalleled empathy, are lucidly expressed in electrifying and vivid language. This book is a captivating tale of struggles against terrifying memories, the healing of grief, and the return to life. With great love the author demonstrates how the fight for survival can be won, thanks to the power of people who were shaped by – and acted from – a standpoint of Jewish culture.

At a time when hostility against the Jews is once again rearing its ugly head in Scandinavia and in all of Europe, perhaps the result of a general complacency toward extremist anti-Semitic factions, it is a relief to have Chana Sharfstein remind us…of a period, during and shortly after the Second World War, when [Scandinavians] had the courage to stand erect in the battle against the beasts who spread lies and persecuted our Jewish population. This book empowers us to carry on the fight for life in being a 'mentch'.

Ben Olander
CEO, Buttericks, Stockholm, Sweden
Member of Wallenberg Foundation, composer and folk artist

☙

Chana Sharfstein's revelatory book, *It Was Evening, It Was Morning: Scandinavia in the Aftermath of World War II*, is an unusual and important addition to the literature that relates both to the Holocaust and to Scandinavia. It contains a highly personal account of her devoutly religious Jewish family's life in Sweden before, during and after WWII. Chana explores the psychological and the physical challenges that are present in a society that is both highly accepting of *differences* and is, at the same time, so homogeneous that the family must set its own boundaries if their family's religious integrity is to survive.

I could easily understand the struggle that the warm and open Swedish acceptance caused her family, and the unceasing need to find a "safe haven" for both their religious and cultural traditions. I learned so much about the beauty of the traditions of Orthodox Judaism from this book…I came away with a deeper understanding and a richer appreciation of the traditions that shaped my own Jewish heritage.

For me, the Ice Menorah was the defining moment of this beautiful book. The light in the darkness of the Holocaust was how I have always visualized Raoul Wallenberg; Chana's Ice Menorah fully embodies the beauty of her wonderful book and the glorious men and women who fill its rich pages. It is a must-read on so many different levels: for Scandinavians, for survivors, for Jews, for Holocaust and World War II scholars and for those of us who simply love reading a joyous and well-written book.

Thank you, Chana, for this gift of Light in my own life.

Rachel Oestreicher Bernheim
Chairman Emerita,
The Raoul Wallenberg Committee of the United States

Contents

Foreword

That this charming book both enriches and enlightens the reader should come as no surprise since its author, Chana Sharfstein, has been a gifted teacher her entire adult life: first in the Boston public school system, then in New York's and, most recently, as a volunteer Gallery Educator at the Museum of Jewish Heritage – A Living Memorial to the Holocaust in Lower Manhattan, where I have been privileged to observe her passion and her skill. As a practitioner of the noble art of teaching, Chana pursues the incomparably important mission not only of imparting knowledge, but also of equipping others with valuable life lessons.

The subject of this book, Scandinavia after World War II, is little known among the general public, and the experience of Holocaust survivors in the immediate postwar period has received far less attention than it deserves. Chana addresses both of these subjects in this book through the lens of her own experience and brings to the narrative not only important information about an ignored history, but also the illuminating authenticity of the first-person voice. While I am certain that this book is the product of the totality of Chana's life experience, I would like to believe that her service as Gallery Educator at our museum provided a model for the profound power of the individual story. Just as we in the Museum explore the complex history of Jews in the 20th and 21st centuries through the experiences of the individuals who lived it, so does Chana examine her subject through the lives and experiences of those who lived it and those whom she has encountered.

The Holocaust marked perhaps the darkest period in human history, but within that history, and emerging from it, are uplifting stories of courage, resilience and commitment to life. In this book, Chana Sharfstein provides us with inspiring examples of these and throughout, true to form, she is the skilled and stimulating teacher.

David G. Marwell, PhD
Director,
Museum of Jewish Heritage – A Living Memorial to the Holocaust
New York

A Letter to My Mother

Initially, when you asked me to collaborate with you on your magnum opus, *It was Evening, It was Morning: Scandinavia in the Aftermath of World War II*, I was intrigued. I had scant knowledge of your childhood and I longed to know more. Perhaps working on the book with you, I thought, would fill in the blanks. You seldom discussed your teenage years with me, content to allude to mysterious snippets about your life before your arrival in the States.

I recalled fuzzy images, disjointed nostalgic anecdotes, and I frequently pondered the missing pieces. I remember sitting on a couch with you, exploring the pages of a hard-cover book with glossy, colorful pictures, featuring children from around the world. Even as a child you imbued me with a love of travel, a desire to learn about other people.

I listen to your sad voice as you tell me about the red bicycle that you left in Stockholm, my fingers splashing in a proverbial pool of unshed tears, mourning an abrupt ending of a carefree childhood. That anecdote was all I knew about your childhood, that helpless gesture as you bade farewell to the shiny, mysterious red bicycle, left on the island of Sodermalm, before reluctantly boarding the ship that would transport you to the United States. You rarely meandered down memory lane, your childhood remaining an unvisited topic, almost forbidden in your consistent desire to keep the past hidden.

Your invitation to collaborate on this novel became all the more alluring, for it provided an opportunity to venture on paths previously untouched. I looked forward to bonding with you while working on the book and I have not been disappointed.

"There is no frigate like a book," Emily Dickenson insists, and you, a proud Bostonian, identify with your New England sister. Typing and editing pages of content was a privileged journey I would not have traded for anything.

My personal connection to the manuscript occurred when I accompanied you on a family pilgrimage to Sweden, a trip commemorating fifty years since my grandfather had been viciously and fatally attacked on the streets of Boston. Many relatives participated in the event; we wandered the streets you had walked, visited the schools you, your sister and your brothers had attended, entered the apartment where you had lived with your family and *davened* in the shul where my grandfather had maintained a pulpit for more than three decades. We even visited the island where you had spent languorous summer days, and the park where one hateful woman had muttered that you should move to Palestine where you belong.

This book is important to me on a personal as well as on a professional level. On a personal level, it has answered questions and filled in some gaps in my knowledge of family history. On a professional level, it differs from most books of this genre, which provide glimpses into varied war experiences. This particular book goes far beyond the scope of a typical survivor's memoir, in that it elucidates much of the history and geography of Scandinavia, addresses the salient role played by Danes who rescued their Jewish neighbors and discusses how survivors acclimated to an unfamiliar society and rebuilt their lives after the war.

I hope that all your readers enjoy traveling the pages of this book as much as I enjoyed working on it, truly a labor of love.

Sterna Maline

Preface

After a long period of silence, the Holocaust emerged as a major force in all areas of creativity. There was an outpouring of literature, an intermingling of fact and fiction, which dealt basically with the Ghetto, the concentration camp experience and the destruction of European Jewry. Insufficient attention focused on "The Aftermath," the period from 1945 until 1952, when large numbers of shattered survivors were literally abandoned in Displaced Persons camps because they had nowhere to go. They had survived the turbulent Nazi era; now, adrift and forgotten, this was an additional tragedy.

It was Evening, It was Morning: Scandinavia in the Aftermath of World War II explores the lives of survivors who settled in Sweden after the war and rebuilt their lives. These accounts, based on personal interviews, radiate inspiration and hope. They fill us with pride and give us strength.

This all began in the spring of 1950, when I was required to submit a biography for the final project of my Freshman Composition class at Boston State Teachers College. In a palpable quandary regarding my choice of topic, I longed to select a captivating subject who would generate interest. A teenager, I never considered my father, Rabbi Y. Y. Zuber, as a viable choice. After all, he was my father. And my mother, well, she was merely a housewife. My sister-in-law Yenti became my choice; I knew her story as a Holocaust survivor was interesting.

The day our reports were due, we sat in a circle instead of in the usual straight rows. The professor suggested that we randomly exchange term papers. After reading them silently, we were asked to read aloud those that we thought were particularly well written, and of particular interest. My paper was selected and I remember being very uncomfortable as it was read to the class.

English composition was definitely not my easiest subject. I had only been in this country for two and a half years and English was my fourth language, the second foreign language of my schooling. I was the only foreigner, submerged in a totally American classroom.

While my paper was being read, my eyes remained downcast. After a while, I surreptitiously gazed at my classmates. The room was absolutely silent and everyone was listening intently. Some pupils seemed on the verge of tears, while others were actually wiping tears from their cheeks. There was applause at the end punctuated by a barrage of comments and questions.

I was astounded. Yenti's story was special, but I had heard similar accounts numerous times in Sweden. My home in Stockholm had been a center of activity, and Holocaust survivors had visited frequently. My father was faced with the agonizing task there of providing a Jewish divorce to the countless *Agunot*, women who did not know whether their husbands were still living. This necessitated lengthy narratives of the murderous Nazi era. I would sometimes overhear parts of their somber tragic accounts.

Overnight guests would awaken me with their loud cries and screams, night terrors that pierced my tranquil dreams, shattering the silence of the night, and I would hear my mother's soothing words, "*Vein nit mein kind*" – Don't cry, dear child – calming them into a sound sleep. I had never imagined that in the United States, an affluent society known to be the trendsetter of the world, amidst an intelligent group of college students, there would be this lack of awareness of the cataclysmic events of World War II.

I did not become fully recognizant of Sweden's incredible involvement in the aftermath of WWII until many years later. This small country opened its doors and heart to provide the survivors with an opportunity to be restored to health physically, mentally, socially and spiritually. The first group arrived on the White Buses before the end of the war, and were followed by thousands more. Survivors were stranded in Europe after the war – free, with nowhere to go. Indeed, it was tragic that the world was so incredibly slow to provide help.

The role of Sweden and Scandinavia during that era of darkness must be remembered. Today, in 2009, I still encounter numerous individuals who have scant knowledge of the geographic location of Sweden or that Scandinavia consists of several countries. Many lack awareness of Sweden's role after World War II. The history of the humanitarian acts in that part of the world should be shared and remembered,

My inspiration for writing this book was the enthusiasm generated by hundreds of wonderful tourists who participated in my Scandinavia Trio

Preface

Tours during summers from 1980 until 2006. Their delight in the magnificent scenery, the sculpture gardens, the museums and castles and most importantly, their interest in Scandinavian Jewish history, specifically Sweden's response to the survivors of the Shoah, spurred my creativity. That is the purpose of this book.

May we continue to be warmed and inspired by the stories of survivors in Sweden and may we all remember the importance of the healing power of kindness, and fight to eradicate hatred in the world.

Acknowledgments

To The Rebbe:

Rabbi M. M. Schneerson inspired me with his great interest in my Scandinavian tours. His enthusiastic response was the impetus for organizing these tours. Yearly he would provide directives prior to each tour and request complete reports upon my return. His great love and concern for the Jews of Scandinavia was clearly evident.

To all the wonderful members of Scandinavia Trio Tours:

Your enthusiasm for the beauty of Scandinavia and interest in the Jewish history in this part of the world inspired me to write this book. Those tours were truly memorable.

To Suzannah Warlick and Nachum Michael Schwartz:

Thank you for believing in me and following me to Scandinavia to film our documentary of Scandinavia in the Aftermath of World War II. Your faith in me sustained me. Without you, my dream might never have become a reality.

To Dvora Friedman:

My dear friend of many many years, I appreciate your encouragement to write this book, your interest and concern and your great help in editing. And great special thanks for introducing me to my publisher, Yaacov Peterseil.

Acknowledgments

To Sterna Maline:

My firstborn, my daughter, your input was invaluable. Thanks for the endless hours of typing and endless hours of editing, and more hours of typing and more hours of editing. It was great working with you. This book is as much yours as it is mine.

To Nathan Ib Bamberger:

Your careful review of the history of Scandinavia and your useful suggestions were very much appreciated. There are few people who possess your expertise in this area.

To the wonderful people who read my manuscript and offered suggestions:
Cyrel Deitsch, Adina Feder and Charlene Drobney

Section 1

BACKGROUND OF SCANDINAVIAN
LIFE AND HISTORY

CHAPTER 1

Dreams

Hesitantly, with gentle motions, I smoothed the straight bangs away from his eyes, to try to uncover the mystery behind his decision. My grandson Dovi – a casualty of the computer era – in his desire for isolation, prefers the predictable tapping of the keyboard to mediocre conversation, and homeschooling to classroom interaction.

His choice is foreign to me; I thrive on communication. Memories of my family's immigration to the United States resurface once again. A scant fifteen years old when I arrived in the States, an awkward teenager, I spoke hesitantly, my exuberance temporarily stifled, due to the unfamiliar language. Endless evenings were spent in solitude, anxiously perusing the dictionary in an attempt to devour the language and be able to communicate with my classmates. Yet here was my grandson glibly forfeiting classroom camaraderie for the freedom to learn at his own pace – incomprehensible! I would never have done that.

We sat together in the kitchen – he, comfortable with his decision, and I, his grandmother, attempting to piece together the puzzle.

"What do you plan to do with your life?" I queried. A member of a different generation, I longed to bridge the gap, to comprehend why a teenager would choose isolation over socialization.

"I plan to be a film director," he announced enthusiastically.

Sensitive by nature, I was reluctant to put a fifteen-year-old on the spot. A seasoned mother, I had encountered indecisive children, barely able to choose what they want to eat for supper. Yet Dovi had deliberately sabotaged his high school career. I figured he had plans.

"My interests are fantasy, primarily," he continued, eagerly offering ideas and storylines. Apparently he had pondered this matter in depth, this choice to be homeschooled, and then become a famous director of films. Mature beyond his years, his fingers navigate the keyboard more avidly than mine thumb the Yellow Pages.

"But what will you do if it doesn't work out?" I wondered. A product of life experience, I wasn't so easily seduced by grandiloquent aspirations. "Surely you have a contingency plan. I mean, a lot of people want to direct films but very few actually succeed."

"*Bubby*," he interrupted forcefully, eyes gleaming with purpose, "if I don't succeed at first, I will keep on trying. I have a dream and I intend to follow that dream. I will always want to do this. I will dedicate my entire life to this because that is my dream. That is what I want to do."

He picked up his head and stared at me intently. I could feel the heat from his smoldering eyes. "Didn't you ever have a dream, Bubby?"

An innocent question, casually uttered, and I gasped, speechless. I had never given it much thought. The past five decades had been a struggle to survive, to make ends meet. I had neither the time nor the inclination to focus on dreams. *Dreams are for sleeping*," I mumbled to myself sarcastically.

Suddenly, I animatedly blurted, "Actually, when I was little, I loved to read books about explorers – Columbus, Magellan, Vasco da Gama and Robinson Crusoe. When I got older, I longed to see the world, to befriend children my own age in strange and exotic places. I wanted to be a steward-ess, to fly all over the world and visit other countries. But being a stewardess wasn't practical for a Rabbi's daughter," A sigh escaped. "Anyway, after exam-ining it more carefully, I realized that a stewardess was only a glorified wait-ress who serves demanding customers in the air instead of on the ground."

Listening curiously, a faint smile on his lips, Dovi was seeing a different side of his grandmother. The domestic woman who welcomed him into her home and served him tantalizing meals at her homey table had been trans-formed into a travel-hungry youngster.

"We moved to the United States when I was fifteen," I reminisced. "That particular journey wasn't especially enjoyable, but I did travel halfway across the world. Then, after my children married, I returned to Sweden, founded my own travel company, Scandinavia Trio Tours, and traveled extensively."

I looked at my grandson and, this time, was able to meet his pierc-ing gaze. "Yes, I did have a dream, and I am fortunate to have realized that dream."

Dovi nodded and placed his hand on my arm. "I am glad, Bubby," he remarked earnestly. "Dreams are not just for sleeping," he quipped and I could almost imagine that he was able to read my mind. Though I did not agree with his decision to be home schooled, I was beginning to understand.

As I review my life, alone in my dream apartment in Rechavia, an affluent neighborhood in Jerusalem, Israel, I feel content, relieved to retreat into a cocoon-like tranquility and escape the mayhem of family and friends. Solitude is necessary, almost preferable sometimes.

Some memories, gossamer thin, stretch all the way back to childhood, to first grade, when I was told to memorize the Swedish national anthem. Inherently obedient, I planned to fulfill the assignment with aplomb. My older brother Mendel heard me reviewing the poem and advised me to only mouth the words to the final lines: *I want to live and I want to die in the North*. "Do not give credence to them," he stated emphatically. "You don't want to live and die in Sweden. Sweden is not your country. Your land is Palestine. You are a Jew."

Young and innocent, his attitude bewildered me. Sweden was my country, the only place I knew. I loved my life, my friends, my school and my environment. Only later, when the survivors arrived in Sweden from the camps, and I heard countless tales of horror, experiences that no man should have to endure, I began to realize that my people needed a safe haven, a land of our own. And so, having a home in Israel became another part of my dream.

I had never thought about it much before, but now I realize how fortunate I am to have been able to fulfill my dreams – dreams so far-fetched, they seemed too incredible to be put into words. For twenty-five years I have been able to travel every summer to Scandinavia, conducting tours, organizing my own tours, being president of a company, as well as vice president, secretary and treasurer, figuring out the itinerary, locating interesting places in the fjord country and so on. I happily told my grandson, "My life has truly been a magnificent, wonderful dream."

I turned to Dovi: "You should have dreams and try to follow them. Hope and pray that they can be fulfilled because life can be an exciting experience."

CHAPTER 2

On Being Different

I did see myself as different – a square peg in a round hole, a brown-haired girl surrounded by blonde schoolmates – but I didn't feel isolated. I fit in. I was accepted and invited everywhere, even though I was strikingly different.

As far back as I can remember, I knew I was different. I mean, you don't have to be Einstein to circle the picture that doesn't belong with the others. Nobody told it to me explicitly. I just knew. I cannot pinpoint precisely when I became aware of myself and my surroundings, consciously comparing myself to the other children in my neighborhood. I had always known I was different. My chestnut brown hair, dark brown eyes and petite stature contrasted dramatically with the appearance of my tall, blonde-haired, blue-eyed classmates.

Growing up in Sweden, a Jew in the midst of Nordic individuals, I developed a taste for Scandinavian fairy tales. After all, that was the literature most readily available. One didn't need therapy to analyze why Danish author Hans Christian Anderson's short story "The Ugly Duckling" was one of my favorites. I often read that story to my own children. No, I had never felt inferior to the other children, a brown duckling in a sea of golden haired swans, just different.

"No. It's a story about belonging," I insisted, when my daughter asked if the duckling was really ugly. "It's about perception. The duckling thinks it's ugly because it doesn't look like the other birds. But then the duckling becomes a swan and realizes it was beautiful all along. Not ugly," I remind my child, "just different."

The need to belong has always played a central role in my life, maybe because my features were so undeniably different from those of my peers

– on the fringes, yet accepted. This would have been an oxymoron, maybe even an impossibility had I lived in Europe proper, especially during the World War II era; but then, fortunately, I didn't.

Swedish was the spoken language in the homes of all my friends, whereas in my house, Yiddish, a foreign language, was the preferred tongue. My immigrant parents, having relocated from Russia, spoke the language of the country in which they found themselves with great difficulty, a hesitating, halting, heavily accented Swedish.

The neighborhood children boasted extended families: grandparents, aunts, uncles, nieces, nephews and cousins. We were a painfully small nuclear family, consisting of parents, two older brothers, Mendel and Shalom and my sister, Leya. Everybody else's parents were tall, blonde and blue eyed. My parents were short, their heads covered in dark hair, and my father's chin hidden by a black beard. The beard was markedly unusual; nobody else's father had a beard. Nobody else's father was a Rabbi. In fact, none of my friends were even Jewish.

It was difficult growing up in a totally homogenous country that lacked a visible group of immigrants. But it didn't really affect me because I had a lot of playmates. Wholesome, peaceful people, Scandinavians never exhibited xenophobia or distrust. They did not regard minorities as inferior, just different. Open and accepting, to them everybody was equal; everybody was worthy of consideration.

I only realized how fortunate I was after the war, when survivors arrived in Sweden en masse, destroying my pristine childhood with their indescribable tales of horror. But that came later.

My idyllic childhood began on the island of Sodermalm, the largest of the fourteen islands that comprise the beautiful city of Stockholm. Daily, I walked around the corner to the neighborhood grammar school, Katarina Norra Folkskola on Tjarhofsgatan. During the first four years of my schooling, we progressed from grade to grade with the same group of children and the same teacher, Miss Danielson.

I developed a strong and lasting friendship with two classmates, Alice and Margareta, and this friendship continued, not just through the primary grades, but in secondary school as well. I still contact them from time to time and retain a warm space in my heart for them, my first friends.

If I concentrate really hard, I can picture the scene in the flimsy, hazy film of life – an incident that occurred more than six decades ago, during the last few days of summer, just before entering second grade. The episode has been shelved in the deepest crevices of my mind, repressed in a memory closet. Intuitively, I must have known that if I told my parents, it would upset their equilibrium, shattering their tenuous foothold in the country in which they lived.

I can visualize myself in Bjorns Tradgard, my favorite park, together with Alice and Margareta, jumping rope in our favorite playground, double dutch:

It is the last few days of summer vacation and we want to squeeze as much playtime as we can out of the long summer days. My family has just returned from vacationing on our beloved island, Skarpo, in the archipelago, and this is a special day – our first outing to the park by ourselves. Later, I mark this page on the calendar of my mind, but for different reasons.

While jumping, the ropes get tangled and Alice and Margareta proceed to unravel them while I walk away, absent-mindedly bouncing a ball to pass the time. The ball rolls away under a bench, and as I bend down to retrieve it, I notice an elderly Swedish woman sitting nearby. She gazes at me intently, shakes her head and mutters, "You poor, poor child."

I stop in my tracks, my brow wrinkled, trying to decipher the cryptic message. It is a beautiful summer day. I am in the park with my friends having a wonderful time, anticipating the beginning of second grade. Why does that old woman describe me as a "poor child"?

The woman continues her senseless murmuring. "You should not be living here. You should not be in a foreign country, in a foreign place. You should be in Palestine. That's where you belong. That is your home. You should be in your own country, like everyone else is in their country. You poor, poor thing, you should go to your own country." Then she departs, like a character in a play – reciting her lines, and then going offstage as mysteriously as she had initially appeared.

I am dumbfounded. The woman's message shatters my world and I feel the earth shifting, my own private earthquake, leaving in its wake an unfamiliar landscape. It marks the end of childhood – not the exciting rite of passage, of being able to venture to a park unaccompanied, but a tainted transformation, founded on superficial judgment, on prejudice.

I had learned to read in school last year, but I cannot decipher the hieroglyphics on that woman's cryptic Rosetta stone as easily as Alice and Margareta untangle the jump rope. I ponder: *What does she mean, I don't belong here? What kind of advice is she dispensing, suggesting that I travel to Palestine? Where is Palestine? I have never heard of it. Why am I supposed to go there? This is my home town. I speak Swedish like everybody else. This is my school, my park, my friends. Why does the woman say that I don't belong here?*

I back away and look around stealthily, relieved that my friends have not heard these words. The ropes untangled, they call me to resume the game and I run to rejoin them, but my mind remains tangled by the experience. I swallow the memory, gulping it down quickly like unpleasant medicine, ignoring the taste. A victim mentality, I blame myself. I am a child, too unseasoned to analyze why I am embarrassed. I do not want my friends to witness my discomfort. Temporarily paralyzed, I hear their voices call me, as if from a long distance, summoning me back to my previous life. But there is no going back. I run, geographically distancing myself from that woman, but something in her words has irrevocably changed me. The memory is stuffed in the archives of my mind, a frightening skeleton in the closet.

Memories cannot be controlled. They lie dormant, sometimes exploding when you least expect it. This seemingly insignificant memory comes back to haunt me during my first visit to the Museum of Jewish Heritage in Battery Park in Lower Manhattan.

That day is etched in my mind. It was a gloriously sunny fall day in 1997. I felt free, meandering through Battery Park, thirstily imbibing the scenery, the Manhattan skyline across the water, the Statue of Liberty, Ellis Island, the lush vegetation and the trees and flowers in their apex of glory. The museum had recently opened and the lines to enter were abnormally long but, deeply interested in the Holocaust era, I was really looking forward to exploring the museum.

I purchased my ticket and, after what seemed an interminable wait, entered the museum's bowels. Impressed with the layout, I spent a great deal of time on the first floor, the floor of the Jewish heritage. Solitary exploration is an enjoyable activity for me. It is always a treat not to have to contend with impatient people urging me to hurry, to proceed to the next exhibit. I reveled in reading every label, viewing each artifact, matching descriptions to items.

The first floor displayed the symbols of Jewish life: the *chuppah* canopy for the wedding, the fabulous Steinberger Sukkah and various articles associated with Jewish holidays. The Jewish Shabbat is described and the two different Torah scrolls – the Ashkenazi in its velvet mantle and the Sfardi Torah scroll enclosed in an ornate metal case – are displayed near videos of synagogues throughout the world. I then perused the story of immigration and studied an exhibit entitled, "Opposition and Opportunity," highlighting situations that impacted Jewish life, whether in a positive or negative manner, such as the Dreyfus Affair.

Wandering the first floor left me somewhat fatigued. I had been at the museum for more than an hour and really needed to be rejuvenated. I was parched, dehydrated and beginning to feel lightheaded. The crowded throngs lurched forward and I experienced a surreal feeling; was this intended by the architect who designed this museum? In some way, I was internalizing the Holocaust experience! Is that the reason for the lack of water fountains, even of places to pause for a rest? No benches, no seats. And nowhere is there a soda machine or snack bar!

I felt the thirst of the inmates as they stood at *appel.* I felt their fatigue as they were forced to participate in the endless death marches. I almost felt guilty looking for a solution. Reluctantly approaching a guard, I was embarrassed to ask if I might go outside to purchase something from a vendor. He informed me that it would not be possible, that I would have to go back to the long line and purchase another ticket.

Somewhat annoyed, I shrugged my shoulders, decided to forego food and continued viewing. In retrospect, I realized that it may have been hunger that induced me to be so affected by the exhibit, but that is getting ahead of the story.

As I stood on the escalator, allowing myself to be propelled upward, to the next portion of the museum journey, I noticed that the second floor looked dark, simulating a bleak period of Jewish history: the Shoah, Nazism, the ghetto and the destruction of the six million.

I stepped off the escalator and was swallowed up by a huge display entitled, "The Rise of Nazism." It features an oversized portrait of Adolf Hitler, flanked by his book, *Mein Kampf,* smaller black-and-white posters recollecting the elections in Germany and a big flag, the hateful Nazi swastika emblazoned on it. In the first exhibit area, immediately to the left, on the opposite wall of this foreboding panoply of images, was a huge photograph of Hitler youth – healthy, young children dressed in identical Nazi uniforms: pressed shirt, short pants and a tie that resembles a scarf. One can sense the discipline, the paramilitary spirit. Marching, hiking and sports are essential areas of their life. All are blonde, blue-eyed Aryans, resembling the Swedish children with whom I have grown up. They look happy and content holding musical instruments, Hitler's hope for the future.

I continued to view some artifacts on display, and came upon a game, an ordinary board game, similar to Checkers, Chutes and Ladders or Candyland, well-known children's games…

Pressed up against the window, I began to read the game's instructions. Suddenly I am transported back to the park, to that mysterious woman on the park bench. Childhood experiences, buried for more than six decades, erupt with such force that I reeled from the impact. Vertigo has always puzzled me; now I was experiencing it firsthand. The room began to tilt and shift. *The floor is no longer solid and I am suddenly a young child with Alice and Margareta and the Swedish woman admonishing me to go to Palestine.* The museum was crowded and I wondered what might have transpired had it been less claustrophobic. It is very possible I might have fainted.

The game, devised to indoctrinate innocent youth, has rules. One begins in any of the four corners at the perimeter of the board and advances toward the center. There are two sets of players. The cute, little, chubby blue-and-red wooden pieces represent the Germans, while the yellow, upside-down cone-shaped pieces with ugly, pronounced features drawn on them represent the Jews.

The game's objective is to rid the board of Jews because Jews are not wanted. The large squares on the board are called *Zammelplatz*, gathering place. The player rolls the dice, advances toward the center, and as he proceeds, he removes yellow pieces – signifying Jews who are blocking the way – and places them at the *Zammelplatz*. The aim of the game is to clear the board of yellow pieces, to rid the town, to make it *Judenrein*. Then the Jews are shipped to Palestine.

The poem describes the game succinctly: *Zeige Geschick in Würfelspiel, damit du sammelst der Juden viel* – "Show your skill and gather the Jews." On the bottom left-section of the board are caricatures of three or four Jews burdened with luggage; the German text reads, "Go to Palestine." My deep memories, etched within me, exploded like a bomb, leaving me totally shattered. Thunderstruck, it is my private storm.

That was exactly what the woman in the park had told me decades ago. At that time I had lacked knowledge. I had not known about the Nazis, had not known that Jews were not welcome in other countries. I thought Nazis only appeared as distinguished men clad in spotless uniforms, cap perfectly placed on the head, and wearing tall, shiny boots. I had never known that a Nazi could be camouflaged as an elderly woman, an ordinary Swedish woman.

* * *

When I was a teenager, my family immigrated to the United States. My first day in the new school in Roxbury Massachusetts was a pleasant revelation. Boston, a very Catholic city, mandated that schools be separated by sexes. I attended Jeremiah E. Burke High School, an institution for girls only, similar to the gymnasium in my hometown in Sodermalm. When the teacher called attendance, I was in heaven. The roster of names was music to my ears. No longer was I the outsider among Andersson, Peterson, and Svenson. Now the names were Schwartz, Cohen, Goldberg and Fleisher. It was fantastic.

Fascinated by my presence, my classmates demanded to know where I hid during the war, and what terrible things happened to my family. They asked me to describe horrific conditions of brutality and deprivation. They crowded around and bombarded me with questions, hungering for drama and tales of woe. But my cupboard is bare. I have been living in a neutral country, partaking of a lifestyle similar to theirs, attending school, enjoying leisure time and vacations. I may not have eaten a lot of pineapples and bananas because they were imported, but we always had an ample supply of local fruits: apples, peaches, plums, cherries and berries. We may have lacked rice, but there were always plenty of potatoes. Sugar and coffee were rationed, as were some other items, but I believe there was rationing in the United States as well. We always had plenty to eat. We were warm and our house remained intact. Life was quite normal.

Bored with my unexciting descriptions, their offers of friendship declined and they quickly lost interest. However, I developed a friendship with Marilyn Freeman and her sister, Natalie, who took me to parties, introduced me to their friends, brought me to social events and, most importantly of all, they introduced me to *HaShomer HaDati*, an organization that later evolved into *Bnei Akiva*, a very enthusiastic, idealistic organization that inspired its members and instilled in them a love for Israel and building the land of Israel. I became very active and involved. I participated in marches down Blue Hill Avenue, proudly wearing the blue denim shirt with the Bnei Akiva emblem on the sleeve. I overcame my shyness and walked through subway cars with a *pushka* collecting money for JNF.

My summer experience in Camp Moshava, a Bnei Akiva camp – living in tents, walking to bathrooms and showers – was a wonderful, unforgettable teenage experience. Lifetime friendships were formed, still maintained today: Ada in Phoenix, Shully, Hedy, Judy, Helga and numerous other Bostonians, all now living in Israel. This is something I now understood to be of great importance, especially after World War II and the tragedy of my people not having a home. Perhaps I connected to the organization more passionately because of that old woman on the bench so long ago, as well as because of my brother Mendel.

In approximately half a year, I became acculturated and high school took on pleasant overtones. Fond memories include the high school ring, the special Honor's pin, walking down the aisle at graduation in a white dress and then applying to college.

I was accepted to Boston University with a substantial scholarship for my freshman year. Worried that the scholarship might not be renewed, obligating my father with great financial burdens, I opted to forgo private university and enroll in a less expensive college, Boston State College, part of the University of Massachusetts. I was delighted that one of my Bnei Akiva friends, Rivka Epstein Merzel, was a student there also. I noticed a difference in the student body. The majority of students were Irish and Italian Catholics with a small number of Jewish students, less than five percent. Having been a minority of only one in Sweden, I felt prepared to contend with what I assumed would be a familiar experience. It wasn't.

A serious and dedicated student, I was immediately invited to participate in a study group. The sessions were held in the homes of different students. After several meetings, I was asked why I never participated in Newman Club meetings, an organization for Catholic youth. I explained that I had little time for socializing, but that if I would be inclined to join an organization, it would probably be the Hillel Club.

"Why would you go to the Hillel Club?" one girl asked nervously. "That's an organization for Jewish youth."

I answer calmly, "Well, I am Jewish."

My words were met with total silence. "How can you say you are Jewish," another girl asked wonderingly. "I don't see your horns."

I had never encountered such provincialism. I had no idea that Catholic schools taught that Jews had horns. The conversation then faded, the discomfort dissipated. I completed the assignment, but there were no more invitations for study sessions. Being different in Boston, Massachusetts, I quickly realized, was tantamount to being excluded. In Sweden, though I had been the only Jew in my class, I had never felt isolated.

Once my stability recovered, I began socializing with the Jewish students in the college, getting involved in other activities, and life went on. I realized, too late, that I would probably have had a more positive academic experience in Boston University, but no one took the time to explain to me, a newcomer to this country, the different student bodies that are present in universities. College proved to be a dissatisfying and somewhat bewildering experience.

After graduating from college, I approached the Board of Examiners in Boston to apply for a position. Again, I encountered rejection. It was the McCarthy era and I was questioned regarding my political affiliation.

After strongly emphasizing that I had no Communist allegiance, I was asked, "But Sweden, well, you come from Sweden. That's right near Russia, isn't it?"

I looked at them in amazement. True, Sweden is close to Russia, but I never was given the opportunity to visit neighboring Finland, much less Russia. I told them that Russia is not a part of the world in which I had ever lived. Disillusioned with the bigotry of Boston society, and the sense of not belonging, I landed a teaching position in Chelsea, Massachusetts, at Carter Junior High School, a wonderful introduction to teaching.

The following summer I got married and relocated to Crown Heights, in Brooklyn, New York, to a *Lubavitch Chabad* community. I was certain I would fit in, that now there would be nothing to differentiate me from the other people in the group. Again, I was wrong.

I was viewed with distrust because I had not attended the same schools they had attended. They'd studied in Yeshivas in New York, but there were no Yeshiva day schools for girls outside of New York City. They viewed me strangely because I had attended college. Once again, I suffered from a sense of alienation. My parents were Russian, like the parents of all the other young people in Crown Heights. Yet, since I had lived outside that community, I was viewed as different. However, there were other people in the neighborhood, graduates from Stern College, who lived on my block. We became acquainted, and I developed my own circle of friends.

We shared similar interests: the library at Maple Street and Grand Army Plaza, Brooklyn Children's Museum, Brooklyn Botanic Garden and the playground on Lefferts Avenue. Some of us became substitute teachers at neighborhood public schools and enrolled in graduate courses at Brooklyn College.

Eventually I became a public school teacher at PS 167, then in PS 161, in Crown Heights, Brooklyn. Once again, I experienced a sense of not belonging. The staff at PS 167 was riddled with cliques. An ESL teacher, I became quite friendly with the Hispanic teachers in the bilingual department. The male teachers, helpful and kind, would come into the room to remove unruly students and offer helpful suggestions. The student body was very difficult and principals kept leaving. In contrast, the majority of female teachers were unkind; they teased me about my way of dressing, of being Orthodox and Jewish, I always wore skirts and dresses, exclusively – never pants, an item of clothing that recently had gained acceptance in the school system.

After transferring to PS 161, my experience became much more positive. The school was professionally run, with uniforms required as the attire for all children. In this orderly ambiance, my ESL position was very rewarding. The staff was cohesive and the principal, a strong leader. I remained there until retirement.

After retiring, I became a docent and volunteered at the Museum of Jewish Heritage in Battery Park. Once again, I was labeled 'different'. The docents are divided into two distinct groups: the American-born ones, and the survivors from Europe. Though I had emigrated from Europe, I am not a survivor. I belonged in neither group. It was as though I was back in high school that first day, being questioned about my war experiences. Over and over again, I explained that though I am European, my war experiences were non-existent.

I have encountered many situations where I have been labeled different, and have been forced to overcome many hurdles. But throughout my journeys, I have had to analyze myself, to grow from within, to develop a sense of self-knowledge and self-awareness, to stand alone without the padded protection of a group. Learning to think for oneself is a very enriching, albeit sometimes lonely, experience. There is a sense of security in being part of a group, yet also a loss of independence. One must conform to the group or risk being excluded.

I may not always have chosen to be different, yet isolation is also a blessing. I would not have evolved into the person I am today had I not been forced to stand alone, to develop a sense of self. Cocooned in a group, I would never have searched for new experiences, taken chances or pioneered into new fields. Strength, courage and independence are the awards one receives when one is given the opportunity to overcome challenges and forge ahead.

CHAPTER 3

In the Beginning

My parents were both native Russians. My father hailed from Schedrin, a city boasting an innovative history. The Tzemach Tzedek, a Lubavitch Rabbi, had been instrumental in founding the community. A revolutionary thinker, he believed Jews should be permitted to engage in agriculture. Unfortunately Jews were not allowed to own land in most of Europe and that was a major problem. Thus, Jews became traders and moneylenders – even the guilds were closed for Jews.

This type of thinking was contrary to Russian law, which explicitly prohibited Jews from owning land. Russia also enacted strict laws, restricting Jews to the Pale – specific areas set aside for their habitation. A Jew's inability to acquire land indirectly became a financial death sentence, since Russia was primarily agrarian.

In 1844, the Tzemach Tzedek arranged to purchase a tract of land from Prince Schedrin, in the Minsk Goberno, and invited three hundred Jewish families to join in his venture. Each family was granted a free plot of land upon which to build a home and erect farm buildings. For the first time in history, Jews were landowners. Schedrin – so named in honor of the prince – evolved into a productive, vibrant society, lasting until World War II, when the Nazis cruelly decimated it.

Czar Nikolas, ruler over a vast country spanning two continents, initiated a plan to unify Russia, through a process known as Russification. The Czar wished to unite the diverse population, fragmented by varied languages and cultures, under one common banner, but soon realized that the Jew, inherently different, would be an obstacle.

After careful deliberation, the Czar devised a strategy to prevail over Jewish resistance to assimilation to Russian culture by appointing *chappers*, kidnappers. These chappers were sent into Jewish communities for the express purpose of snatching youngsters, sometimes even boys just eight years old, from the hearth of their family, and placing them in mandatory military schools, *Cantons*. They subsequently continued their military service in the Russian army for a total of twenty-five years. It was hoped that after this long absence, they would be full-fledged Russians. A group who wanted to return to Jewish life settled in Finland, at that time a Grand Duchy of Russia, where they developed the Finnish Jewish community.

Inhabitants of Schedrin managed to circumvent this terror; they protected their children and exempted them from attending the military schools. In 1897, when a census was taken from the forty families who had originally settled in 1842, those Yeshiva families had flourished into 4,022 inhabitants with seven different shuls.

My grandfather settled there; Reb Menachem Mendel, a Renaissance Jew, served as a *melamed*, a teacher of young children and a *shochet*, a ritual slaughterer. Thus, he provided the community with knowledge and food, spiritual and material sustenance. They had eleven children initially; two died in infancy, and my grandparents were occupied with raising their remaining nine children.

During the period before Pesach, my grandfather earned extra money by traveling to nearby communities to slaughter chickens for the upcoming holiday. Unfortunately, on one of these travels, the last night before he was scheduled to return home, the young father was staying overnight with an affluent family, when robbers descended upon the household. In the wrong place at the wrong time, my grandfather sacrificed his life for the sake of his family.

A young widow, my Grandmother Sheina was left with a houseful of young children. The plan was that the older children would immigrate to America one by one and she would eventually join them, traveling with the youngest children.

Rose, the oldest daughter, left for Scranton, Pennsylvania. Her husband, Benny, was a businessman with a horse and cart, a real Yankee peddler. Sophie had been contributing to the family finances by peddling wares in neighboring towns, a dangerous occupation for a young, attractive woman, no more than seventeen years of age. Walking alone on lonely country roads, carrying heavy bags was quite a formidable task. At the age of seventeen, she departed for the United States, settled in East Flatbush and married Uncle Kalman, a bagel baker. Her home was a great place to visit, always filled with fresh bagels, lox and cream cheese.

The next sister, Chanah, settled in Brownsville with her husband, a house painter. His work was seasonal, as the heavy odor of the oil paint made it difficult to paint in the winter. He wielded that thick brush, painting with rapid strokes, covering the walls with tan or gray paint, splashing the floors and windows in the process. Nosson Nota Zuber, a brother, arrived in the United States and became a Rabbi in Rosselle, New Jersey, where he remained at his pulpit for forty years, until he retired. He became a legend, a Talmud scholar with a photographic memory. He was consulted by many individuals and would respond immediately with the exact page, verse and line.

One time, a visitor surreptitiously jotted down the information of the source provided and upon his return home, checked inside the Babylonian Talmud. The response had been, as always, very rapid and he thought that perhaps the source was inaccurate; however, it was exactly correct.

Yaacov Peterseil, a disciple of Rabbi Nota Zuber's, related the following incident: "Rabbi Zuber's son, Mendel, collected baseball cards, the kind with a picture on the front and lots of personal and professional information on the back. Rabbi Zuber had no knowledge of baseball but asked his son to see the cards, wanting to share his interest. The next day, he displayed to his son all the information, batting averages, positions and all other details. That was truly amazing," concluded Yaacov, smiling as he recalled that incident.

My father continued his studies in the Yeshiva in Lubavitch, where he was ordained and received *Smicha*. His uncle, an inhabitant of Streshin, introduced him to my mother, Zlata Golbin, a young woman of means, whose father, Reb Chaim, owned a grocery store.

I was greatly surprised regarding what was considered a sizable dowry: three sacks of flour, a sack of beans and a barrel of butter. Actually, this was worth more than jewels during those days because food was scarce. Stalin was in power and hunger was pervasive. The dowry enabled Grandmother Sheina and her children to stay alive.

In 1922, my father, Yacov Yisroel, became a Rabbi in a city called Satchchere in Gruzia, Georgia. Both my parents had come from small towns in Belarus in the province of Minsk, but were totally unprepared for the poverty in this mountainous region of Georgia.

The people lived in huts with mud floors, without electricity or running water, but they probably did not have those amenities in their own villages either. Though superstitious and primitive, the people were kind and loving. Despite his youth, mid-twenties or thereabouts, my father established himself as a superb leader. He learned their *Gruzinish* dialect, and became a great orator, charismatic and popular. Yet, he longed to travel to America, to join his other siblings who were already settled there.

In 1928 they left for Riga, Latvia, which was, at that time, an independent Baltic state. Later it became a satellite of the USSR but today, once again, Latvia is independent. My parents settled there, albeit temporarily, awaiting passage to America, but they were discouraged from coming. Though nobody expressed negativity explicitly, it was right after the depression. Perhaps the relatives feared that a family with three children would be a financial burden. FDR's fireside chats had not yet warmed the financial hearts of the country – it was hardly an opportune time for immigrants.

One day a representative from the community of Stockholm came to Riga, looking for a spiritual guide for their synagogue, the Adas Yisroel, on the island of Sodermalm. The requirements were manifold: an effective speaker, someone able to conduct services in the synagogue, a good teacher, a leader able to take charge, a *shochet* and a *mohel*. My father could perform all those tasks.

The Lubavitcher Rebbe at that time, Rabbi Yosef Yitzchak Schneerson, the *Frierdike Rebbe*, encouraged my father to accept the position in Sweden. Yacov Yisroel knew nothing of Sweden and envisioned it a totally uncivilized area, a country of ice – dark and uninviting, and dominated by polar bears grunting through the streets. He did possess one piece of accurate knowledge: most Scandinavians had scant knowledge of Jewish life.

My father left for the interview by ship. Today it takes approximately forty-five minutes to fly from Riga to Stockholm; at that time, it was a journey of more than twelve hours. Upon his arrival in Stockholm, he was pleasantly surprised. The city was magnificent, and Adas Yisroel was a cheerful little synagogue on the quiet residential street of Sankt Paulsgatan, off busy Gotgatan, a major shopping street in Sodermalm.

The members of the congregation, mostly Polish and Eastern European Yiddish-speaking Jews, welcomed him warmly. Comfortable with the congregants, he agreed to stay there a few years, until the situation in the United States would improve and he and his family could join his siblings in the United States. So, in 1931, he accepted the position in Sweden.

Life rarely turns out the way you expect. The sojourn in Sweden actually became the longest time period of his married life that he remained settled in one place. The Zubers lived in Sweden from 1931 until 1947, a crucial period in Jewish history.

Nazism was on the rise. Doors were closing everywhere. Immigration into Sweden was becoming more difficult with each increasing day; eventually, the doors closed completely and it became impossible for my parents to leave Sweden. My father, Yacov Yisroel, communicated with his mother, Sheina, faithfully, but soon, that also became hazardous. People in Russia were not permitted to receive mail from other countries. His communication with his mother severed, my father remained in Sweden, isolated from his family.

Bubby Sheina spent the remaining years of her life with her youngest daughter, Leah, in Siberia. It was incredibly difficult; starvation was rampant and the cold seeped through their undernourished bones. Bubby Sheina had photographs of the children who had gone to America, and of my father, my mother and us children. She would look at the photographs periodically, her paper children. She referred to her sons Nosson Nota and Yacov Yisroel as "my Kaddish sayers" – the two rabbis that would recite the special prayer after her death. Bubby Sheina would talk to the photos and pray that someday they would be reunited, but that never happened.

An inspirational story featuring Bubby Sheina encapsulates the power of strength and sacrifice. One Passover a drought had rendered flour exorbitantly expensive and without flour, one could not bake matzoh.

The situation dire, Bubby Sheina rose to the task. Bravely, she approached the dentist, requesting that he extract the gold fillings that protected her teeth. The dentist acquiesced, and she unhesitatingly sold the fillings to obtain money for flour. That year she had matzoh, not just for herself, but the entire community. She had heroically sacrificed for the sake of a Mitzvah.

Bubby Sheina longed to travel to Sweden to join her son and his family, but that never happened because entry to Sweden was prohibited. Bubby Sheina lived with her daughter Leah throughout the war years and died in 1961. Several times, Bubby Sheina's children collected money, diligently saving their earnings, penny by penny, from their meager salaries. They would send the money to Bubby Sheina so that she could apply for papers to come to the United States. Yet somehow the government workers always misplaced the papers and "lost" the money. In Russia it was not uncommon for documents and payments to mysteriously disappear. After three disappointing and fruitless attempts, she became discouraged and told her children that she no longer wished to come.

Bubby Sheina kept the letters from her children – bundles of letters lovingly wrapped in an old kerchief, tied with a cloth belt – in a box placed in a secure area under her bed, and read them and reread them, until the pages were tattered. They were the greatest treasures in her life.

These days, with mass communication, phones, cell phones and instant messaging, we can contact each other easily and immediately. In those days, there were only letters, and every letter was treasured. We cannot conceive of parents and children separating, realizing they might never see each other again. Today, traveling is easier. It's a different world. That poignant song, *A*

Brivele di Mamma, about a letter from a parent to a child, encapsulates the nostalgia of those letters. Our hearts ache for the difficulty people underwent. There was something very special about writing and receiving letters, an event this generation will never experience.

Coming to America to begin a new life was a very big step, suffused with the angst of separation, knowing one could never return to visit family, friends and familiar places. When returning to Sweden after an absence of thirty-three years, I was elated with the joy of visiting the house in which I had grown up, the school I had attended, the familiar streets, my classmates. To be denied that opportunity must have been overwhelmingly difficult, yet my parents had to endure the permanent separation from their parents and childhood home.

Chapter 4

My Childhood

We lived on Katarina Vastra Kyrkogata number six in Stockholm, on the island of Sodermalm. A large, heavy, ornate oak door flanked the entrance to our apartment building. I remember how difficult it was to open that door because it was so heavy. Thoroughly amazed, upon my return to the neighborhood more than thirty-five years later, that same door was still guarding the entrance. So much of my world had changed, yet some pivotal markers remained the same.

The little elevator inside had remained unchanged as well. Though we lived only on the second floor, as a child I always liked to press the buttons, to enter the small chamber and watch the inside metal door open and close like an accordion.

The most important room in the house was my father's study. A large mahogany desk covered with glass dominated the area, and behind it, an imposing chair. The side of the room housed a chocolate-colored couch and the brown velvet curtains were accented with heavy, brown and gold, braided silk rope with tassels. A lush carpet blanketed the floor and in the corner stood the glossy, polished, mahogany piano with ivory white keys. We were mandated to scrub our hands meticulously before practicing our lessons.

The top of the piano featured beautifully framed photographs, portraits of the extended family. These black-and-white pictures were the only tangible evidence of their existence. There were beautifully carved wooden figures that my father had received when journeying to different areas of Sweden to perform a circumcision. In lieu of payment, if there was a shortage of funds, they would present him with these beautifully hand-carved figures.

My Childhood

The focal point of our apartment was the dining room. A large, sturdy table, surrounded by eight chairs, occupied the center of the room; here, the family ate supper daily and this is where we gathered for Shabbat meals and holidays, usually with guests.

Bookcases laden with books lined the dining room walls. My father possessed an extensive collection of Judaica, mainly books from Poland and Russia, including some hand-written manuscripts dating as far back as Maimonides. A genuine bibliophile, he taught himself the art of bookbinding, painstakingly lining the inside covers of his books with decorative wallpaper.

I loved to watch his fingers plunging the needle in and out through the heavy pages of the books, rebinding them so that they would be in good condition. He placed labels on all his books and treasured them, because that was the most important thing in his life, to study Torah. In the margins and on the sides of the pages, he would write his comments.

In the alcove area of the dining room nestled a table with an oversized radio, the size of a clumsy, old-fashioned television. This radio could receive frequency from stations in all the European capitals. My parents would sit close to the radio, reluctantly listening to Hitler's strident, angry, brash voice, his speech constantly interrupted by exuberant cheers of *Heil Hitler* from an intoxicated audience. My father would stroke his beard mechanically, sadly nodding his head, eyes filled with fear and worry.

Those were the famous speeches broadcast from Tiergarten in Berlin. Unable to decipher all the content, I only knew that Hitler sounded hostile, enraged, spouting messages of virulent hatred, saturated with an ideology about the parasitic Jew, and the destruction that was destined to follow. German was my first foreign language in school and although I was not fluent, it was obvious his aim was to kill all Jews, clearly and frequently stated in his speeches.

The couch, hugging one wall of the dining room, introduced a living room portion. The apartment did not contain a separate living room; that room was a combined living room and dining room. I enjoyed relaxing on the couch, either reading books or chatting with school friends. Assorted guests were also entertained there.

Father's study was totally off-limits. A formidable room, it was reserved for important people who came to discuss climactic events. I remember something strange that occurred with the couch. A silent observer, I never told my parents what I had seen. My mother opened the seams of the pillows on the couch. The youngest, I was the only child at home. My siblings were all in school. I saw them take out rolls of money, lots and lots of paper bills, nervously stuffing them into the pillows.

My father took out gold medals from a hiding place – solid gold medals, three or four inches in diameter, shiny, large coins – and he pushed them carefully into the pillows. Intuitively, I knew this was something that should not be discussed, a secret; I never let my parents know that I had seen what was happening. I was only a child bearing a burden too large for my immature years. They sighed while performing this operation. Their sighs might have deepened in intensity, had they realized I was watching.

The hallway connecting the dining room and kitchen held my mother's most cherished possession, the Singer sewing machine. I liked watching my mother press the pedal rapidly back and forth with her tiny feet, sewing long, even rows to make quilt covers for the family's fluffy, warm quilts. Evenly spaced button holes, neatly fastened, strategically protected the quilts. She also made decorative throw pillows and curtains with fancy ruffles and lace. Her personally designed aprons were constructed from cheerful cotton material, embossed with colorful designs of zigzag ribbons and borders.

I was almost ten years old when my baby brother was born. For so long I had been the youngest, longing for a baby sibling. My mother created the most beautiful white shirts for him, large, ruffled collars trimmed with lace, items featured nowadays in glossy museum catalogues, and we marvel at their beauty. My mother reveled in being a homemaker, as the focus of her life was home and family. Our father was a king and she, his chief assistant.

She enjoyed cooking and baking, her expertise – Eastern European food with a sprinkling of Scandinavian recipes. Her *kneidlach*, soft and fluffy, her chicken soup, golden in color, rich and delicious and her chicken, served exclusively on Shabbat and *Yom Tov*, spicy and tantalizing.

Food preparation was a major task in those days, particularly arduous if one maintained a kosher house. My mother baked her own bread, delicious black bread. She also made yeast cakes, soft, fluffy sponge cakes and fabulous Danishes. She mastered the Scandinavian yeast cake that consisted of a loaf into which one inserted partial cuts and then placed the pieces in alternate directions, creating a leaflike effect.

She made her own noodles, from a simple dough of flour and water. With a rolling pin, she would roll out the dough very thin, neatly fold it several times and then cut the flat piece with a sharp knife to make exceedingly thin noodles. During the summer, my parents would pick blueberries and my mother would make jam, special pudding desserts, blueberry soup – a typical Swedish dish – or cake with blueberry filling. She pickled cucumbers, placing them in glass jars and later stored them for the winter, placing them into large, wooden barrels in the attic of the apartment building.

My favorite dessert, a tangy lemon meringue pie, was made without benefit of prepackaged items. The taste of the lemon filling, made from real lemons, still lingers on my tongue, along with the fluffy topping of egg whites, beaten into cloud-like softness.

On Passover, potato puffs, sweet *chremslach* and a popular Swedish year-round dish called pittypanna, delicately fried leftovers, graced the table. My mother enjoyed company; she loved feeding her guests and would constantly implore them to *"Ess noch a bissel"* – eat a little bit more – continuously plying their plates with food until they would laughingly protest that they could not eat another morsel.

A kind and compassionate woman, my mother also entertained people who were not welcome anywhere else, like the disheveled, unkempt man who often came for meals. She would seat him at the table and treat him as an honored guest by serving him first. When noting my discomfort, she would quietly gesture, vigorously shaking her head, admonishing me to make sure the guest was treated respectfully.

Impoverished musicians from southern Europe gathered in the courtyard of the building entertaining us with musical extravaganzas on violins or guitars. My mother would wrap some coins carefully in newspaper, open the window and instruct me to toss down the little packets.

In those days, children began attending school at the age of six, entering first grade. Preschool and kindergarten were attended only by unfortunate children who had working mothers or families plagued by severe illness. My formative years were spent in the comfort of home. My sister and brothers were in school, and I treasured those carefree years – a marvelous childhood.

I have fond memories of grinding meat in a special grinder attached to the table. I grew proficient at using a special tool to push the food down, in that particular apparatus. I became quite an expert at assembling the machine myself, and disassembling it to prepare it for washing.

Thursday was my favorite day of the week, when I accompanied my mother to Kornhamstorg, the open market, to buy fish and vegetables for Shabbat. I learned how to check the freshness of the fish by the glossiness and clarity of the eyes, and I watched my mother open the flap to view the color of the gills.

Purchasing fruits and vegetables was another important learning experience. I always received a special treat during these excursions. On the way home, we would take Katarinahissen, an exciting elevator, outside in the street. It traveled from Slussen up into the heights of Sodermalm. I loved watching the riveting view through the large glass windows as the elevator climbed upward.

On Shabbat afternoon, I amused myself with my dolls in the proximity of my mother, who perused the Yiddish version of the Bible, the *Tzena Urena*, in a soft, singsong tune. The Torah portion of the week came alive with her

reading, because she was a superb storyteller. I possessed a myriad of luxuri-
ously illustrated Swedish storybooks, but Swedish was a foreign language to
my mother. Instead, I would listen to her stories, captivated by old Russian
folk tales, like "The Fisherman and His Wishes," variations of Cinderella or
stories about poor Jewish children and their trials and tribulations.

Many of my fondest childhood memories were associated with the
carefree summers in Skarpo, the island in the archipelago, which was previously mentioned. My parents loved it there; perhaps it reminded them of
their *shtetl* in Russia. The island lacked modern conveniences like electricity
and running water. Kerosene lamps provided light, but we really didn't need
electricity because the days were very long, with just a few hours of twilight
at night. Summer nights were vastly different from the heavy, black winter
nights: the sky would begin to darken at about eleven o'clock at night and by
about four o'clock in the morning, it was already light.

The primitive conditions on the island were truly enchanting, giving us
children a first-hand insight into life of long ago. We had a lot of fun. My
brothers learned to use an axe to chop wood, fuel that filled the bowels of the
old-fashioned wood-burning stove for baking. We would walk into the forest
to gather pinecones for a bright fire with a wonderful smell for the ceramic
heating elements in the corner of every room, the kakelugn. Frequent rains
in the summer would make the house feel chilly. My sister and I ventured
to the well to draw water, carefully transporting full pails of water to the
kitchen. Sometimes we would obtain water from the local pump.

The summers were truly wonderful, away from the noise and distur-
bance of the city. Cars were significantly absent, so bikes were used instead.
Every Thursday, punctually like clockwork, our father arrived from the city,
bringing meat and chickens for the following week. We would gather at the
harbor to await his arrival. A small store on the island provided for our immediate needs. Mail was also delivered to this store, brought by ship daily,
for the inhabitants of Skarpo. There were no phones.

During the war years, we were forced to find an alternative vacation
spot because the island of Skarpo was near Waxholm, a strategic island.
Though we were Swedish citizens, we were naturalized, not native born, and
this status precluded us from inhabiting that area. Many years later I realized
that numerous important meetings, between German Nazis and Swedish
politicians, had taken place near Waxholm.

Excursions to Skansen, the outdoor museum and Nordic zoo on the
island of Djurgarden, were always a highlight of spring and fall. The small
ferry departed from Gamla Stan – the Old Town – or Nybroviken, for the
ten-minute ride across the water. One could also walk there across the bridge,
or take a bus, but the ferry was the transportation of choice.

At Skansen, one could walk on cobblestone streets and visit old-time shops of glassblowing or candy production, a smithery, a bakery and shops of other crafts. The zoo was filled with foxes, bears, polar bears and other popular Nordic animals in their natural habitat. There were buildings of long ago, and entertainment – folk dancing and communal singing of old Swedish Bellman tunes. A day at Skansen was always a treat.

I was the only Orthodox Jewish girl in my elementary school. There was one Jewish classmate from a very assimilated home. In the entire city of Stockholm, a metropolis of one million people, there were only three Jewish girls in my age bracket. One of them, in the northern part of Stockholm, Norrmalm, came from a family of German lineage. We had little in common.

There was only one boy my age. The girl from Norrmalm would tease me mercilessly, threatening that when it became time to marry, she would marry that boy, because they both came from German background. A bit perturbed, I wondered what would happen to me. We attended regular Swedish schools because there were no day-school Yeshivas or Talmud Torahs, afternoon Hebrew schools.

When the Danish Jews fled to Sweden, the situation improved greatly. A Danish young woman, a teacher in Copenhagen, now became the teacher of a small Talmud Torah that met twice a week. A Norwegian Jewish girl, daughter of Rabbi Samuel of Trondheim, who had been captured and killed by the Nazis, escaped to Sweden with her mother and siblings. Thus the small student body consisted of a sampling from all the Scandinavian countries.

I did not really comprehend the enormity of the tragedy that was taking place and just thought it was exciting to have an injection of more young Jewish people in the community and that life was improving for me, socially at least.

Content as a student at my school, Katarina Norra Folkskola, I experienced no differentiation between myself and the other students and felt a sense of belonging. Deep down, though, I was always acutely aware that I was not like all the others. Once or twice, in fact, there was an uncomfortable incident. One time, a classmate lost something. It might have been taken or misplaced. The teacher asked the students to disclose any information. Nobody volunteered. Later she approached me, specifically, asking for additional information. I was not happy to be singled out. I guess it's only natural to suspect somebody who looks visibly different from the rest of the group.

On another occasion, a photographer visited the school. He wanted to photograph the class to illustrate an article about education in Sweden. Surveying the room, he noticed me sitting in the front row of the classroom, where I usually was placed because I was so short. The photographer consulted with the teacher in an impromptu whispered discussion. Then the teacher approached me, a trifle uncomfortable. Apologetically, she asked me to change my seat, explaining that the photographer wished to capture the group from a certain angle and preferred that I not be in the picture. Even though I was very young, I understood that he wanted the classroom to represent a homogenous group of Swedish youth, tall, blonde and blue-eyed, and my presence would mar the picture.

There was food rationing during the war years, but our family always had plenty to eat. We had a specific problem with bread coupons. A staple in our diet, we needed a lot of bread. Coupon exchanging easily resolved the dilemma. Our Swedish neighbors drank a lot of coffee and were very pleased to exchange coffee coupons for the bread rations.

Although there was only one other Jewish family in our building, and we were the only immigrants, my mother maintained good relations with our Swedish neighbors. In addition to the language barrier, there were religious and cultural differences as well. All the girls in those days wore big bows in their hair, but my mother's bows always looked limp. The problem was solved by bringing me to a neighbor who would make a beautiful bow with a flourish. My mother was always ready and eager to help her neighbors and gratefully accepted their assistance as well.

Bananas were one of the items that were scarce and once during these years, a shipment arrived. I was the only one in my family allotted bananas, and was rather upset that I had to share them with my siblings. The precious bananas were cut into pieces and distributed to all the family members. It was a novelty; I did not even know they had to be peeled.

I will never forget the shipment of rice. My mother happily sent me to the store to buy the allotted amount. I placed the rice in the basket of my bike. Taking the shortcut through the park, I noticed, to my great horror, that the bag, poorly constructed from wartime paper of inferior quality, had come undone and small grains of rice were seeping out from the bottom of the bag. Stopping my bike, I jumped off and scurried around on all fours, retrieving the small grains of rice from the ground, carefully brushing away the sand. Each grain of rice was valuable; people were only allowed one small bag per family.

Shortages of materials resulted in interesting innovations. A gas substitute, Gengas, was invented. Cars looked strange as they sputtered along the streets with their portable gas generators attached to the outside of the car, burning charcoal or wood. Sweden's attempt at producing chewing gum without gum arabic was a dismal failure. Within moments, the gum hardened into a tasteless solid clump. Worn woolen sweaters were carefully ripped up and then recycled, knitted into new garments.

My Childhood

Leather was scarce, but I loved the new style of summer shoes with the thick, wooden platform base and the attractive upper part, stylishly fashioned from brightly colored denim cloth. To prolong the wear, my father skillfully cut strips of leather from discarded shoes and placed them strategically across the sole of the shoe.

My older sister, Leya, hated the blackout, the special black curtains placed in front of the regular shades, to darken the homes. Civilians were instructed to keep the city totally dark during the war years, for protection, in the event that the enemy would attempt to bomb the beautiful city of Stockholm.

My mother informed us that a new boy would join our family. Excited, I assumed that it was going to be another baby brother. Instead, it was a foster child, a boy my age whose parents shipped him to Sweden for safekeeping while they remained in Finland. For two years, Avi lived in our household. He was eventually reunited with his family and later they immigrated to the United States. We all met later in Boston, Massachusetts, where all of us settled.

We had a letter from school asking my parents' permission to be evacuated along with my classmates to a secluded, well-hidden area in case we would be occupied by the Germans. That was a very real danger. I overheard my parents discussing this situation. I remember my father saying that he was going to sign the paper. He said, "At least let this child remain alive if no one else can be saved."

I found it rather exciting, because I didn't understand all the consequences. We had to prepare a blanket, heavy pajamas, a warm sweater, utensils for eating, cutlery, extra underwear and socks. Everything was rolled together in a bundle, tied in such a way that we could carry it on our backs. It was placed in the closet.

Then a list was made of all the students in the class and if, God forbid, something happened, there would be a chain call. We would meet at a specific location, probably the school, and from there, we would be evacuated.

Sometimes I would go to the closet to check if my bundle was still there. A child, I thought that this might be an exciting school excursion. Thank God it never happened.

When the Danish Jews came, we frequently hosted guests at our house. This was the first time in my life that I saw corn flakes. A young man, who remained in Stockholm to complete his studies after the Danish Jews left, was supervised by my parents. He received boxes of corn flakes from relatives in the United States. He sat with a big box eating his flakes, enjoying the taste. It looked to me like candy, like chips of some kind. He didn't eat it with milk, just dry out of the box. We thought of corn flakes as a tasty snack. I remember asking him if I could try some and he said no, that it was his special treat from America. I just stood there watching him, listening to the crunchy sound and observing his obvious enjoyment. Years later, while conducting tours to Spain, I met him and reminded him of this episode. Corn flakes was my introduction to American food.

The war years did not mar my childhood. My life continued as usual. I was quite unaware of the serious destruction that was happening to my Jewish brethren, to our neighboring countries and all around Europe.

During the spring and fall, I would spend time outside after school with my friends, playing hop scotch, jumping rope, playing ball or going to our beloved Bjorns Tradgard with the swings, slides, jungle gym, sandbox and the wading pool for water play.

In the winter we would go almost daily to the skating rinks in the neighborhood. They were all free of charge and we had our own skates. In the skating rink there was a little building with a fire burning so we could stop in to warm up. I loved sledding and skiing. I had my own skis and my own sled, all the things needed to keep a child happy.

Regardless of the seasons, my dearest, most important treasure was my beautiful, shiny, red, Swedish-made Husqvarna bike. All my siblings had second-hand bikes but I begged and pleaded with my parents to get me a brand-new bike. I did not want to put it in the basement where everybody else had their bikes. My parents allowed me to keep it in the living room for the first year or two. I was constantly polishing my bike and was greatly distressed by every tiny scratch. The bike was not used just for fun and games, but also to perform errands and a means of transportation to school. All year round, the bike was a very important part of my life.

I always spent a lot of time reading, doing homework. I was a perfectionist in school, a quiet child. If there were too many erasures on the paper, I would redo the entire page. In our family, we had an extra incentive for top-notch performance, for really working hard: In Sweden there were six days of school, and we did not attend on Saturdays because our father was a Rabbi; however, we were required to obtain permission to remain home that day, and this was dependent on our school performance.

We started foreign languages already in fourth grade and our first one was German. When the war had started, our German teacher, who taught us songs and poems to enrich our understanding of the culture we were studying, told us that we were no longer going to sing the song that we usually sang, "Deutschland, Deutschland uber alles" (Germany, Germany above all). I didn't understand why, but if that was the instruction, I simply accepted it.

After the war I never wanted to hear German or speak German and when I heard that language, I just froze and felt uncomfortable after all that had happened. My parents, much like the parents of the other children in my class, I'm sure, did not get us involved in any of the worries and concerns that had to do with World War II. Obviously we had newspapers at home every day. My father would anxiously ask my brother Mendel to carefully share the news with him. After all, Swedish was a new language for him and he wanted to clearly comprehend all the details of the events of the war. I would read the headlines, but none of it had much meaning for me. I didn't understand what war was all about.

In school we were taught hobbies: knitting, sewing, embroidery and crafts, so we always had activities to occupy ourselves at home, in our spare time. Thinking back upon that time, I recall a carefree childhood. Life was normal, filled with games and purposeful activities.

Mendel, my oldest brother, who was about nineteen years old at the time, was very concerned with the situation. He was a very great artist. He never attended art school, but had a natural talent. I remember his set of charcoal drawings that portrayed anguish; tortured figures on a gray background. He was keenly aware of what was going on. He spoke a lot to my father about the situation and expressed it in his art.

My mother felt literally unable to look at the paintings. They were so well done, so powerful and striking, that she could not tolerate them, and one day she simply pulled them off the wall and tore them up. That was very out of character for her, but it caused her great unhappiness to see those pictures. This upset my brother a great deal and afterward, he was no longer interested in creating art.

The Jews that came from Denmark had no tales of horror. They were saved before anything had happened to them. The Jewish population in Norway suffered great losses. Those that escaped by a dangerous, hazardous trek across the border, through the forests separating Norway and Sweden, were only aware of the difficulties of the resettling as refugees in a new location. Of the one thousand five hundred Jews – the total Jewish population of Norway – fifty percent were rounded up, placed on boats and taken to concentration camps. After the war fewer than thirty Jews from that group returned.

My father was deeply concerned, but faced a difficult dilemma. We were not yet citizens and having the status of an alien was a very precarious situation. He could not jeopardize his possibility of procuring citizenship papers. Becoming Swedish citizens was very valuable, particularly in those days, protecting our lives and providing safety.

My father had grown up in Russia during the Stalin era. He was very uncomfortable, almost panicky about dealing with authorities. Every six months he had to go to a government office to report our whereabouts. That was the rule of the country, to know the whereabouts of all non-citizens. He was tense every time he had to file that report.

My brother Mendel found out that he could save the lives of young women by marrying them, for then they were placed under the protection of the Swedish crown. He married several women from Holland, just paper marriages, and when they were safe, he immediately divorced them. One of the women, Anna Orgel, actually came to Sweden. Of course he gave her a divorce immediately. Unfortunately, Anna came with an advanced case of tuberculosis and after several months, she died. She was probably no more than twenty-two years old.

The day we received the citizenship papers, there was very joyous celebration in our home. My father felt relieved, secure and safe in this new position. He became actively involved in assisting Yeshiva boys traveling from Poland to Japan. Chiune Sugihara, the Japanese ambassador in Lithuania, issued passes so that these young men could travel via Kobe to Shanghai, where they were saved during the war.

America supplied the funds for these Yeshiva boys. Because America was at war with Japan, money could not be sent from the United States My father, living in neutral Sweden, transferred the money so that it arrived safely in Japan. He also became involved in supplying individuals, the fortunate ones, with visas to go to South America via South American Embassies that had offices in Sweden: Dominican Republic, Cuba, Costa Rica and others.

In April,1945, two weeks before the war was over, the White Buses arrived in Sweden. Count Folke Bernadotte, grandson of King Oscar II, vice president of the Swedish Red Cross, was very actively involved. Concerned about political prisoners of the Scandinavian countries in concentration camps, he supplied them with food packages and negotiated their release, which involved bringing them to safety with the White Buses.

Sweden opened its doors and let in thousands of survivors. When they came to Sweden, they were placed in what we call Displaced Persons' camps, for rehabilitation. These were actually large buildings that had been used for dormitories, hotels or hospitals that were no longer in use. There were a large number of similar places throughout Sweden to accommodate the thousands that continued coming after the war was over. There were many Displaced Persons camps throughout Sweden to accommodate the thousands of survivors.

That country played a pivotal role in assisting with the rehabilitation. My brother Mendel became deeply involved in helping these young survivors. He would go to the camps to visit them, to socialize with them and encourage them. He organized meetings between the men and the women who were in separate camps so they would have an opportunity to see each other. Many marriages subsequently took place here in Sweden.

I remember one beautiful summer day when he invited me to go with him on a bike trip. That was always very exciting, to have my older brother spend time with me. He brought me to one of these camps to visit the people. I had no idea what I would encounter. It was an overwhelming experience. The women were bald because the Germans had shaved their heads in order to dehumanize them. The Germans attempted to remove their dignity and beauty, to make the prisoners feel uncomfortable with their very existence. Emaciated, almost skeletal, most of them were young, only in their twenties, but they looked old. Weak, they clung to the walls, leaning up against the sides for balance, sad and forlorn.

When I came in, they all stared at me, these women from Poland, Hungary, Czechoslovakia, France and Romania. They spoke Yiddish, their common language, but when they were together with people from their own country, of course, they would speak in their native language. I knew Yiddish from my home.

I overheard them saying to each other, "That's strange. She looks like a Jewish child." And so I responded in Yiddish, "Yes, I am a Jewish girl." And then there was an outburst of hysterical screaming and crying. People could not believe that there were any Jewish children alive. Their experiences had been so horrific, they could not envision that a mere hour's plane ride from where they had undergone hell, there had been a country where people had lived normal lives, safe and secure. So extreme a contrast, it was difficult for them to absorb it.

I was quite frightened by all this. My brother Mendel was pleased that I had come along. Eventually he met a very beautiful young woman at one of the camps. Her name was Sarah Einhorn and she became my sister-in-law. Sarah had a friend, Yenti Ganz, whom she knew from her home town. They had reunited in the camp, in Auschwitz.

During Sarah's engagement, she introduced Yenti to my brother Shalom, and eventually they married. Yenti describes how, upon her arrival in Auschwitz, she noticed Sarah walking in the yard. "Even in a prison uniform, in those miserable conditions, Sarah carried herself like a queen," she told me. "She still looked beautiful."

My parents accepted Sarah fully and she became an integral part of our family. She loved my parents, especially my father. There was always an aura of happiness about her. She would tell stories from the camps that were inspirational, that demonstrated the love and caring of the *Lager Schwester*, sisters from the camps, how they would help and protect each other.

Sarah was very strong in her religious beliefs. She said that in the camps, they would find a match and strike it so that they could say the prayer for Friday night, to remember that Shabbat was coming. They would trade recipes and speak about the delicious foods their mothers had made at home to take their minds off the starvation. For a few moments, they were back home in their thoughts and just thinking about the food would make them happy. It gave them hope and encouragement that some day, normal life could resume again.

Their wedding was at our home on Katarina Vastra Kyrkogatan. It was a very emotional event, with my father performing the ceremony. Mendel was the first child in our home to marry. Thinking about the experiences that had led Sarah to our home in Sweden, the tragic events that had taken place in her life, created a special atmosphere at this wedding.

The chuppah was placed in the dining room and all the furniture had been moved away to make place for long tables, so the wedding guests could be seated for a festive dinner. Two women came to help my mother cook because all the food had to be kosher and there were no caterers or restaurant services in Sweden. Our sleep-in maid was also a big help for special events like this.

A trousseau was prepared for Sarah's wedding and Yenti was asked to come to our house to prepare beautiful pillowcases, quilt covers and linen. Yenti was skilled in sewing and embroidery, her hobby from her home in Hungary. Now it became her livelihood. She was a proficient seamstress, adept at any activity that involved handiwork. My mother would view her masterful work and with great admiration, she would say, "Hands of gold, *goldene hent.*" My parents became acquainted with Yenti before she met my brother Shalom and became my other sister-in-law.

Sarah and Yenti reacted very differently toward becoming members of our family. Sarah was happy, excited and enthusiastic. She quickly integrated and became part of our family. When Yenti came to us for Friday night dinners in Boston, she was rather quiet. One time, she actually told me she found it difficult to join in gatherings for Shabbat and holiday meals. It made her sad. I was quite upset by her remarks because we loved her and thought she loved us. She explained that she was happy to be part of our family but at the same time, it reminded her of what she had lost, of home and family that she would never see again.

The only survivor of her entire family was her sister Miriam. One day, in Boston, years after the Holocaust, they sat down to recall all the family members they had lost in the Holocaust – aunts, uncles, nieces, nephews, cousins, in-laws, extended family on both sides – and when they had reached one hundred fifty-four they were totally drained and exhausted. Miriam and Yenti were the only survivors from that Ganz family.

Yenti related that on her first visit to Stockholm, on Rosh Hashanah, she came to my father's synagogue with several young women from her Displaced Persons' camp. "I remember coming out of the synagogue and noting your sister Leya happily conversing with her friends, socializing, laughing, having a carefree, wonderful time, her beautiful, wavy, brown hair flying in the slight breeze. I then realized that the carefree joy of youth had all been taken away from me, that my experiences in the camps had changed me forever. Never again would I have that zest for life, that joy, because the Germans had forever deprived me and taken that part of youth away from me."

During the war, Sweden brought in Kindertransports from Germany. Those children were fortunate, but their experiences in Sweden were beset with many difficulties. There weren't enough Jewish homes to receive the children, so oftentimes, they were placed in non-Jewish homes. They stayed with strangers and were often taken advantage of with household tasks, babysitting and errands.

The adjustment period for these young teenagers away from home, having to fend for themselves, was not easy. Often, close friendships were formed, as they had been lonely and finding each other gave them great reassurance. I remember in particular Rita and Fred, who decided that when they would get a little older, they would get married.

After the war, their parents reappeared. Rita's family immigrated to the United States and insisted she join them to be reunited. She had to separate from the close friends she'd made and start life all over again. Fred's mother joined him in Sweden and eventually they made *aliyah*, immigrated to Israel. The marriage plans for Fred and Rita never materialized. Once again they were confronted with a major readjustment in life, a great life change. The first blossoming of young love, to end with the geographic separation – that was very sad. They had been forced to leave the security of their homes and build new lives in a strange country. And after being on their own, they now had to readjust to become members of their families again.

Those life experiences, as these adolescents were forced to readjust to many different situations, must have been very traumatic. Yet, Jewish people live with hope. We have an indomitable spirit, a zest for life. As soon as the young men and women had regained some of their strength in the DP camps, their first thought was marriage and starting a new family. They wanted children to name after dear lost ones. They wanted to rebuild their lives and have a home and family, to enjoy the security of being part of a family once again.

Many weddings took place at this time. The birth rate among the survivors was the highest the Jews had experienced in many centuries. This was in and of itself a beautiful testimonial to the resurgence of life, of hope reborn. Hitler had caused havoc in the Jewish world. He had separated families, broken apart communities, and the most important nucleus of Jewish life, home and family.

In the Displaced Persons' camps, people had no idea if there were any survivors from their communities: spouses, relatives, siblings or friends. They felt adrift on an endless ocean, isolated and alone, longing for some verification of their past. A newsletter was published on a weekly basis listing the survivors by name, date of birth and place of origin. These sheets were circulated in all the DP camps, not only in Sweden but in the American and British zones in the center of Europe and every place where survivors were gathered. In that way, spouses could reconnect and siblings, relatives and friends from the same community could find each other.

When the papers were distributed in the camps, everyone eagerly stretched forth his hand to scan the names. They were tense, filled with emotion as they were searching for something familiar to appear. If they were successful, tears of joy and screams of excitement could be heard everywhere. Once again they were able to know where they belonged in the world. With superhuman effort, they embraced life and worked toward a goal, to once again have a normal life situation.

From 1945 till 1952, displaced persons attempted with great difficulty to go to the country of their choice to begin a new life, find a job and rejoin the human race. It is a very sad chapter in world history that these survivors, who had been through a living hell, the worst experiences ever visited upon mankind, had to wait for years until roads would open up for them, to clear obstacles, to restart a normal life.

My childhood memories are filled with the sorrowful tales of the survivors. The aftermath of WWII was an abrupt ending of my childhood. Listening to the anguished words of the survivors impacted sharply on my life. They needed to unburden themselves and would speak endlessly about their war experiences, but no one could endure the tales of unspeakable nightmarish experiences. The uncomfortable listeners would interrupt the speakers and attempt to change the subject or offer a glass of tea and cake. This was followed by decades of silence. Today, we are witnessing a great outpouring of literature, music, art and drama focusing on the horrors of Nazism.

May we Never Again experience such sorrow.

CHAPTER 5

Scandinavia - A Different World

Overview

In the northernmost part of Europe, the Scandinavian Peninsula stretches forth like a lion, with the kingdom of Norway as the head, and the kingdom of Sweden the extended paw. South of Scandinavia, extending from the mainland of Europe, is the peninsula of Jutland. East of Jutland is the island of Sjælland (known in English as Zealand or Sealand), the site of Copenhagen. Together these areas comprise the kingdom of Denmark. The term "Scandinavia" basically refers to these three kingdoms.

The term "Nordic Countries" includes Finland, which belonged to Sweden for several hundred years before it became an independent republic, as it still is today. Iceland and the Faroe Islands used to belong to Denmark; in 1944, with Denmark under German occupation, Iceland seceded and, after achieving independence, was promptly occupied by the United States, who established a NATO base in Keflavik. This was of strategic importance, done to protect the North Atlantic from German submarines and secure the waterways to Murmansk, Russia. The U.S. base at Keflavik was closed in 2008. The Faeroe Islands still belong to Denmark. Greenland, the largest island in the world, is also a Danish province.

Finland and Norway are approximately the same size as Poland; however, Poland's population is eight times as large as the population of these countries. Sweden, the fourth largest country of Europe, has a population density – the term that refers to the number of people per square mile – of eighteen. Iceland's population density is two, Finland's, fifteen and Norway's twelve. In Denmark, the population density is one hundred nineteen.

Finland, the most eastern of all the Scandinavian countries, borders Russia on the east and is separated from Sweden by the Gulf of Bothnia. On the west, Sweden borders Norway. The entire northern part of Norway, Sweden, Finland and Russia, above the Arctic Circle, is called Lapland. This is the country of the Lapps or Samis, historically a nomadic people who traveled with their herds of reindeer.

The Lapps, visibly different from Scandinavian, shorter and dark haired, are probably related to Eskimos or tribes from Central Asia. This part of the world has twenty-four hours of daylight during the two summer months and total darkness in the winter. Some tribes were fishermen and some were farmers. This entire northernmost region is rich in natural resources, with the area of Gallivare, in particular – located in Sweden near the Finnish border – well known for its production of iron.

The languages of Sweden, Norway and Denmark are in the Germanic group of the Indo-European family, related to English and German. The Finnish language belongs to the Uralic-Altaic group related to Hungarian, Turkish, Mongul and Manchu, a totally different language category. A tribal dialect, Finnish may have originated in the Ural Mountain Region.

Finland

Finland, the Land of Lakes, belonged to Sweden for 600 years. In 1809, at the end of the Napoleonic Wars, Sweden surrendered Finland to Russia. From 1809 until 1917, Finland was a Grand Duchy of Russia. Finland became independent in 1917 and has remained a republic ever since. In the Winter War of 1938–39, Finland lost the city of Viborg to Russia; that area was never returned.

Finland borders Russia on the east, the Gulf of Bothnia on the west, Norway on the north and the Gulf of Finland, which extends to St. Petersburg, on the south. South of the Gulf of Finland are the Baltic States: Estonia, Latvia and Lithuania, strategically located, bordering the Baltic Sea. Estonia was once a possession of Sweden. Many wars were fought over these countries, due to their importance in commerce during the time of the Hanseatic League.

The Finnish personality differs from that of their Scandinavian neighbors; Finns tend to be brooding, gloomy, inward and moody. Finns go to great lengths to attend social dances. Yet, though they enjoy dancing, the socializing that usually accompanies this activity is distinctly absent. The sauna is an essential part of Finnish life and many private homes have saunas, in addition to the numerous public ones.

The Jewish population lives mainly in Helsinki, with a minority in Turku, a city geographically closer to Sweden. The total number of Jews in Finland never exceeded 1,400. After the war it remained unchanged.

Jewish life in Finland traces its beginning to the era of Czar Nicholas, who yearned to unify Russia in a process called Russification.. Young Jewish boys were seized from their homes by chappers during his reign.

The children were forced to participate in the Russian army for twenty-five years, in the hope that they would become so indoctrinated with love for mother Russia that they would never return to their Jewish way of life. But Jews are a very stubborn people! At the end of twenty-five years, many young men still remembered their Jewish roots and strove to settle as far away from "mother Russia" as possible, to begin a new life where they could embrace their Jewish values. Finland became inhabited by these Cantonists. The cemetery outside Helsinki houses gravestones embossed with magnificent Hebrew writing and Jewish names, a testament to their love and attachment to Judaism.

The history of Finland during World War II is fascinating. Jewish soldiers fought alongside Finnish soldiers, on the side of the Germans against a common enemy, Russia. General Mannerheim, of the Finnish army, treated Jews and Finns equally. In turn, the Jewish soldiers were devoted and dedicated to him and to Finland. The veterans of World War II, close-knit and proud of their army service, proudly retell the story of a Jewish soldier from Finland who had distinguished himself in military service and was awarded the Iron Cross, a great honor for active duty of the highest degree. When this Jewish soldier was summoned to the tent of the German officers to receive the award, he told them, in beautiful Yiddish, "*Ich darf das nicht,*" I don't need this. "*Ich bin ein Jude.*" I am a Jew.

The military cemetery, part of the Jewish cemetery in Helsinki, in addition to their beautifully maintained graves, includes a special monument for soldiers who died in action, whose bodies never were recovered.

The Jews of Finland led a very active communal life. They established a school, hired a Rabbi and built a synagogue that recently celebrated its centennial. The Russian-style synagogue, with its onion dome, used to be visible from afar. Nowadays, the SAS Radisson Hotel obscures the view. Located on Malminkatu, the synagogue, school and old age home are adjacent to each other and surround an inner courtyard. It is pleasant for the seniors to sit outside, watching the children at play or the people coming to shul. Recently, a Chabad Rabbi moved to the area to revive and invigorate the Jewish community.

Many Finnish Jewish children were sent to Sweden for safekeeping during World War II, while most Finnish Jews remained in their homes in Finland. Though they did suffer typical deprivations, they were never deported to concentration camps because they were fighting on Germany's side.

Sweden

Sweden, the largest of the Scandinavian countries, is the fourth largest country in Europe. The USSR, the largest by far, is followed by France, Spain and then Sweden in fourth place. Sweden is roughly ten percent larger than the state of California. A third of Sweden extends beyond the Arctic Circle, with no daylight during the winter, virtually uninhabitable. Sweden's rich natural resources, particularly iron ore, protected its neutrality during World War II.

Iron ore was very much coveted by the Germans, and Sweden allowed them shipments for their war industry. The Crown Princess of Sweden at the time, Princess Sybilla, a native German, facilitated Swedish-German relations. The Queen today, Queen Silvia, is also of German descent. The King met her during the Olympic Games in Munich, Germany.

Jews came to Sweden in 1774, invited by King Gustavus III, known as the theater king. murdered while attending a theater performance. The famous Italian composer Verdi memorialized the event in the opera *The Masked Ball*.

A progressive monarch, interested in art and culture, Gustavus III established the Swedish Academy of Art, which awards the Nobel Prize of Literature every year. Alfred Nobel, a Swedish scientist, experimented with nitroglyceride and became very affluent when he invented dynamite in 1867. He patented this explosive, important because it was used to extract iron ore from the mountains. The steel industry, which was of great importance in Sweden, was revolutionized by his invention. Dynamite was effectively used in construction, mining and railroad development, yet as a negative force it brought destruction and death in warfare. Alfred Nobel, wanting to be remembered as a humanitarian, set aside funds for the purpose of awarding prizes to individuals who distinguished themselves in medicine, science, literature and economics, engaging in activities to make this world a better place. The Peace Prize is presented in Oslo, Norway and all others in Stockholm, Sweden.

Aaron Isaac, the first Jew in Sweden, was invited to come from Mecklenburg, Germany. An engraver, an important skill in those days for signet rings, seals and other important items of throne and government, Aaron Isaac agreed to come, provided he would be able to bring ten other Jewish families. The government granted his request, and with a minyan, quorum, he established the first Jewish community in Sweden.

At first, Jews were permitted to reside only in specific cities in Sweden: Stockholm, Gothenburg and Norrkoping. Their rights limited, they could not become professionals, own land or join guilds. With only a few options available, they became peddlers and eventually built department stores. The history of their economic rise is similar to that of other countries, including the United States.

Sweden limited immigration. In 1840, there were 900 Jews in Sweden. The first settlers were German-Jewish big businessmen, followed by a scattering of both Polish and Russian Jews who came in the 1920s, after the Kishinev Pogroms, a difficult period for Eastern European Jews. The restrictions worsened. During the prewar years, people were anxious to come to Sweden, but were not allowed to enter. From 1933 until 1938, three thousand Jews were admitted. One thousand Jews were allowed on transit visas. Before the war, there were 6,000 Jews within the total population of six and a half million inhabitants.

In October and November of 1942, eight hundred Norwegian Jews escaped across the border between Norway and Sweden, through the woods and mountains, and in Sweden they found a safe haven. Unfortunately, the remaining 763 Norwegian Jews were captured by the Nazis and taken to concentration camps. On November 26, 1942, the largest group was transported on the Donau ship from the Oslo harbor to Stettin, where they arrived on November 30. Then they continued to the concentration camps. In Norway's Resistance Museum at Akerhus Castle, there is a copy of the official receipt from the commandant at Auschwitz acknowledging the delivery of 532 Norweigan Jews on December 1. On February 24, 1943, another group of 158 Jews was shipped on the Gotenland ship. Only twenty-four survivors from all those captured by the Germans returned to Norway after the war. Thus, Norway lost nearly fifty percent of its Jewish population in the Holocaust.

In 1942, one hundred fifty Finnish children found refuge in Sweden during the war, eventually reuniting with their parents. A Kindertransport from Germany brought children for safekeeping to Sweden.

On April 19, 1945, a few weeks before the war's conclusion, through the Red Cross and the White Buses, with the intervention of Count Folke Bernadotte and a fascinating Jewish man named Gilel Storch, 3,500 inmates from Ravensbruck were transported to Sweden for rehabilitation. Later, an additional 4,500 came on the buses. The Danish Jews who had been interred in Thereisenstadt were also brought to Sweden on the White Buses. Among them were Chief Rabbi Max Friediger and the Dayan Josef Fisher. The group in Thereisenstadt had been fortunate to receive special care packages from the Swedish Red Cross through Folke Bernadotte, who had special permission to alleviate the difficulties of Scandinavian prisoners.

Today there are 18,000 Jews living in Sweden, several thousand descendants of the Forty-fivers, the survivors who came to Sweden from the concentration camps and remained after 1945. They did not want to leave the country that had offered refuge and accepted them. After the years of terror, they were content to live in a peaceful country, a country that had not been involved in war since Napoleonic times.

Jews arrived from Hungary in 1956, following the Communist revolution, and another group of Jews came from Poland in 1962 after the Communists changed their laws.

Today 450,000 to 500,000 Muslims live in Sweden. Muslims began entering the country forty years ago. Their presence has changed the climate considerably. The population in Sweden today is 9.5 million people, with an immigrant population of 15 percent. Pre-WWII, the immigrant population was 3 percent, with the Jewish population at 0.1 percent, one of a thousand. Today that figure is 0.2 percent.

According to Swedish government rules, the Great Synagogue on Wahrendorffsgatan, dating back to 1870, is a historical landmark and may not be altered in any way. The intricately carved wooden balustrades, banisters and pillars of imported cedar wood, the red and blue colors of the Ark evoking the Biblical description of the Temple and the ornate ceiling design contribute to creating this magnificent edifice. The forty-foot-high building seats nine hundred people. On the eastern wall, which faces a courtyard, is a magnificent Rose Window with a six-petal flower in white and deep blue. The length of the building faces the street, with the main entrance on the left side. There is a balcony for women upstairs, but during the past ten years, an additional area for women was set aside downstairs. Services, truly a spectacle, are accompanied by a choir and organ.

Along the back wall of the synagogue's courtyard, is a forty-two-meter memorial wall, inscribed with 8,500 names of people who perished in the Holocaust. Their relatives who were living in Sweden submitted the names. Lacking a gravesite, this wall, completed in 1997, memorializes them. King of Sweden at that time, Charles XVI Gustav, attended the dedication of the memorial wall, an impressive Holocaust memorial.

People place stones in remembrance of the victims of the Holocaust on a ledge along the bottom. The wall includes the name of the person, place of origin, year of birth and, if known, place of death. They are listed in groups, according to the concentration camp in which they perished.

There is a separate section for those people who arrived so debilitated that they could not survive and actually died in Sweden. The archive of the synagogue displays a tattered notebook with a brownish cover. In that book are the identities of the aforementioned Forty-fivers, listed by name, city of origin, the name of the concentration camp and family members' names. Lost relatives could be traced through this book.

On a pedestal, in the garden outside the synagogue, stands the statue Flight of Torah by the famous Swedish sculptor Willy Gordon, born in Courland, Latvia. A man in flight, his arms encircle the Torah, his most important possession. The sculpture is an expression of gratitude from the Jews of Denmark for their rescue, through the Danish underground, to a safe haven in Sweden, where they could continue to experience Jewish life undisturbed.

Willy Gordon and his father were among the people who greeted the Jews that were rescued on the Danish fishing boats. His father, who had served as a cantor in Helsingborg and later in Malmo, conducted services on Yom Kippur that very year, 1943, right after the rescue, at the synagogue in Malmo – a very emotional experience.

Near the synagogue is Nybroplan, a place at the harbor where the fashionable street Birger Jarlsgatan, with its beautiful boutiques, meets Strandvagen, the most exclusive street in Stockholm, which runs alongside the water. In this area, renamed Raoul Wallenberg Plaza, is a sculpture group dedicated to Raoul Wallenberg, the Swedish diplomat who was sent to Hungary toward the end of the war. He was there for only a six-month period from July 9, 1944 until January 17, 1945, when he mysteriously disappeared and was never again heard from. During his short time in Hungary, he saved between thirty- and sixty-thousand Jews by giving them a *Schutz-Pass* – a protective passport – and by establishing Swedish "safety houses": thirty-two buildings where up to 10,000 people were saved at various times. Three hundred fifty people were involved in this operation.

In a contest to find the best sculptor to prepare a fitting memorial for Wallenberg, Kerstin Ortwed from Denmark was awarded the honor. In 2001, the completed sculpture was dedicated in the marketplace area. The monument consists of twelve separate sculptures spread along the ground, and symbolizes people rising from concrete – individuals rescued by Raoul Wallenberg, from death. The figures are abstract and evoke minimal emotion. Wallenberg's signature in patinated bronze, spread among the sculpture group, gives meaning to this scene. The dedication was attended by King Charles XVI Gustav and Koffi Annan, married to the niece of Raoul Wallenberg.

In April 2006, an impressive memorial dedicated to Raoul Wallenberg was placed in Lidingo, a suburb of Stockholm, where he was born. The artistic sculpture by Willy Gordon portrays a headless man standing erect, high up on a small hill, hands behind his back, holding a safety pass, a Schutz-Pass. On the safety pass, one can see the three crowns, the symbol of the government of Sweden. The headless statue connotes a man who, guided by his heart, allowed his emotions to dictate his actions.

Between the synagogue and the memorial at Nybroplan, a large globe pays tribute to Aaron Isaac, the survivors of the Holocaust and the Jews who found freedom in Sweden. The phrase "Never Again" is prominently displayed in Swedish, Hungarian, Yiddish, German and Hebrew on the surface of the globe. The walkway leading from the Great Synagogue on Wahrendorffsgatan past the globe to the memorial for Raoul Wallenberg is called The Aaron Isaac Walkway.

Stockholm's oldest synagogue was located in Gamla Stan, The Old City, on Sjalgardsgatan 19, at Tyska Brunnsplan. Originally an auction house, it was rented from 1795 until 1821, when it was purchased. It served as a synagogue until 1870 and then became a police station. Today there is no sign to indicate that this once was a synagogue.

There are currently two Orthodox synagogues in Stockholm with daily services. Adas Yisroel, on Sankt Paulsgatan 13 in Sodermalm, is located inconspicuously, amidst an entire block of apartment buildings. A short flight of stairs leads up to a nondescript white door with no indication that this is a synagogue. One enters a small hall where the restrooms are located as well as the stairs leading to the women's balcony. This small hall leads into a larger room with a coat rack, a small refrigerator and a kitchen area on the side. There are chairs and a table in the center of this room, and here, the members share a daily breakfast after morning services.

One walks through the room, opens the large doors and, the first time, the visitor is overwhelmed. This beautiful synagogue, more than one hundred years old, is in very good condition. The oversized windows are set into deep frames. When I was a child, there were lovely blue wildflowers painted inside the frames, encircling the windows. Unfortunately, they disappeared when the shul was renovated. There is a carpet on the floor near the Bimah, with the original brass fence surrounding this area. The blue dome, held up by heavy white columns, stands on a platform in front of the *Aron Kodesh*. There is a pulpit, near the surrounding fence, where my father, Rabbi Zuber, would dramatically adjust his *Tallit* before beginning his eloquent speeches. The furniture for the shul, including the benches upstairs in the women's balcony, was purchased from Kibbutz Lavi. The majority of current members are from Eastern Europe, many of them Holocaust survivors.

The second Orthodox shul, the Adas Yeshurun, was brought from Germany, from the Heinrich Barthstraze Shul of Rabbi Carlebach in Hamburg. The shul's furnishings were dismantled and the boards were sent to Sweden in 1939, in the presence of the Gestapo. Placed in an apartment building on Biblioteksgatan on the island of Norrmalm, it was arranged exactly as it had been in Germany. The shul was housed among the tenants of the building: lawyers, doctors and businessmen. A large room was reserved for the men, a smaller area for the women, a kitchen and dining room for *Kiddush* plus an entrance hall and coat room. It was very private, known only to the initiated. The Aron Kodesh, the *ner tamid* and all the original pews are still in use today.

After the boards were carefully reassembled, it was a great surprise to discover that underneath the camouflage of plain brown paint, the pews had beautiful hand-painted designs. This is one of the only synagogues from Germany still in existence. The shul was relocated to Nybrogatan, across the street from the Jewish Center. When a school of the aristocracy on Riddargatan was purchased by the Jewish community, the shul once again was moved and relocated to the top floor, with one of the few Shabbat elevators in Scandinavia. The lower floors are occupied by the Hillel School, the Jewish school in Stockholm.

Sweden was neutral during World War II. This small country extended itself to help the poor Jewish survivors at the end of the war and afterward. Some criticize Sweden's shortcomings, but if one compares Sweden to the United States, a country twenty times its size, Sweden undoubtedly played a significant role and should be remembered.

It is tragically true that FDR could have saved countless lives by bombing railroad tracks that facilitated the deportation of thousands of unfortunate Jews. There was the incident with the passenger ship St. Louis, which sailed from Hamburg, Germany in 1939 with 936 passengers. The ship was bound for Cuba, but upon arrival, Cuba refused them entrance. Their visas were supposedly not acceptable. Hitler had said that if the ship returned, the passengers would be brought to concentration camps. Jews from all over the world protested this outrage and begged the president to allow this unfortunate group to find asylum in the us. They were refused. They passed Miami and saw the lights, but were not allowed to dock. Four countries in Europe offered help, so the passengers went to France, England, Belgium and Holland. Hitler was very pleased because he now could show that Jews were not desired in most European countries.

A group of Orthodox Rabbis, 400 to 500 of them, came to Washington on October 6, 1943, three days before Yom Kippur, to seek an audience with the president, but unfortunately he never met with them. FDR left the White House through a rear door to avoid meeting them. Rabbi Stephen Wise from New York was against this protest march as he was concerned about arousing feelings of anti-Semitism in America.

Buried by The Times, by Laurel Leff, demonstrated the miniscule attention given in the *New York Times* to the destruction of European Jewry during the Holocaust era. This was never headline news. There were small news items, maybe an eighth of a column on page twenty-four or thirty, stating that thousands had been transported from ghettos to concentration camps. Only those with great interest in the plight of the Jews would be cognizant of the enormous tragedy. And the Jewish people in America thought of FDR as a best friend; many had photos of him proudly displayed in their homes.

In the aftermath of WWII, the situation was likewise bleak. General George Patton of the US reported from the American Sector in Europe that the survivors were sub-human. Of course that is how they appeared – starved, in prison clothing, unkempt. He stated they had to be kept behind bars and not be allowed to walk around freely. In his diary, the description of Jews was demeaning. He was, however, compassionate to and concerned about the German civilians.

Large numbers of survivors remained in DP camps in Europe from 1945 until 1954 because they had no place to go. The road to America was beset with problems of immigration restrictions/quotas and visas. The British did not allow Jews to enter Palestine, as the State of Israel had not yet been established. Sweden certainly stands out as one place that offered rehabilitation for survivors with a wide, welcoming door at the end of World War II.

The United States was not especially generous with its immigration policy. From 1933 to 1942, 175,000 Jews were permitted entry. From March 1938 to September 1939, there were 120,000 applicants, out of which 85,000 were admitted. In late 1938, there were 125,000 applicants. The quota only allowed 27,000. In June 1939, there were 300,000 applicants, but hardly any immigrants.

Between Pearl Harbor and the end of the war, ten percent of the revised quota of twenty-one thousand was admitted. At one point, 70,000 Jews could have been rescued, but the United States brushed aside the offer. In 1943, Sweden offered to accept 20,000 children from Nazi-occupied countries, provided that the United States and Britain would cover the cost – the infamous Wagner Rogers Bill. The United States flatly refused.

The United States allowed a miniscule 1,000 people to Fort Ontario, Oswego, NY in August 1944. There, they remained in army barracks until January 1946. Out of a total of 140,000 survivors, 35,000 came to the United States.

The Abandonment of the Jews: America and the Holocaust, by David S. Wyman, published by Pantheum, reveal United States' failure to facilitate Jewish immigration during those crucial years between 1941 and 1945. At the Bermuda Conference in April 1942, with Roosevelt and Churchill attending, there was no effort to welcome people who tried to escape the horrific situation in Europe. Shanghai admitted 17,000. Bolivia, between 1938 and 1941, admitted 20,000. The Dominican Republic extended a warm welcome to Jews, but only a small number accepted the offer.

The White Paper in 1939 severely limited immigration to Palestine, not yet Israel, to 75,000 in five years. In 1940, the tragic situation with the ship Patria occurred; two hundred people died and eventually the ship was blown up. The year 1942 marked the tragedy of the ship The Sturmer. At the end of the war, the limitation on immigration was 1,500 people per month. The tragedy of the Exodus occurred in the summer of 1947, with the ship returning to Europe, back to the DP camps. The ship never even reached Cyprus, the island where many ships were detained in the British blockade, because the British would not allow entrance to Palestine.

Sweden had dealings with Germany during the war. An investigation exposed the transfer of thirty-eight tons of Nazi gold, equal to $430 million. Sweden also supplied Germany with paper, wood and iron ore. On one occasion, SS soldiers were allowed to cross Sweden from Norway so that they could return to Germany for furlough, a black page in Sweden's history. A major betrayal of the brotherhood of the Scandinavian countries, this ugly incident was long remembered.

The accomplishments of Sweden, in providing refuge for the remnants of the Jewish population after the Holocaust, are overwhelming. Today, Sweden is a pioneer in Holocaust education. Living History, a government-sponsored educational program initiated by the Prime Minister, Goran Persson, in 1997 aims at educating Swedes about anti-Semitism. They published *Tell it to Your Children*, a book delivered gratis to every household in Sweden, and translated into different languages to educate minority group members. This book recaps the horrors of World War II and encourages the movement to be human, to fight racism, so that these tragic events should never be repeated. More than a million copies have been distributed.

Uppsalla University, one of the oldest universities in Sweden, possibly in the world, has a website with a section on Holocaust studies, as well as an Institute of Holocaust and Genocide Studies. In 1998, they hosted an International Holocaust Conference.

In January 2000, Sweden hosted an international forum on the Holocaust with forty-five heads of state in attendance. Subsequently, in 2001, they developed Paideia, the European Institute of Jewish Studies in Sweden, which focuses on Holocaust education and Jewish revival. The institute offers a one-year program of studies and participants from all over the world are welcome. The program emphasizes the reawakening of an interest in Jewish culture and heritage, a response to what was lost in the Shoah.

Norway

The most western of the Scandinavian countries, Norway borders Sweden on the east and the North Sea on the west. Shaped like a spoon, the largest portion of the population live in the bowl, with the handle extending upward all the way to the North Sea. The majority of the population of Norway live in the southern part of the country, one third of the total area. The entire west coast of Norway is cut up into deep, long fjords, inlets of water that extend as far as 120 kilometers. Sogne or Hardanger fjords and their tributaries are the most frequently visited fjords in Norway.

Norwegians were known as sea-faring people. This was the country of the Vikings because almost everywhere in Norway, one is in close proximity to a waterway. There is a scant amount of land suitable for agriculture, though the valleys between the mountains are very fertile and have superb growing conditions, an abundance of grains, vegetables and fruit orchards. The Hardanger area is beautiful in the spring when the apple trees are in bloom.

During the summertime, when the days are very long, the additional amounts of light and heat is absorbed into the mountains, then reflected back into the valleys, providing optimum growing conditions. In addition, there is plenty of rainfall. Winds come in from the west – from the North Sea – cross over the mountains and bring the rain. Norway has a large wood industry, which is comprised mainly of paper production, construction of prefabricated houses and ship building.

The mountains themselves are another important natural resource, rich in minerals and semi-precious stones. Production of aluminum is important in Norway. Once a poor country, it has become one of the richest of the world since the discovery of oil under the Atlantic Ocean. The economic growth of Norway has been phenomenal since then.

Norway is very popular among tourists because of its scenic beauty: the fjords, mountains and glaciers. Tourism is one of the most important industries in this country.

Jews were not admitted to Norway until the 1850s. Henrik Vergeland, an author, praised the Jews and stated that he could not understand why these honest, hard-working people should not be allowed residence in Norway. As a result of his writings, Norway allowed Jews to enter, but nobody was anxious to immigrate because this country was far from mainstream Europe.

In 1875, there were only twenty-five Jews living in Norway. There was never a huge influx of Jews who rushed to immigrate to this cold, faraway country. The small Jewish population never exceeded 1,400.

During World War II, fifty percent of this miniscule population was rounded up by the Nazis – who had occupied Norway – and were taken to concentration camps. Sadly enough, only a handful returned.

Norway's strategic location was of great importance during World War II. From the west coast of Norway, one could easily reach Great Britain. The

Germans were interested in the heavy water produced at a plant in Vemork, in northern Norway. Heavy water was of value for nuclear energy projects. Members of the Norwegian Resistance, in a series of actions, destroyed this plant to prevent atomic warfare. Norway had the second-largest merchant marine corps during World War II, which was important for the Allies.

Germany invaded Norway in 1940. Quisling, leader of the Norwegian Fascist Party, was considered a traitor by the majority of Norwegians. There were few Nazi sympathizers and the Resistance movement was strong and powerful with many highly courageous people. Many lives were lost in the battles, property was destroyed and there were severe shortages of food and basic necessities. The Norwegians fought a valiant battle at Narvik, but experienced heavy losses.

On the grounds of the Akerhus Castle in Oslo stands Norway's Resistance Museum. The persecution of the Jews is powerfully presented in this museum. There is an interesting petition signed by nearly all Norwegian clergy to protest the persecution of the Jews. It eloquently states that the Jews have been good citizens and should not be discriminated against because of their religion. The exhibit about the Norwegian teachers refusing to indoctrinate their students with Nazi ideology is well displayed.

Nearby is the memorial for patriots of the Norwegian underground who were executed on that spot. King Haakon fled to England while the fighting continued. Several concentration camps were established in Norway and nine thousand Norwegians were sent to German prison camps.

At the harbor in downtown Oslo, where ships transported unfortunate Jews to the concentration camps, a memorial to the Holocaust has been established with empty chairs signifying that the citizens who were taken away left a void in the country.

There is a small synagogue in Oslo on Bergstien, near Waldemar Thranes Gate, which was built in 1920. The Jewish community is referred to as Det Mosaiska Trossamfund, meaning people of the Mosaic Faith. One of the synagogue walls was made into a Holocaust Monument, for those lost during the war. The wall is divided into two sections: the upper part is filled with approximately 700 dots, each signifying a Norwegian Jew who was sent to a concentration camp and never returned. The lower part commemorates those that escaped to Sweden or managed to escape the roundup. The divided wall is a visual representation of the community sliced in half.

Norwegian Jews who returned from Sweden, where they had experienced sanctuary during the war, reestablished themselves. The government regretted what had happened to the Jews of their country and invited 500 displaced persons to come to their country, people who, for medical reasons, had nowhere else to go. The climate in Norway was especially salubrious for those with tuberculosis, a very common, and oftentimes fatal, disease among the survivors. The survivors were offered free treatment, transportation, housing and jobs and the opportunity to become citizens in half the time, five years instead of ten. However, very few people took advantage of the invitation.

There has been a large immigration to Israel from all the Scandinavian countries. Trygve Lee of Norway, the first Secretary General to the United Nations, was very actively involved in helping Israel become an independent country.

The Norway-Israel Association was formed to forge good relations between Norway and Israel. In 1949, this organization invited a group of children from Tunisia to come to Israel on "Youth Aliyah," stopping first in Norway for eight months for rehabilitation. Unfortunately, the Dutch aircraft crashed en route leaving only one child who survived. The Norwegian people collected money and, in memory of this tragic incident, established Kibbutz Norway in Israel for North American immigrants. Outside Oslo, the Norwegian Boy Scouts also established a Jewish Memorial Park.

The synagogue in Norway is active. Rabbi Michael Melchior, son of Chief Rabbi Bent Melchior of Denmark, was the Rabbi for a number of years. He instituted an interesting concept to encourage attendance at the synagogue. At the end of services, the young children in the congregation, those too young to walk, carried by their fathers, line up to sing the last part of the services. They stand in front of the Aron Kodesh, the Ark where the Torah Scrolls are housed, up a tall staircase, at the front of the synagogue.

The parents became so enthusiastic about the participation of their children, seeing them high up on the platform outside the Ark, that they started to attend the services more frequently. With reparation money from Germany and help from the Norwegian government, extensive repairs have been made to the Jewish Center quarters, in the complex where the synagogue is located. To the left of the synagogue is a beautiful old age home where the elderly people live, adjacent to the synagogue so that they can see the congregants coming in and out of services.

A second congregation, one of the northernmost in the entire world, existed in Trondheim. That congregation was established in 1905. Rabbi Samuel, leader of that congregation, was captured by the Germans and sent to a concentration camp. He never returned. After the war, Rabbi Fruchter officiated in Trondheim until he immigrated to the United States.

During the past few years, a Chabad house has been established in Norway. Rabbi Shaul Wilhelm, using the internet, actively seeks out Jewish people who live isolated in small towns or in mountainous areas. He arranges activities for Jewish holidays: a Passover Seder, a Lag B'Omer outing, a Purim masquerade, a Shavuos ice cream party or a Chanuka menorah lighting to connect estranged Jews to their Jewish heritage.

Denmark

Denmark, the smallest of the Scandinavian countries, is the only one of the Scandinavian countries that borders on the mainland of Europe. This is the area of Schleswig-Holstein, which is mainly German, with the most northern part belonging to Denmark. The largest part of Denmark in terms of area is the peninsula of Jutland. The most populous part is the island of Sjælland, where the capital city of Copenhagen is located. Denmark is the same size as the Dominican Republic, half the size of the island of Hispaniola, and approximately double the size of the State of Israel.

Denmark was the first of the Scandinavian countries that welcomed a Jewish presence, during the reign of King Christian IV in the 1620s. A capable leader, he built many of the important buildings of Denmark: the Stock Exchange, the Rosenborg Castle and the Christiansborg Castle. In the seventeenth century, he invited Jews to come from Amsterdam, Sephardi businessmen, to promote business in his country. These Jews were actually descendants of the Jews who had lived in Spain before the Expulsion.

Among the very first Jews to come to Denmark were Albertus Denis, a mint maker, and his physician and friend, Yonah Charizi. The second group of immigrants that came from Hamburg included businesspeople as well as professionals. Niels Bohr, a Nobel Prize winner famous for atomic energy research, and Victor Borge, born Borge Rosenbaum – a famous pianist, television personality and entertainer – are notable Danish Jews of the twentieth century.

Victor Borge founded the organization "Thanks to Scandinavia" to help the world remember what happened in the Scandinavian countries with regard to the Jews during World War II. This organization aims to build bridges of understanding and friendship among Jews of Scandinavia and America and Jews worldwide. The organization includes a student exchange program that provides scholarships to Scandinavian youth, enabling them to come to the United States to study, and to Americans, allowing them to attend the Niels Bohr Institute in Norway, University of Oslo, University of Copenhagen or the Aarhus University in Denmark.

Before World War II, Denmark had the most active Jewish community in all of Scandinavia. They were first to publish the Siddur (Jewish prayer book) and Chumash (the Torah) with Danish translations, and to establish a Jewish Day School. Many young Jewish Danes have left to settle in Israel.

The current main synagogue, the first one built in Scandinavia, was erected in Copenhagen in 1833 by an architect named Gustav Hetch. This synagogue – known as the White and Gold Synagogue of Krystalgade in Stroeget, the walking street area – is still a magnificent building. It is an impressive structure with very tall columns of white and gold; the wall surrounding the Ark is also white and gold, as are the large doors of the Aron Kodesh. Within this Aron Kodesh there is a breathtaking treasury of Torahs in splendid velvet covers and heavy, ornamented, embossed silver crowns.

The women's balcony, several flights up, affords a splendid view of the synagogue. The length of the building, which faces the street, is quite unimpressive. The entrance on the left side, a large door on street level, differs greatly from the prominent entrances to large houses of worship in the United States. Congregants enter through a metal security door at the far right, walk into a courtyard and then enter the building through a small, unobtrusive door.

April 9, 1940, a black day in the history of Denmark, was the day that Germany occupied Denmark in a swift tri-part invasion by air, land and sea: the Blitzkrieg. Denmark, a small, peaceful country, had no way of defending itself. Germany did not wish to fight with the Danes; they liked the Scandinavians, who personified the Aryan race: tall, blonde haired and blue eyed, the quintessential example of the ideal human, according to Hitler.

In addition, it was beneficial for Germany to maintain peaceful relations with Denmark and derive benefit from all their produce.

Denmark, known as the bread basket of Scandinavia, is extremely fertile, producing vegetables and grains, and also famed for its livestock and dairy products. King Christian X was well aware that small peace-loving Denmark was no match for Germany. Not wanting to lose brave Danes in a doomed fight, he capitulated. Therefore, they permitted King Christian X to remain as head of state and allowed the courts and parliament to continue to function; however, a German government was set up alongside the Danish one, under the auspices of Werner Best, the German Ambassador to Denmark. Life proceeded normally for the first two years; children attended school and went to services at the synagogue, no major changes occurring.

In 1941, an attempt was made to set the White and Gold Synagogue on fire, but fortunately, no major damage was done. In 1942, there was another attempt. King Christian X sent a personal letter to the Rabbi at that time, Chief Rabbi Max Frierdiger, telling him that he had heard about the attempted fire and was relieved that there was no major damage. He added wishes for a good year to the congregation. The Danes were always very accepting of the Jews and treated them fully as citizens.

Many stories circulate about King Christian X wearing the yellow star, but these are mere legends. What is true, however, is that the Jews of Denmark were never forced to wear a yellow star. The King of Denmark publicly stated that his Danish citizens would not be singled out. If Jews would be forced to wear a star, he would wear one himself – and many Danes would probably have followed him. A leader of that caliber was able to influence an entire country, to make them understand that there should be no separation between citizens, and that everyone was entitled to the same rights. His attitude made the rescue of the Jews a possibility in Denmark. King Christian X is an outstanding example of one single person making a difference.

A book of nonfiction titled *Why the Holocaust Failed in Denmark* describes the king frequently riding through the streets of Copenhagen on a horse, encouraging his subjects to have hope. No bodyguards were required, for all Danes protected him.

In October 1943, the situation in Denmark changed rapidly and the active underground intensified its sabotage efforts, destroying ships and railroad tracks and engaging in a variety of other actions to thwart German victory. The Danish landscape became riddled with strikes and riots.

On August 29, the Germans established martial law and King Christian X became a prisoner in his castle, Christiansborg, in Copenhagen. The Germans, enraged, decided to enforce the Final Solution in Denmark.

Dr. Werner Best, German Ambassador to Denmark, was very uncomfortable about the situation. He realized there would be an uproar in Denmark were he to deport the Jews to concentration camps. He thought of a different way of getting rid of the Jews.

A major roundup was scheduled on the first two days in October, Rosh Hashanah, to transport the Jews by ship to concentration camps. Instead, Ambassador Best preempted this by informing George Duckwitz, the German director of shipping operations in Denmark, that ships were needed to transport Jews to concentration camps.

George Duckwitz immediately contacted Sweden, pleading with the Swedish Prime Minister to accept the Danish Jews. Sweden agreed. News of imminent deportation reached the ears of the Rabbi at the Krystalgade Synagogue, the White and Gold Synagogue. When Jews arrived at the synagogue for *Erev* Rosh Hashanah services, the Rabbi implored them to return to their homes, share the information with Jewish friends and ask their Danish neighbors to hide them and transport them out of Copenhagen, up the coast of Sjælland, to the fishing villages that face Sweden on the east of the Sound of Oresund.

Denmark became free of Jews swiftly, bloodlessly. The Danes cleverly shipped out the Jews in a peaceful manner and made their country *Judenrein*. An evil mind might wonder if this was a clever plot of getting rid of their Jews without force. The miracle of this operation, the humanitarian aspect of it, was witnessed when, twenty-two months later, in May 1945, the exiled Jews returned.

The war over, the Danish Jews returned to reclaim their homes. The temporarily exiled group experienced something remarkable: their homes had been left intact, the table still set for Rosh Hashanah as they had left it, the luxurious tablecloth, the place settings, the porcelain and crystal. Flowers had been watered by neighbors, businesses had been overseen. There had been no theft, destruction or vandalism of property. The returning Jews were joyfully greeted and welcomed by their Danish neighbors.

This incredible rescue is one of the most moving tributes of all the humanitarian activities that transpired during World War II. This event was successful because the entire country cooperated to help their Jewish brethren. It is important to remember that Sweden played an important part in the rescue by accepting and welcoming the Danish Jews. Without their cooperation, the rescue would not have been possible.

The Resistance Museum in Churchill Park in Copenhagen depicts all aspects of the resistance: the invasion of Denmark, the sabotage activities, the underground, the rescue of the Jewish people and the events at Gilleleje.

The Memorial Pillar, for those that perished in the Holocaust, stands in the cemetery outside Copenhagen, near the Tuborg plant, where the popular Danish beer is produced. Surrounding the pillar is a square area with four cornerstones connoting major disasters in Jewish history: the Egyptian experience, the Babylonian exile, the Spanish expulsion and World War II. Fifty-seven names, one percent of the Jews in Denmark, the total number of people who perished in the Holocaust, are inscribed on the pillar in the center.

Many of these people perished from sickness and old age. The bulk of the Danish Jews were saved, and those deported to Thereisenstadt were able to receive packages during their stay through the activities of Folke Bernadotte and the Swedish Red Cross. A total of four hundred sixty-four people were deported to Thereisenstadt. Forty-eight persons perished from by natural means – old age or sickness. Two children were born there, living happily today. Four hundred twenty-five survivors were brought to Sweden on the White Buses.

The Jewish Community Center in Copenhagen on Ny Kongens Gade houses administrative offices for numerous Jewish organizations. This is also the location of a kosher restaurant. Extensive renovations were made with German Reparation Money.

The Royal Library of Denmark contains one of the largest Judaica collections in the world. In 1932, Chief Rabbi David Simonsen donated his private collection of twenty-five thousand volumes and numerous manuscripts to the library. In 1999, the new Royal Library was dedicated, The Black Diamond.

The new Danish Jewish Museum of 2004, situated within the Royal Library of Denmark, was designed by Daniel Libeskind, architect of the Jewish Museum in Berlin, the Wohl Center at Bar Ilan and winner of the competition for the Memorial Tribute for the Twin Towers in February 2003. The museum's form contributes to the function. Designed with slanted walls and floors, patrons who walk through the museum experience unsteadiness, an unpleasant loss of equilibrium. Libeskind wished to impart the idea that Jews have always lived on unsteady ground. He also strove to simulate the experience of the movement of the ships during World War II, effectively done through this museum's structure.

The rescue of Danish Jewry is a glimmer of hope from the tragic era of World War II, one bright experience of what can be accomplished when individuals cooperate and act in a humanitarian way to protect their fellow citizens.

CHAPTER 6

Brief History of Scandinavian Trio Tours

In the fall of 1980, my world was definitely altered – at least as far as my summer plans. For twenty years, I had spent my summers in bungalow colonies in the Catskills, in different parts of the mountains. Though names and places differed, the basic venue was identical: primitive, bedraggled huts containing the barest of essentials, a decrepit refrigerator and stove, an ugly bathroom with outdated tiling – never a bathtub or air conditioner – large iron beds and rickety kitchen table.

But I relished those summers, the sounds of crickets chirping and birds twittering, the beautiful butterflies that nestled on my arm, the small critters, ladybugs, slimy frogs and salamanders and the spacious, luxurious, verdant grass. Socializing at the pool, games and lectures for women, knitting and crocheting, the exchange of recipes and child-rearing ideas were a welcome diversion from the burning asphalt – true family time.

Everything changed when my youngest daughter, Raizel, chimed, "No more bungalows for me. That's for babies. Next summer I am going to camp and that is non-negotiable." It was time for a new beginning.

"What will I do all summer?" I lamented. "I don't want to remain in the city, I certainly don't want to contend with the tumult of children in a bungalow colony when I have no children." Briefly I contemplated a camp position, but quickly dismissed the idea. "I teach all year," I told myself. "I need a vacation from children."

One day, while perusing the Jewish Press, I came across an advertisement for a Jewish Experience Tour to Scandinavia. Never had I considered returning to my childhood paradise in Stockholm, especially after the tragic demise of my father. Memories of childhood, for me, were too painful, too raw. I lived in a conspiracy of silence, similar to Holocaust survivors who had been unable to confront their memories for decades.

And then, like a flash of lightning, I had an idea. I could become a tour guide. I am experienced in conducting groups, I convinced myself, bringing groups of school children to Brooklyn Academy of Music and Madison Square Garden. I know the languages, history and culture of Scandinavia. The idea germinated, and slowly the possibility became a probability. Our financial budget prohibited the luxury of touring, but returning as a guide was a novel idea.

Contacting the tour company, I was told that they had no need for escorts; local guides were hired in the capital cities. "Should I call you at a later date?" I asked, not wanting to accept a definite refusal. "You might change your mind." Never in my life had I pleaded for a position, but this was an opportunity of major importance.

"Fine, OK," was the noncommittal reply.

A few weeks later, I phoned and again was confronted with negativity.

"Don't you get it? He doesn't need you." Many people, including my husband, discouraged me, but I persisted.

In May, the groups filled up, a meeting was arranged and I was hired. My dream of returning to the city of my childhood was becoming a reality.

As the day of departure drew near, my excitement increased. I frequently woke up during the night and began dreaming of childhood. My longing to return – to gaze upon my father's shul, to reconnect with friends, meander in my favorite playground, enter the apartment where we had lived – overwhelmed me. In the morning, my pillow would be drenched, from tears shed as the memories rushed forth.

Holocaust survivors tried to protect me. "Going home is never what you expect," they warned me. "You will be disappointed." They unanimously concurred that they would never return to their homes.

"It's different for me," I insisted. "My childhood was idyllic. I was never betrayed." Refusing to let their barbs burst my bubble of enthusiasm, I continued to anticipate the experience and was, gratefully, not disappointed.

In Denmark, the first leg of the journey, I met a man who had spent a portion of his teenage years in our home in Stockholm during the German occupation of Denmark. He was one of the Danish Jews rescued on a fishing boat. It was a heartwarming reunion in the courtyard of the magnificent synagogue on Krystalgade. Aside from that meeting, however, I felt like an outsider. Few people remembered my father, though he had lived in Scandinavia for almost two decades.

In Helsinki, I encountered the relatives of Avi, who had joined our household in the World War II era. One of many Finnish Jewish children, he had been smuggled across the border during that turbulent time. This was another connection with the past.

Not many Jews live in Scandinavia, so a special brotherhood exists among the Jews there. This bond of kinship tightened during the war years, with neutral Sweden lending a helping hand to the less fortunate neighbors.

Upon finally reaching Stockholm, the climax of my journey, I found my home intact, though strangers were living there. It was a never-to-be-forgotten experience to walk through the home of my childhood. I contacted friends, visited my father's shul and happily retreated into childhood. The business area of Stockholm had been totally updated, barely recognizable, but the Old Town of Stockholm – the City between the Bridges – remained unchanged, the same as when it was founded by Birger Jarl in 1250. My island, Sodermalm, was also untouched, preserved in the reality of my memories.

Coming home was cataclysmic, and launched my new career. I became a guide in 1980. In 1987, with the blessings and encouragement of the Lubavitcher Rebbe, I founded my own tour company, Scandinavian Trio Tours, alluding to the three kingdoms of Sweden, Norway and Denmark. The Rebbe provided specific instructions prior to the tours and in the fall, he requested a detailed summary of the experiences. In those years there were no Chabad Houses in this part of the world and thus, I felt that I was fulfilling this role with my tours.

My goal was to give tourists an appreciation of the starring role Denmark and Sweden played during the Holocaust years and their aftermath. These tours offered a unique and rich blend of places of Jewish interest, intermingled with the scenic beauty of waterfalls and glaciers as well as castles and museums. The tour members were delighted to become acquainted with the Jewish history in this quite unknown part of the world and the Scandinavian Jews were inspired and strengthened by these visits.

In 2006, the Scandinavian Trio Group was formed. At first glance, we appeared to be a rather unlikely combination, and yet we quickly developed great rapport and became a solid unit, interacting closely with one another, displaying mutual respect and admiration. It began with Suzannah's visit to my home for an interview for her documentary on matchmaking. During the taping I commented that I woiuld be guiding a tour in Scandinavia that summer. I met Nachum, her assistant, for a follow-up taping and that is when I expressed my cherished dream – actually, this was the first time the thought was expressed in words – to produce a documentary of Sweden during World War II and in the aftermath.

I was delighted at their interest and in the summer of 2006, at the end of my tours, we met in Copenhagen to begin the filming with a visit to

Gilleleje. In January of 2007, we spent a full week in Stockholm with interviews scheduled around the clock. In August 2007, we met in Berlin for the Potsdam Film Festival for the presentation of Suzannah's documentary, *Match and Marry*. We visited Wannsee and Ravensbruck for continued filming of the documentary. We had frequent reunions on the East Coast for presentations of the *Match and Marry* documentary, and a particularly joyous one on June 7, 2009, when we celebrated Nachum's wedding to Ilene.

As the senior member of this group, I became the resident historian, providing information on people to be interviewed and places to visit. Suzannah Warlick, a young mother of three – vivacious, charming, petite and attractive, a filmmaker from California – was the head of the project, the Director. She contacted the people to be interviewed and prepared the schedules. Nachum Schwartz, a California transplant from Crown Heights – a handsome, pleasant, easygoing highly eligible bachelor – became chief assistant to Suzannah. It was a fabulous experience for us to film the documentary on Scandinavia during World War II and the aftermath.

The project of filming the documentary became the inspiration and springboard for my book. It is important for the world to become acquainted with Sweden's role during World War II and develop an understanding of how the survivors acclimated to life.

The entrance door to our apartment building, Katarina Vastra Kyrkogata 6, has remained unchanged since my childhood. It gave me great joy to open that heavy oak door in 1980, more than thirty years after we immigrated to the United States. Left, above the entrance door, the alcove area of the dining room is jutting out from the building. Photo: Richard Graber, Tour member, 2003.

My father, Rabbi Y. Y. Zuber, always engaged in the study of Torah, his favorite activity. Stockholm, 1944.

My mother, Rebbetzin Zlata Zuber, looking elegant in her classic, timeless, black outfit. Stockholm, mid-1930s.

This photograph with my big sister, Leya, was displayed on our piano. Stockholm, 1934.

The four of us. Back row: Shalom (left) and Mendel; front row: me (left) and Leya. Stockholm, 1937.

The grandparents and family members in Russia and the USA appreciated our photographs; unfortunately, we never had the opportunity to meet many of them in person. Left to right: my sister, Leya; our mother, holding me; Mendel and Shalom. Stockholm, early 1930's.

In our fourth grade class, I was the shortest one. I am standing left of my teacher, Miss Danielson, and on her other side is Margareta, one of my best friends. My other best friend, Alice, is also in the back row, third from the left. Stockholm, 1942.

My parents outside our home, 31 Howland Street, in Roxbury, Massachusetts, with their first grandchild, Henie Zuber Fialkoff, 1948.

The Great Synagogue of Stockholm, located on Wahrendorffsgatan, has been declared a national landmark. Erected in 1870, during the reign of King Gustavus III, this synagogue seats 1,000 people. Stockholm, 2005.

Adas Yisroel, the Orthodox synagogue where Rabbi Y. Y. Zuber, my father, was the Rabbi during that critical period when Nazism destroyed six million Jews. Stockholm, 2004.

Adas Yeshurun, the second Orthodox synagogue in Stockholm, was brought from Germany in 1939 in a miraculous rescue. Riddargatan, Stockholm, 2004.

On Rosh Hashanah 1943, the announcement was made that the Germans planned an Aktion. Krystalgade Synagogue (aka the White and Gold Synagogue), Copenhagen. Photo: Dr. Ivan Nelson, Scandinavia Tour, 2005.

The only Holocaust memorial in the entire world where the names of all victims are inscribed in one location. Jewish cemetery at Vestre Kirkegardsalle in Copenhagen, summer, 2005. Photo: Dr. Ivan Nelson, Scandinavia Tour, 2005.

In 1998, King Karl XVI Gustav attended the dedication of the forty-two-meter-long wall located in the courtyard of the Great Synagogue. The names of eight thousand five hundred Holocaust victims, all related to survivors living in Sweden, are inscribed on this wall. Stockholm, 2005.

Section 2

ORDINARY PEOPLE IN
EXTRAORDINARY CIRCUMSTANCES

CHAPTER 1

Father

Rabbi Yacov Yisroel Zuber, my father, commanded respect and attention in all situations. He was short, of slender stature and quite good looking. His clothes were always immaculate – white, crisp shirts, black well-pressed suits, polished shoes, black hat and conservative, tasteful ties. His smooth, black hair and black beard were always properly brushed. He had good features, but most compelling were his dark brown eyes, sparkling bright with intelligence, with depth, producing a highly intense look. This was a no-nonsense man.

In a crowd, he stood out despite his being short, for there was an aura about him, something that caught your attention. When he walked down the street, strangers and acquaintances, Jews and non-Jews, greeted him respectfully. When my brothers were engaged in play activities with their friends, the moment he called them to come inside for Torah study, they left the game. Their friends were intimidated by him. Words were not necessary, just a sharp, intent look and the recipient shriveled. At the Shabbat table, there was no loud talk, no improper language or actions; it was a dignified meal with well-behaved, respectful children. When he ascended the pulpit in Adas Yisroel, his synagogue on St. Paulsgatan, as he stood there adjusting his Tallit, the prayer shawl, looking out at his congregation, there was total silence. And during his sermon, no one left his seat and no one uttered a word. He was the ultimate Rabbi, the ultimate scholar.

He was born in Russia, in Schedrin, a well-known settlement in the pale, an area reserved for Jews. He attended Yeshiva in the town of Lubavich. The students were very poor and all week, they looked forward to Shabbos, when they were hosted by local families. That was the only time they could fill their empty stomachs. All week long there was hardly anything to eat and no packages came from home, where poverty ruled. He became a chain-smoker, rolling his own cigarettes to still the pangs of hunger. He carefully saved stumps of candles and melted them together to have a few more hours of light for learning through the long, dark winter nights. He was cold and hungry, but the study of Torah filled him with the greatest pleasure – that was his life. He distinguished himself in his studies and received Smicha from the Rogotchover Rebbe, of world fame.

He married Zlata Golbin from the nearby town of Streshin. The first year, the couple lived in Streshin and then, as was a new custom of the Lubavitch/Chabad community, he was sent as a *shliach*, a representative, to Gruzia, Georgia, to the isolated, mountainous town of Satchchere. Great bravery and courage was required for this. They left family and friends, familiar surroundings, to a place with a different language and different customs. There were no visits from family members, as the travel was cumbersome, and there were no visits to the hometown. For a young bride, this was quite difficult, but that was – and is – the life of a shliach.

The dream of America was still burning strong within my father, but when the Lubavitch movement departed with the *Rebbe Rayatz* for Riga, in independent Latvia, on their first step in the journey to the New World, he joined them with his wife and three young children.

Life in the United States at this time was very difficult, as this was the time of the Great Depression. People were jumping out of windows as they saw their resources dwindle and disappear. There was no social security and everyone struggled to try to save any of their hard-earned money for sickness and old age. When an offer came for a position as a Rabbi in Stockholm, Sweden, with the encouragement of the *Lubavitcher Rebbe*, he accepted the position.

My father's education from the age of three was one hundred percent Torah related. Being highly intelligent, he was also proficient in math and geography and familiar with European Jewish history. However, he was totally unfamiliar with the Jewish history of Scandinavia. That was definitely not surprising, since the history of Jews in these countries was brief and quite insignificant. The combined Jewish population of all these countries was far less than that of a large city in Poland or Russia. No Yeshiva had ever existed there and no great Talmudic scholars had ever lived there.

The Jewish population of Sweden was only six thousand out of a total of six and a half million inhabitants. However difficult the situation was, there was absolutely no desire to return to Russia; as a matter of fact, one drew a sigh of relief at having left that country. The United States was not a tenable option, so Sweden became the new residence of the Zuber family. This was supposed to be a temporary stay, just a stopover en route to America, but the old Yiddish expression is quite applicable here: *Der mentsh tracht un Gott lacht* – in other words, man proposes and God disposes – for we are not the rulers of our destiny. The Stockholm experience became, by far, the longest period of time in their married life in one place: one year in Streshin, four years in Gruzia, three years in Riga and then, after eighteen years in Stockholm, they spent a brief five years in Boston, with an unexpected tragic end.

Life in Stockholm, physically and economically, was quite outstanding. Stockholm is a beautiful city built on fourteen islands, connected with bridges, with clean streets, plentiful parks and lots of museums and places of interest. The city was very modern, with all the latest conveniences – elevators in the buildings, escalators in the large department stores – and the whole country was filled with a large variety of food items, in addition to an abundance of all the essentials and luxuries of life: clothes, household goods, furniture, even toys and sporting goods, and so on.

Our family lived on the largest island, the island of the working class, Sodermalm. The first apartment was on Mariagatan near the shul, and later we moved to a larger home on Katarina Vastra Kyrkogatan, an apartment building with a small elevator. Many years later, when the family arrived in the United States, relatives displayed with great pride the string hanging from the ceiling that could be pulled to turn on the light. In Stockholm this was controlled by buttons in the walls. And in the homes of the relatives in Brooklyn, there were no elevators. Sweden was, indeed, a completely modern, extremely advanced country.

A live-in maid assisted my mother, and for *Pesach*, special holidays or social events, additional help was hired. We had private tutors for Hebrew studies, as there were no day schools or Talmud Torahs. There were piano lessons for the girls and violin lessons for the boys. Summers were always spent out of the city, for my parents were firm believers in the importance of unpolluted air; the fresh air of the islands in the archipeleago, where the only means of transportation was the bicycle, was the perfect choice. There, we had swimming lessons and enjoyed badminton, ping pong and other sports.

My father was always occupied with Torah study, constantly pursuing his learning, engrossed in the large *seforim* spread out on the dining room table. In the margins of these books, and across the top and bottom of almost each page, he wrote his original thoughts. In notebooks, he added additional material, finely written in his beautiful script with a pen dipped in an inkwell. He had a quill for writing *Mezuzos* and other specific documents. Posthumously, his sefer, *Zichron Yacov* was published by Mosad Harav Kook. It was a text dealing with specific problems and questions pertaining to

Jewish Law applicable to the Scandinavian countries. One of the concerns was the earliest time one could begin *Shabbat* during the longest days, in the end of June and beginning of July.

He traveled extensively through the Scandinavian countries, limited to Sweden during the war, to perform circumcisions. To do so, he wore a sparkling white doctor's coat and used the finest precision instruments enclosed in a stainless steel case wherein all was sterilized. He was also a *shochet*, and when the organization for animal rights in Sweden outlawed *shechita*, Rabbi Zuber, an uncompromisingly law-abiding citizen, would dutifully pay his fine at the police station prior to performing that illegal act.

The ultimate intellectual, he rarely displayed emotions. Though he would smile quite readily, his laughter was seldom heard. Self-confident, respected by family and community, secure in his lifetime contract with the synagogue, he knew his role in life and was aware of his goal, striding forward, assured of his future. In one area of life, however, he displayed a discomfort that almost bordered on fear. When encountering a policeman in uniform, he would freeze. His brisk walk would slow to an almost hesitant movement. He would turn pale, almost white, his facial muscles tightening with visible distress.

At night he sometimes had nightmares that would awaken us children, who slept soundly in the adjoining room. There would be heavy breathing, like someone running away, being pursued, in fear of his life. Then there would be moans and groans, sounds of fear intermingled with words of protest or pleading, in Russian. He would be awakened by my mother calling his name in soft, gentle tones. She would whisper words of comfort and reassurance, and eventually his peace of mind would be restored. The house would become quiet as everyone went back to sleep. During the day, he never spoke of life in Russia in the Stalin era; the frightening memories of that brutal time would never break through his reserve during the day, but they would make their appearance in dreams. We children never asked questions; it was a closed topic.

Extremely law-abiding, he paid his taxes in full, to the last penny. Streets were always crossed at the corners, bills were paid on time, report cards were scrutinized and signed and all legal documents were always handled with great efficiency. Every January he would appear at the appropriate government office for the alien registration, and that day, he would be visibly nervous. With the spread of Nazism and the increasing animosity and threat of Bolshevism, a Russian passport was quite definitely not desirable in Sweden.

There were whispered secret reports of Hitler's plan to destroy the Jews. There were reports of resettlements, ghettos, even death camps, but the rumors could not be substantiated. My father was deeply concerned, quite overwhelmed, but, feeling powerless, he was afraid to be noticed, to be actively engaged. However, all of that changed on his day of personal liberation, the blessed day when he became a Swedish citizen. The step from shaky immigrant status to citizenship was a very important one, especially with the threat of Nazism becoming stronger day by day.

He involved his oldest son, my brother Mendel, an enthusiastic supporter of activities involving the plight of European Jewry, to participate in rescue missions. My father did not want undue attention, with his heavily accented Swedish, so Mendel became his spokesperson and interpreter. The father-son team, with great difficulty, located so-called Honorary Consuls – businessmen who served as diplomats when career diplomats were unavailable – from South American countries, and enlisted their help in providing visas for fellow Jews in Nazi-occupied countries. The recipients did not always leave for Haiti, Honduras or Costa Rica, but were often shipped to a camp for political prisoners in Vittel or a special separate section in Bergen-Belsen. Tragically, the Vittel inmates eventually ended up in Auschwitz; however, numerous families escaped and were saved with these visas.

My father worked extensively, secretly and quietly, to relocate Yeshiva students and bring them to Sweden, to safety. In 1939, Chiune Sugihara became the Vice Consul of the Japanese Embassy in Kovno, Lithuania. After the Soviet takeover of Lithuania in 1940, Polish and Lithuanian Jews attempted to acquire exit visas for Japan. The situation was difficult because funds were required and there were numerous stipulations.

From July 31 until September 4, 1940, Chiune Sugihara arranged ten-day transit visas through Japan, in direct violation of the Japanese Foreign Service rules. Arrangements were made to travel across Russia on the Trans-Siberian Railroad at prices five times the cost of the standard tickets. The visas were produced at a feverish pace, handwritten, with a normal month's worth of documents prepared each day. Even after Sugihara was dismissed from his post, during his departure, while in the transit hotel and even after boarding his train, he continued writing more visas for the throng of desperate people. He understood their plight and responded in a most humane fashion. In total he, saved between six- and ten-thousand people.

These fortunate refugees arrived at Vladivostok and then continued by boat to Kobe, Japan, to join its Russian-Jewish community. When the political climate worsened, they were sent to Shanghai to join the sixteen thousand Austrian and German Jews in the International Settlement. Among the refugees were the entire student body of Mir Yeshiva and a number of Yeshiva students from *Tomchei Temimim* who had fled from Otwock, Poland to Vilnius, Lithuania, an independent Baltic state at that time. With great perseverance and fortitude, their administrators procured the visas.

The Japanese government was pressured by Germany to dispose of the Jews just like in the Nazi-occupied countries in Europe, but because the Jewish banker and philanthropist Jacob Schiff had given a $196 million loan to fund the Russo-Japanese War in 1905, the disaster was prevented. Russia was viewed as the formidable foe, the undisputed conqueror, and Japan's efforts to obtain funds to fight that war had been futile. Mr. Schiff's courage in engaging in this risky venture precipitated the development of Japan's favorable attitude toward Jews and Sugihara's readiness to sacrifice his diplomatic career to issue the lifesaving visas years later in World War II.

The situation was precarious, however, so my father located a large estate in Sweden and began making arrangements to bring the group to Sweden. The Swedish government cooperated and provided a collective visa for the hundreds of students involved, but the Russian government refused to allow passage from Japan by rail to Sweden. The students remained in Shanghai throughout World War II. The economic situation was critical and Rabbi Zuber became an important intermediary in providing essential funds for the Yeshiva boys. The project was financed from the United States through *Va'ad Hatzalah*, the Joint and wealthy Jews from Sweden and America. His responsibility was to transfer the funds and make them available to the students

In the spring of 1945, when the first group of survivors arrived in Sweden, with the help of Folke Bernadotte and the White Buses, Rabbi Zuber's life became forever altered. He aged visibly, day after day, as he patiently and compassionately listened to the unbelievable horrors of the Nazi death camps. In our home, there was no night or day. There was an endless stream of visitors requesting advice, wanting to unburden themselves, needing hope, inspiration and encouragement for the future. My father's black hair became tinged with gray. His eyes were saddened and red from crying in the still of the night. During his meetings he would excuse himself, voice breaking, holding back tears, to regain his composure. Whatever rumors there might have been, whatever cruelties he might have envisioned, nothing – absolutely nothing – prepared him for the unspeakable, nightmarish horrors the survivors had endured.

The Displaced Persons camps were located outside the city and visits to embassies in Stockholm were essential for making plans to resettle. Overnight guests filled every part of our house, with us children doubling up to provide space. Our mother, the Rebbetzin, prepared endless meals as we watched the visitors devour slices and slices of bread, even hiding some in their pockets. The Swedes always placed small portions of food, attractively arranged on the plate, with a can of sardines to serve at least two people. The visitors would fill their plates with an entire can and consume it with great

haste, as if afraid the food would disappear. The kitchen was constantly busy to fill the needs of the guests and my mother never uttered a word of complaint. With great warmth and tenderness, with kind, comforting words, she mothered the unfortunate souls. Unable to hear the stories from the camps, she focused on bringing some joy into their lives with the familiar dishes from home.

The most difficult task confronting my father was the issue of *agunot*. An *aguna* is a married woman who has not obtained a Jewish *get* and therefore is not free to remarry. The problem was that only a husband could grant the get. World War II had wreaked havoc in the Jewish world, separating and destroying families. Husbands had been taken to labor and concentration camps and there were no death certificates to prove that they were no longer alive.

Young women, married before the deportations, had no knowledge of the whereabouts of their husbands. Weekly published lists of survivors appeared in all the Displaced Persons camps. These lists were carefully scanned in the hope of finding missing dear ones. After a few months of no success, however, they wanted to be free to marry, to begin life anew. Hope of finding their respective mates was gone. My father consulted with leading authorities in the Jewish world, Rabbis from Israel and the United States. He researched books of Jewish law discussing situations in other times of great tragedies in our history – the Crusades, the Inquisition and the Pogroms.

My father became a leading authority in this field. Regarding the halacha of agunot, he corresponded extensively with leading Torah scholars of that era: Rabbi Shlomo David Kahane of Warsaw and Jerusalem and Rabbi Yechezkel Abramsky of London. In the absence of actual, official reports of death, it became essential to interview survivors as witnesses to the atrocities. Throngs of people were interviewed, providing eyewitness accounts of the person in question. When witnesses reported that they had seen the corpse of the individual, that he had died from starvation, a brutal beating or gunshot, a get could be procured. There could be a group response regarding an incident in a labor camp, a march into the gas chamber or an incident in the yard at appel, during roll call. The witnesses cried brokenheartedly as they related the tragedies, reliving them in the telling.

Rabbi Zuber's heart ached for them, he was speechless. There were no words with which to respond to the brutality of the Nazis. The unimaginable, the whispered warnings of the "Final Solution," the attempted destruction of European Jewry was now exposed in its visible, naked horror. There was an intermingling of tragedy and joy, of determining death and freeing the aguna: that was the ultimate goal of this project. The ultimate goal was closure, which was needed to begin life anew. Marriages were frequently performed within the DP camps. With the indestructible spirit of the coura-geous survivors, the desire to rebuild and establish Jewish homes and fami-lies, life slowly emerged from the ashes. At this time, there was the highest birth rate ever recorded, for the survivors wanted children to name after dear departed family members.

Devastated about the overwhelming loss of European Jewry, numerous communities nearly annihilated, my father was heartbroken that the world had allowed these atrocities to occur. His interest in fulfilling his dream of long ago to settle in America now reemerged. He wanted to resettle his fam-ily in a new place to provide a safe foundation for future generations. Anti-Semitism in Europe had destroyed six million, and in Sweden there was another serious threat: assimilation. The Swedes were kind and accepting, so the rate of intermarriage was very high – more than sixty percent. My siblings were of marriageable age, and he was concerned. The Jewish youth in Sweden, especially among the Orthodox, were few in numbers.

The situation now changed with the influx of the survivors. My broth-ers were in the Swedish army, but within a short time after their discharge, they both married survivors from the camps. Though my father welcomed them into our family with great warmth, he still was concerned about the spiritual continuity of their future families and believed that they should not stay in Sweden.

At age fifty, living in modern, comfortable surroundings, with a safe, secure future, with a life contract at the synagogue, he courageously packed all his belongings to start as a newcomer in the United States. Relocating to an uncertain financial situation, to a new language with new customs, for the sake of securing a spiritually safe world for his offspring was very courageous.

Life in the United States was an economic step down. He had accepted a position as *Rosh Yeshiva*, essentially the Dean, of the Central Lubavitch Yeshiva in America, which was located in Brooklyn, New York; however, plans were changed when the previous Rosh Yeshiva from Europe reappeared unexpectedly, after having been presumed lost in the war. My father then became a Rabbi in a small Lubavitch shul in Dorchester, Massachusetts, on Bradshaw Street, and Dean of the Lubavitch Yeshiva for elementary school students, nearby.

The family settled in a small attic in Roxbury, on Intervale Street, in an apartment that consisted of just two bedrooms, a kitchen and a bath. There was no living room, dining room or study. The walls were so slanted that during the summer, the apartment was like a hothouse. The physical sur-roundings were quite a comedown from life in Stockholm. Within about a year came an appointment as Rabbi of the Crawford Street Synagogue and membership at the Rabbinical Board of Boston. We then moved to a lovely apartment on Howland Street, my brothers arrived with their young wives and in June of 1948, my older sister Leya married an American Lubavitch young man, David Edelman – life was becoming good. Then, after just five years of living in Boston, tragedy struck.

On December 31, 1952, my father insisted on escorting me to a small, informal, impromptu birthday party at the home of a Finnish friend, a cousin of Avi's, who lived in the same building as my brother, on Walnut Avenue. In those days, the world was safe, with front doors left unlocked and street crimes very rare. We often walked alone, even in the late evening. That evening, walking the short distance, less than fifteen minutes, I was happy to have my father by my side. On the way, we noticed a group of teenagers acting boisterous and disorderly. I shivered, thinking how frightening and dangerous this might have been if I had been alone. At first, I had protested to his escorting me but in retrospect, his presence gave my life a second chance.

It was a very dark night, but beautiful, with white snow steadily falling and the street lights separating the tiny flakes as they twirled through the air. The streets were deserted, except for that gang of teenagers, as it was only eight o'clock in the evening, too early for the "New Year's" festivities to begin. We took a shortcut, crossing through the pocket-sized Horatio Harris Park, and stopped at our destination on Walnut Avenue. Unexpectedly, I felt very uneasy watching my father depart for home, in the eerie silence of total nothingness. Was it a premonition, I wondered afterward. Could I have stopped him?

On his return home, my father was mugged in that small park. He was found by some young children at about nine o'clock in the evening, lying in the snow, after having been thrown to the ground by his assailants. Our family was notified by the police, and while revelers were celebrating the arrival of the new calendar year, Rabbi Zuber lay in a coma in a hospital bed. He had suffered a brain concussion as a result of the attack, his head hitting the concrete. The following morning, on a bright, sunny, winter day, he was *niftar*.

This was a great tragedy that affected the entire Boston community as well as the Jewish world at large. Sociologists discussed this incident in text books, stating that this was the death blow of the Roxbury Jewish community, as this became the impetus for departing this area to rebuild in Brookline, Brighton and Newton.

Today the descendents of Rabbi and Rebbetzin Zuber number close to three hundred: children, grandchildren, great-grandchildren and the fourth generation, still in its early stage, constantly growing with God's help. Though his own life was tragically extinguished, his progeny have vindicated his courageous departure from a comfortable position to embark on a new life in new surroundings for their sake.

The light that was lit in Schedrin, Russia, then via Gruzia and Riga, continued to Stockholm, Sweden, where it burst into a large flame of hope, warmth and compassion during the Holocaust, the darkest era of our history. Ironically, it was extinguished in Boston, the Cradle of Liberty, in the country that welcomed the tired, the poor and the huddled masses yearning to breathe free. Life is strange, indeed. Who could have imagined that such a beloved and respected Rabbi would meet a violent death in a cultured city filled with famous universities and hospitals, a death like that of his father, who had been murdered in a Russian village? An ordinary life in an extraordinary situation, his ultimate act of bravery of bringing his entire family to resettle in the United States has resulted in grandchildren that are doctors and lawyers and numerous great-grandchildren that are building Chabad houses in all parts of the world, all contributing to building a better world, a strong Jewish world.

CHAPTER 2

Yenti Ganz Zuber

Portrait of Yenti 2009

Petite, no more than five feet tall, with slender frame, everything about her is delicate: her fine features, delicate hands and small feet. The only oversize thing is her hair, thick curly, puffy, nowadays always covered with a wig. She has aged gracefully and still maintains her beautiful, joyous smile. A celebrator of life, she greets people with a sparkle in her eyes when hearing good news. When retelling her story of life during World War II, she sometimes shakes her head in disbelief. It is sixty years later and she still cannot fathom the experiences of her teenage years.

Betrayal of Innocence

Temporarily blinded by the bright sunlight, Yenti emerged from the train. She turned her head for a moment for a final glance of what appeared, from the outside at least, to be an ordinary train. Yet, its interior was appalling – a vast, empty space. All the seats had been removed completely, creating a surreal vast, dark area.

Yenti gulped, breathing deeply, filling her lungs with fresh, clean air. It felt good after the stale air inside the cramped cattle car. More than a hundred people had been stuffed into an area usually allotted to forty-six passengers. The most horrendous journey of her life, she shivered involuntarily. What a nightmarish experience!

"Kinderlach," her father said, reassuringly, his voice strong and confident, "everything will be fine." Pointing to a sign on the platform, "Auschwitz," he read. "This is good. I have quite a few business contacts here. With God's help, we'll be alright." Yenti's fears began to dissipate as she placed her small hand in his large, protective one. She felt safe and secure with her big, strong father, who had always shielded her from harm.

A handsome, man, he appeared so regal in his black hat and fashionable Shabbat coat, yet so strikingly different without his black beard that had been forcibly, cruelly shorn off. A renowned businessman, he maintained the appearance of a Torah scholar, similar to many of the men in her hometown. He pointed to the sign above the gate of a fence that surrounded a large area. *Arbeit Macht Frei*, it announced. "Well, I have never been afraid of work," was his glib comment.

Yenti remembered the large sacks stamped "Auschwitz," shipped regularly to her father's vinegar factory. The sacks contained wood shavings for the production of vinegar. Her uncertainty and angst disappeared in the face of her father's calm demeanor.

Yenti began to survey her surroundings, clutching her luggage and bundle of bedding. The soft goose quilt, enclosed in a sparklingly white embroidered damask cover, and the light, fluffy down pillow with matching pillow case that filled her arms was hesitantly left on the train as directed by the Nazi guards. During that awful train trip, she had placed the bundle in her lap, for under no circumstances would she have deigned to place it on the floor. The mere thought of this pristine bedding touching the floor filled her with disgust. The SS guards on the platform promised that all their belongings would be distributed to them as soon as they were settled. Yenti had never encountered grown-ups that lied, but now she had been introduced to a new world. Reluctantly, she followed orders and, of course, never saw her bundles again.

On that nightmarish train ride, people had been forced to stand, taking turns sitting on the floor, hunched up in the incredibly crowded railroad car. Her legs felt wobbly, unsteady, when she emerged from the train, after the long hours in a cramped position. She clung to her mother, dressed in Shabbat finery, a classic travel suit befitting a lady. She glanced at her older sister Miriam holding the hand of her oldest nephew, six-year-old Moishele, son of her deceased sister, Sasha Golda, who had succumbed to cancer at the tender age of twenty-nine. Yenti sported her good shoes and dressy coat, suitable for a family trip.

People were milling about with shaved heads and ill-fitting, loose gray garments. Distressed, frightened, her mother lamented. "What is this? Where are we? These women look like the insane people in an asylum!"

Nazi officers, immaculately dressed, accompanied by well-groomed, purebred, snarling canines, were strategically placed near the arrival area. "*Schnell! Schnell!*" they commanded in loud, harsh voices, as the bewildered crowd surged forward.

"Eat your food quickly," whispered the veteran inmates, clad in striped uniforms. Yenti looked at her food bag, tightly clutched in her small hand, still quite full, for she had been too worried and unhappy to consume anything during the dismal train ride. Now she desisted from wolfing down food hurriedly. "I can't eat like that," Yenti mumbled despairingly. "I'll eat later, when I am hungry." Hardly a food enthusiast, she was never able to eat on demand.

Something was occurring at the front of the line. The large crowd was split in half, with each section directed to another area. Her stomach in knots, Yenti was becoming perplexed, terrified of what might happen next.

Suddenly, her vision was blocked by an evil visage with the hardest, cruelest eyes Yenti had ever seen. The notorious Dr. Mengele wielded a baton, an instrument of torture, loosely dangling in his relaxed, white-gloved hand. Conducting an orchestra of cacophony, he capriciously pointed left, then right, dividing the throng of humanity.

"*Links, rechts*" – stridently commanding obedience, his words echoed in the stunned silence of the frightened, bewildered crowd, the only sound heard. Yenti's father failed to react with sufficient alacrity and was brutally pushed by a guard who knocked off his glasses. Yenti held her breath fearfully. Her father's eyesight was poor and his glasses were of utmost importance to him. She longed to rush forward and retrieve them, but her mother, always so gentle and cautious, gripped her wrist like a steel vise.

Helplessly, she witnessed her father, her strong, virile father, stumble, bend down and clutch the damaged spectacles in his fist. The earpiece was hanging loosely, the screw missing.

Comfortably seated on the couch in the living room of her Brookline home, far removed in time and space from these early years, Yenti continued her narrative. Her past was always with her and she never tired of relating incidents from her childhood and youth. Yenti lived in the present and was always pleasant company; however, she never grew weary of recalling stories from her life. Although I had heard numerous tales of her family and shtetl, this time was different: her narrative was actually an interview for this book, thus now there was sequence and details in the recollections. "I knew that I could easily repair them," she told me. "I had curlers in one of the pieces of luggage…"

"Curlers," I repeated, incredulously. "I must have misunderstood you."

"No," Yenti reiterated. "I took my curlers for what I thought was going to be a change of scenery. I wanted to look nice in my new surroundings."

"I still don't understand what you meant about using the curlers to repair the glasses," I asked in surprise. "It doesn't seem to make any sense."

"Do you remember those curlers we used in those days?" responded Yenti. "They were tubular, made of foam, with a wooden tip to close into a circle, to form the curl. Inside, to keep the shape, there were thin wires in a spiral formation." I nodded in agreement.

"Yes, I remember. I had exactly the same type of curlers in Sweden. My hair was thin and absolutely straight. I used the curlers every time I washed my hair. It looked great for a few hours and then it went limp again. So, that makes sense now, to use that thin flexible wire."

Yenti was blissfully unaware that her father would no longer need any glasses. Never again would he be able to study his beloved seforim. Where he was going, inner sight was a sufficient source of vision.

Only a teenager, how could she possibly comprehend what others who were older, wiser, in possession of life experience, could not understand? Hitler's organized plan for the destruction and annihilation of European Jewry – the Final Solution – was most assuredly more frightening than anything she could have ever imagined, beyond the scariest movie she had ever seen, more gruesome than the worst nightmare, more horryifying than any book she had ever read.

That was the last time Yenti saw her father, walking dejectedly to the left, his glasses askew. "Links," she heard, and watched her mother turn left as well. "Links," and away walked Miriam, her hand joined to her nephew, their fate seemingly forever bound.

When Yenti was in front of Dr. Mengele, he pointed in the opposite direction. "Rechts," and she moved automatically to the right. Then, the most amazing thing transpired.

Yenti shakes her head as she relates the memory to me, eyes glazed and startled. "Each time I think of it, I still don't know where I got the courage. Even after sixty years," she states in disbelief.

Soft-spoken and gentle, Yenti rarely loses her temper. Nonaggressive, she never gets involved in argument. Timid rather than brave, she carefully follows rules, not even arguing with a traffic cop.

"I moved away from the line," she admits. "I intuitively knew I was on the 'good' line. The ones surrounding me appeared strong, physically fit. There were SS guards everywhere and I just turned to the left, grabbed my sister Miriam and pulled her into my line, the right."

"You must have been terrified," I exclaimed. "How did you dare?"

"I didn't think of the risk. I only knew that I didn't want to be alone. I wanted to live. I knew I couldn't rescue my mother, who had been rejected because of her age. My nephew was only a child. Only afterward, I was gripped by fear. I realized I could have been shot on the spot, or thrown to the left with my sister."

The Early Years

Yenti and her family lived in Romania on the Millgass, in Oberviso, Marmarosh. The borders were constantly changing: in 1940, that area became Hungary, and after the war, it reverted back to Romania once again. "Our beautiful, elegant home, with six large bedrooms on one floor, was surrounded by a large garden filled with fruit trees, berry bushes and flowers. In this garden, there also was a summer cottage – a small, charming home suitable for vacation time or for guests – the family's summer home."

Their father, a Torah scholar, owned a vinegar factory, which later was converted to an oil factory. He had conducted business with people in Auschwitz. Tragic to note that he was comforted upon his arrival there, thinking he could locate business partners and be safe.

The Ganz family, a well-known, prosperous family, was always ready to donate to charity. Photos of the family depict Mrs. Ganz in a fashionable coat accented by a big, fluffy, fur collar, and Reb Ganz well dressed in a good cloth coat.

Yenti attended the local elementary school and entered *Bais Yaakov* at the age of eleven, where she studied for two years. In 1939, she went to her aunt in Mishara, the second-largest city in Romania, to learn embroidery on her industrial sewing machine.

"I always enjoyed handicrafts and begged my mother to allow me to go there and learn under her tutelage. I mastered the skill in a week and practiced making intricately embroidered items for family members. Monograms and appliqué work were very popular in those days. But the war was approaching, so I returned home after just a few months."

Ironically, Mishara remained unaffected by Hitler's policies and the Jews who resided there were never deported.

"Weren't you sorry that you did not remain there?" I asked. "You would have been spared all the tragic consequences."

"Is that what you think?" Yenti protested vehemently. "I wanted to be with my family. I would never have forgiven myself if I had remained there unharmed. Ach!" she concluded, vigorously shaking her head. "It was fortunate, indeed, that I learned to embroider because now I was able to support the family." She worked for a dressmaker and received staples as payment: flour, oil, chicken. Food was more valuable than currency at that time." My sister Miriam developed a successful black-market enterprise," she continued.

"Miriam," I gasped in disbelief, "your quiet sister? I didn't think she could ever break the simplest law?"

We laughed. "You'd be surprised," Yenti remarked, "how quickly personalities can change in extreme situations. Anyway, life went on more or less normally until Pesach."

From Ghetto to Concentration Camp

"The ghetto was established the day after Pesach ended in 1944 and we were forced to leave our beloved home. Ten thousand people were reluctantly squeezed into an incredibly crowded area of insufficient space. People moved into attics and stables. They gathered Jews from surrounding areas and the situation was horrendous.

"My father, who was a great scholar as well as a successful businessman, prepared a burlap sack," continued Yenti." He cleaned a huge sack that had been used for transporting sugar, flour or grain, tied both ends into a makeshift backpack and filled it with his most cherished possession, his seforim. Imagine the discomfort of carrying that heavy weight – but in his complete faith and innocence, he imagined that he would be able to learn once he arrived at his destination. He was not even allowed to bring it with him when we left the ghetto," recalled Yenti sadly.

A few weeks later, every male was mandated to shave off his beard. "Miriam and I cried when we saw our father without a beard," Yenti recalled tearfully. "We couldn't recognize him. We were devastated."

"How did your father react?" I asked.

Shrugging, Yenti continued. "All the men in the community were saddened. Each change was tragic. And then, three days before Shavuos, we were deported to Auschwitz."

The trip took three days. We were the last transport, which included the *Judenrat* and important Rabbis, seventy in all. The train stopped in Sighet to collect additional people.

"You had your bundle of bedding," I added. "You told me that before."

"Yes, and a bag with food. I constructed the bag out of towels – hand sewn, with a strap – plus I made a backpack out of heavy towels, for my necessities. I sewed these items in the ghetto, using a sewing machine. I had all my essentials in them."

"Like your hair curlers," I quipped.

"Can you imagine?" Her facial expression radiated confusion and disbelief, but her eyes twinkled at the memory. "I was so naïve, so trusting. I wore beautiful Shabbat clothes. Fortunately, I wore my best shoes, and that was very important – a lifesaver."

"Everyone was totally unaware," I said sadly. "They even developed a terminology of euphemisms, to mask their evil intent, and actually were quite successful at camouflaging the facts."

We sit in a companionable silence, contemplating the incomprehensible, attempting to make sense of the senseless, the explosive clash of humanity and evil.

Yenti paused for a moment and refreshed herself with a drink of tea. Then she continued "Now began the real hell. We were stripped of our belongings, and escorted into the camp, straight to a bathhouse. Our clothes were confiscated. We were only allowed to keep our shoes. Stark naked, humiliated, we had no fear of showers, for we had no knowledge of gas chambers." She shudders involuntarily at the memory. "We had actual showers and then they shaved our heads. The SS guard who shaved me complimented me and told me she had never seen such thick, lustrous hair. 'A pity it has to be cut', she said. I couldn't believe she had any human feelings. We were given prison garb – no underwear, not even panties, just a dress. And those dresses, they distributed to us without bothering about size. We could not recognize each other, not even our relatives, with our shaved, bare heads and those ill-fitting clothes." And this was only the beginning, the introduction to a life we could never have envisioned or imagined.

Toileting was the worst. I can't imagine how we ever survived that. No commode, we sat on long benches with holes – no privacy, and no toilet paper…unimaginable. Yenti looks at me in total bewilderment. "How did we wipe ourselves," she says, shaking her head. "I can't recall what we did or how we managed. After a short span of time, we no longer menstruated." Her eyes have a faraway look and her voice drifts off in disbelief.

Yenti continues: "One thousand people were packed in a barrack, fourteen people to a bed, the size of a single bed. We slept head to toe and when one person rolled over, the rest of us had to shift position. Thirty thousand people were in one block. The bottom of the bed consisted of slabs of plain board. During the cold weather, the boards were removed, to be used for firewood, leaving empty slats. Rain would pour in, drenching the beds.

"In the morning, we were served black water. They called it coffee. The thin soup, and everything we were given to eat, tasted like sand. To further dehumanize us, three inmates had to share one bowl. We laughed bitterly about the predicament of a rich, spoiled acquaintance whose pet dog at home would eat bread only when saturated with butter.

"Three months I stayed in Auschwitz. Every day, regardless of the weather, we lined up outside for appel at five o'clock in the morning. The earth, the wet clay, sucked the soles off our shoes. Shoes were our most vital belonging, our dearest treasure. And every day there, was the selection for the crematorium. We tried to support the weaker ones, to shield them, to prevent them from being selected."

Labor Camp

"Three months passed and three thousand of us were selected for work camp. We were permitted to keep our shoes and were given a new dress and one additional dress. We received name plates in lieu of the tattooed number on the arm.

"After a twenty-minute hike to the train, we waited on the platform for twenty-four hours. The train never came. We stood near the wire fence, tired and hungry. Miraculously, the daughter of our laundress at home now worked in the kitchen of the camp across the road. She noticed us and, affected by our plight, tossed in an onion, some bread and a bottle of hot coffee. The bread fell in a puddle and, though we were starving, we would not eat that mud-soaked bread. The coffee, hot and sweet, that was a lifesaver. Never in my entire life have I ever tasted coffee like that. The onion was divided and shared. Then she threw in a clove of garlic."

Yenti uncovered her treasure box, displaying the memorabilia within, the work nameplate, the shoes – the ones she wore throughout those months of hell – and some garlic cloves, saved from that day.

"After a full day elapsed, we were marched back toward the Auschwitz camp, where we lived in bunkers. There were different sections in the camp. Instead of the C lager where we had been, now we were placed in A. You cannot imagine our mood. We had no idea of what would happen next. Our miserable accommodations were now even worse. We had no beds, only a wooden floor upon which we slept. It was so overcrowded that there was no floor space and some of us were placed out in an open field. Fortunately it was August, so it was bearable. The location of the A lager, however, near the crematorium, made us quite uneasy.

"We were ordered to undress, to remove our shoes, and there we stood, stark naked, with people from our hometown, in full view of the penetrating, inhumane, cold eyes of the Nazi SS guards. Hopeless, it appeared that we had reached the end."

Yenti continued with the detailed saga. "After having been selected for the work camp, we had become somewhat hopeful. Then, after just one day, the situation had changed. We were returned to Auschwitz, to those horrendous circumstances. We felt betrayed, utterly hopeless. The situation could not become much worse, except for the total end, the crematorium. Then, surprisingly, we were given clothing once more, and I was fortunate to be able to select my own shoes from the heap of shoes. You can't imagine my joy at finding my own shoes again.

"Once again, we were marched to the train station, and were relieved – almost jubilant – when the train arrived. After a few days, we came to

Fallesleben, a Volkswagon factory, where I worked for seven months in the production of airplane parts – precision work that involved wearing a plastic mask. The conditions were horrific, the work strenuous, yet we lived with hope of survival because our work was essential for the war industry."

End of War: Liberation

"A week before liberation, French POWs roamed the countryside," Yenti relates, "bringing us rice and eggs, items that were very much appreciated. We were scheduled to go to Mauthausen concentration camp, but heavy bombardment rendered the journey impossible.

"Eventually we were sent by train to Saltzverdel, where we were delighted to be reunited with fifteen hundred girls from the original group of three thousand that had left Auschwitz for work camps. After a twenty-four-hour train ride, we were liberated on April 14 by an American soldier who rode in on horseback, opening the gates of the camp. An incredible moment!

"When we arrived, we were placed in a brick building that had previously been a facility for officers' training. We were given regular beds to sleep in, and blankets – total luxury. We were overwhelmed. There was food, a kitchen and a dining room. We were in a normalized situation.

"We were free to leave the camp, and went into the nearby town that had been deserted by the Germans. We entered a store and carried out bolts of cloths, then proceeded to make our own clothes. We pulled threads from the blankets and sewed by hand. To finally be able to wear normal clothing was indeed special. The American soldiers gave us cigarettes, which we carefully saved. I was able to trade some for a toothbrush.

"Cigarettes were a most valuable commodity. The American Chaplain admonished us to leave Saltzverdel, for that area would soon be in the Russian zone. He feared for the safety of young Jewish girls. The Russian soldiers were famed for their brutality, especially their abuse of women. The girls pooled resources and collected one thousand cigarettes. Then we hired trucks to bring us to British or American zones.

"We went to Bergen-Belsen. The scene was indescribable: the skeletal people, the *muselmanner* – living corpses, beings that appeared human but were void of humanity; apathetic, without spontaneity; indeed, living dead." Yenti shuddered as she recalled the tragic sights of these beings with blank, glassy eyes. Then she continued, her voice low and somber: "There were piles of piles of dead, staring, nude bodies; piles of eyeglasses; piles of shoes, hair, teeth and suitcases. Our lives had been hellish, but that sight at Bergen-Belsen was totally nightmarish, even to us. We had not realized the extent of Hitler's destruction. It was completely beyond human comprehension. We had been unaware of the existence of extermination camps and shivered as we noted the vast difference from our life in a labor camp and the devastation of the extermination camp.

"A Jewish doctor came to Bergen-Belsen, telling us that very sick people could go to Sweden to recuperate. I was part of a tight-knit group of six: my sister Miriam, my cousins, Henshe and her sister Frayda and Rebbetzin Ratzelle Hager and her niece Tzipporah. My parents were intimate friends with the Hager family of the famous Vishnitz dynasty. Like a family, we vowed not to separate. Rebbetzin Hager had a heart condition and Miriam, who had just had a slight stomach ache, now exaggerated her condition greatly to gain admission to Sweden. Miriam's groans and grimaces must have been very convincing.

"They were both admitted to the hospital. The Red Cross asked if they wished to leave for Sweden. They wanted to accept, but would not separate from the rest of our small group and thus we were, luckily, allowed to join them. We had no idea where Sweden was, and no knowledge about that country, but we really had no other place to go. We traveled together to Lubeck and then continued by boat, finally reaching Malmo, in southern Sweden. Most of the survivors were on stretchers and a very small group, like us, were not sick. We arrived in July of 1945. We thought we had come to Heaven, could not believe that a short trip from Hitler's insane world there was a place like Sweden.

"We were escorted to a huge hall, as big as a sports stadium, with tables beautifully set with coffee, hot chocolate and assorted cakes and cookies. The tables had bright bouquets of flowers. Students and volunteers welcomed us, offering help and warmth. We were overcome with emotion as we viewed the kind, concerned and friendly faces.

"The healthy ones went to the nearby Linneas School, where beds had been prepared with paper linen for purposes of quarantine. Another group was sent to the Malmo City Museum, an old castle, where mattresses were placed among the statues, paintings and stuffed animals. In Valencia, a small dancing hall, one hundred young Polish girls were placed, thirty-five of them Jewish. We were given a full set of new, clean clothing and underwear, taken from a warehouse. We stayed four weeks in this safe, secure haven.

"We walked out into the fenced-in schoolyard and were greeted by hundreds of friendly, concerned people. We could not believe there were non-Jews in the world who cared abut us. They threw in bags of candy, chocolate and cookies and made us feel loved. We were overwhelmed. We noted the kindness and concern in their eyes. They gave us hope that the future could be good. They made us feel like human beings.

Inga Goldfarb of The American Joint Distribution Committee in Sweden wrote an eyewitness account of her experience in participating in the reception of the White Buses in Malmo. She writes a moving description of distributing combs and lipsticks to make the women feel beautiful. She describes a rather comical scene of the Swedish flag being removed from a flagpole to be cut up by the survivors into bras, a very important garment of which they had been deprived since leaving home.

"After the unspeakable nightmare of our experiences, it was, indeed, unfortunate that there was strife among the survivors, between the Polish and Romanian/Hungarian women. We were now separated in different rehab facilities, and I came to Lovo, a camp for Romanian and Hungarian women. Sara, who later became my sister-in-law, bravely approached the administrators and requested that we be served kosher food.

"There were many other rehabilitation centers all over Sweden where the survivors were sent after the quarantine period. Ronninge was located outside Stockholm. Bollnass was another place. In Farnabruk there was a kibbutz-like settlement to prepare the survivors for the agricultural life of Israel. And for young girls, whose education had been brutally interrupted, there was a Bais Yaakov school with a dormitory in Lidingo."

Yenti continues: "In September, after staying in Malmo for a month, we went to Lovo, one of the rehabilitation camps, located on the grounds of a summer camp. The grounds were beautiful, and there were numerous recreational activities. We were free to come and go at will. Representatives from the Jewish community came to greet us, to check our conditions. We were pleased to receive a radio from them. You can't imagine what that meant to us. We could now hear news and become aware of what was happening in the world. To us, this was a great luxury – freedom."

Stockholm The Beginning of New Life

The Frankel brothers, Jacques and Paul from Romania, followers of the Vishnitz dynasty, had settled in Stockholm. They noticed the name of Rebbetzin Hager on a survivor's list and came to search for her in Lovo. This resulted in the group of six being invited to Stockholm for their first Rosh Hashanah in freedom. Sleeping arrangements were made at a Salvation Army center.

Yenti mentioned her skills in embroidery and was asked by Mrs. Frankel to sew a slip as a sample. The full slip was made of beautiful silk material and Yenti decorated it with embroidery. "I had never made a slip in my life," confessed Yenti, "but I figured out how to make it and created quite a masterpiece." Impressed, Mrs. Frankel assisted her in eventually moving to

Stockholm, where her sewing and embroidery skills enabled her to procure employment. Paul Frankel was actively involved in their move to Stockholm, because this was the place of choice for all survivors. A rule had been established that only those over thirty years of age could acquire residence here and his assistance was essential.

In October of 1945, Yenti moved into an apartment at Hornstorg in Stockholm with her sister Miriam, cousin Henshe and two friends. This small, two-bedroom apartment was the new beginning. They prepared meals in their own kitchen and began a normal life of daily activities. The girls worked in a blouse factory and Yenti sewed for private customers. She was able to obtain an old Singer sewing machine, and now she created her own novel way of embroidery. A hoop was used, and Yenti physically vibrated the machine to create stitches that varied in size and thickness to produce masterful designs. Living in their own quarters was a welcome change from their previous experiences. It is difficult to imagine their joy at having privacy, a place of their own – the joy and pride of being self-supporting.

Fifteen-year-old Frayda became a student at the Lidingo Bais Yaakov school founded for young survivors whose education had been tragically disrupted by the Nazis. As previously described, in this setting the young girls now had an opportunity to resume their studies, to once again feel young. Hensha spent weekends with her sister, and lack of space caused her to share a bed with her. Frayda became ill a year after her arrival in Sweden and X-rays revealed a serious case of tuberculosis. Soon thereafter, Frayda died and was buried in the cemetery at Haga Norra outside Stockholm, alongside numerous other survivors who were too weak to overcome the miserable, inhumane conditions of the concentration camps.

Tearfully, Yenti sewed the *tachrichim*, the burial clothes, for her young, seventeen-year-old-cousin. Hensha, who had shared her bed, also developed a serious case of tuberculosis. She was now hospitalized and remained in the hospital for an entire year. Eventually she recuperated and today enjoys her children and grandchildren in Queens, New York.

Miriam returned to Romania to search for her *chossan*, her chosen groom, a year later. There had been no official engagement because of the uncertainty of the war situation, but they had a clear intention of building a Jewish home. Upon her arrival, Miriam discovered that he already was married, for he had been unaware of her survival. She married and raised her two children in Romania. In August 1946, the Communists took control of the government and Miriam was unable to leave the country until 1963. Before finally immigrating to America, she had to paint her house, pay back taxes and sign the house over to the town – a final humiliating act. Sadly, Yenti and her sister were separated all those years and deprived of the sisterly relationship during their early years of marriage and their children of spending childhood years together.

Within a few months, the situation at Hornstorg had completely changed. With Hensha hospitalized, Frayda gone and the departure of her two roommates to America, Yenti now was all alone. Unable to afford the apartment, she moved into a rooming house on Ostra Jarnvagsgatan where she shared quarters with other survivors: three in one room and two in the other room. There was also a man in a third room. Here she remained until May 1948, when she was married. She found employment at an exclusive boutique, Belleza, where she sewed custom-made intimate wear in the most delicate materials with exquisite embroidery and designs. One of her coworkers, an older, Swedish woman, became attached to her and wanted to adopt her. Yenti was steadfast and strong in her faith. She never faltered. Whenever she had to make a decision, she would always pause and think of her parents, envision what their opinion would have been.

For Pesach, she went to the camp in Farnabruk, where she celebrated the holiday with one thousand survivors. It was heartwarming to be reunited with people of similar experiences, some speaking her home language and many from her own country. That summer, she returned to Ronninge, where she spent her four weeks' vacation with survivors and once again was invigorated with the "touch of home." Life in Stockholm was wonderful, but there was always a feeling of loneliness – of being an outsider – and reuniting with familiar faces was important.

In the most northern part of Europe, in cold Scandinavia, Yenti was brought back to real life. The youngest child in her family, she had been loved and protected, safe and secure in her comfortable home. Yenti had been traumatized by her war experiences; the ghetto, concentration camp and labor camp. It had been a bewildering experience to encounter the brutality and inhumanity of the Nazis. When she was forced out of her home, no tears were shed, for there was an air of unreality about the scene.

In the concentration camp and labor camp, there was no time for mourning and thinking; one had to concentrate all one's strength and energy just to stay alive. One could not really think of it as life, just mere existence: being obedient, following orders and commands and avoiding punishments. Thinking of the past was too painful, for the contrast accentuated the present, making it more intolerable. The future was non-existent, too vague and far-off. How could one contemplate a future when one was surrounded by a crematorium, starvation and illness and was unsure if there even would be tomorrow? In Sweden, where she encountered warmth and kindness, she now began to feel, to reawaken.

Then Shalom entered her life. His attention and interest stirred feelings within her and she became like any young woman in love. The courtship was far from smooth, however. They came from different worlds: Yenti from the insular world of a small Chassidic shtetl, and Shalom from a cosmopolitan world – he was debonair, with an extensive secular education. Yenti was in a quandary. "What would my parents think?" she thought. He was very different from the young men who would have been considered as possible suitors in her hometown. No beard or *payos* and no black hat, just a yarmulke. And though his suits were conservative, European style, they were not black. The relationship developed slowly, for there were numerous misunderstandings. Yenti was concerned about her acceptance into the Zuber family. After all, she was a penniless orphan, a newcomer without family or funds.

Yenti's life was in turmoil, and she discussed the situation with Rabbi Hager. Patiently and lovingly, he told her, "My dear child, the world that we once knew is no longer in existence. We must recreate life. Embrace your opportunity. Rabbi Zuber, the father of Shalom, is a great Talmid Chochom and has raised a beautiful family. Don't be afraid. His son is a fine young man and you can have a beautiful future." The courtship continued, but Shalom's service in the Swedish army, fourteen months' compulsory service, further delayed the progress.

The situation reached a climax when Yenti attended our home for the engagement party for Mendel and Sara. Yenti remembers that day in detail. "I wore a pair of brand new shoes that I had proudly bought from my own earnings. The walk across Sodermalm was quite lengthy and my feet hurt. When I arrived at my destination, I noted that the back of my heels had been rubbed raw and were actually bleeding. The house was very crowded with happy, smiling members of the community. I sat there quietly, when Mendel clinked with a spoon on his glass, the customary way of announcing a toast, and said in a happy voice, 'To Yenti, my future little sister-in-law.'

"Everyone became highly animated and I was embarrassed, but also excited. It was premature, for Shalom had not yet proposed. Within the next few days, however, we had a lengthy, serious discussion and somehow the topic of *sheitel*, wig, was broached. Shalom, always very talkative, grew silent and by the end of that evening, was barely talking." My eyes were glued on Yenti. Yes, silence was definitely unlikely for Shalom. "Continue," I said. "This is exciting."

"Well," said Yenti, "the next day, he called and in a very somber voice, he told me that he had hardly slept that night. He had decided that our differences were too vast and could not be bridged."

Yenti was devastated. She discussed the situation with Rabbi Hager, who once again assured her that the life of her childhood was forever gone.

He told her that wearing a sheitel was not essential, however covering one's hair after marriage was necessary. "Nowhere in our seforim does it state that a married woman must wear a sheitel," he concluded. The connection had been lost, however, and all future plans were canceled.

"I was heartbroken." Yenti sighed. "After all my experiences during the Holocaust, I don't know if I ever cried as much as at this moment. When we were forced out of our home and entered the ghetto, I was overwhelmed and sad, but I don't remember crying a great deal. After all, I was with my family. The concentration camp and labor camp were years of horror I can never forget, but everyday existence was an overwhelming hardship and there was no strength for tears. I had just begun to think of a future, Shalom by my side, my constant companion and protector. I was thinking of a new home, of building a family. I was completely crushed. I did not want to leave my apartment except to go to work. I was embarrassed to meet acquaintances, for everyone was expecting our engagement to be announced."

Her eyes filled with tears, remembering that sorrowful time. "I would go to work, and as soon as I opened the door to my room. I would begin to cry. At first the tears were gentle, like soft spring rain. Gradually they increased in intensity, like torrential rain, like a waterfall cascading down the mountains in the spring, bursting forth from the icy enclosure of winter. Perhaps the tears included those not shed when we left our home and community. Perhaps they included tears buried deep within during the nightmarish time."

She told me how her delicate body would tremble from the tears brought forth from the deepest crevices of her being. "Honestly," she said, "I never knew one could cry so much." Yenti's dreams had been like fragile, shimmering, delicate bubbles of soap, surrounding her with hope. And then, in one moment, they were smashed and her loneliness was more than she could bear. "I was frozen inside during the war years," continued Yenti. "Only now, beginning a normal existence again, could I have feelings and emotions." Then she laughs. "My roommate, Eva Tuchman, when I happen to meet her in New York, always reminds me of the flood of tears I shed at that time. 'Young love,' I say, and we both laugh."

"I spent time in Ronninge with the survivors whenever I felt lonely and I began to eat dinners at the kosher restaurant at Biblioteksgatan where the Adas Yeshurun synagogue was located. I usually sat at the same table with a few older gentlemen.

"And now my story becomes beautiful. One day, Shalom came there for dinner. I was very surprised. For the next few days, he appeared there while I was having dinner, and one day he brought me a gift, a gold *Magen David* with a ruby on a chain."

I interrupted: "Surely you know that had to be made to order. No jewelry shop in Sweden carried symbols of Jewish identity."

"Yes," said Yenti, laughingly. "And guess what?" I refused to accept it. Shalom told me that this was just a Chanukah present, but I still did not want any gifts from him. He then asked me if I would give him a Chanukah gift."

"That's my brother," I said. "That sounds just like him. What chutzpa. Well, what happened next?"

"He asked me to personalize six fine linen handkerchiefs, embroidering them with his monogram and I agreed. Why, I don't know. Then I accepted the necklace, but I did not wear it until much later. And I still have it, you know."

Eventually, the couple reunited and the two were married in Landskrona, a small city in southern Sweden. On Lag B'omer in May 1948, they celebrated their very small wedding with just ten people. "Since the family was in America, Shalom was not interested in a large wedding. I had a beautiful gown that I received from a wonderful Jewish family. I hated the way my hair looked, with a huge, puffy top, so I never display my wedding picture. We had a lovely apartment in the suburb of Solna and furnished it with modern Swedish furniture. Actually, the bedroom set, we brought with us to Boston," concluded Yenti dreamily. The newly wed couple worked and lived happily in their new home until they came to America.

Boston, Mass.

I first met Yenti when she arrived in the United States in 1948. She had married Shalom in Sweden after we had already immigrated. Though she was in the early stages of pregnancy, she still was able to fit into my size nine junior dresses. She remembered me from our home in Stockholm when she came for a week's stay to prepare the trousseau for my sister-in-law Sara, who subsequently introduced her to her brother-in-law Shalom, my brother.

Yenti was rather quiet and shy when Shalom brought her into our household on Howland Street, where they stayed for several weeks until they found an apartment nearby in Dorchester, Massachusetts. I was happy to have a new sister-in-law and very bewildered when she told me one day that it was very difficult for her to celebrate with us on *Shabbat* and holidays. I could not understand her reluctance; after all, we were family.

She explained that this was precisely the reason – surrounded by family pierced her with a palpable pain, recalling what she had lost. The memory of her own home, parents and siblings came into focus, and I ached for her pain and loss. My family was a small nucleus consisting of just my parents and siblings, and I was amazed to learn that Yenti's family had included more than one hundred relatives, all of whom had perished except for her sister and two surviving cousins in Sweden. The youngest in a family of five, with married siblings, nieces and nephews, aunts and uncles, loved, sheltered and protected, she was completely unprepared for the concentration and labor camp experiences.

Yenti loves to read, and Holocaust literature is probably her favorite subject. She laughs at herself as she wonders, "I don't understand it, why I keep reading those books. After all, I lived through it. Why would I want to read about it?"

Then we both laugh because I share her interest in these books; same taste but, thank God, it was not my experience.

In 1948, Yenti and Shalom settled on Glenway Street in Dorchester and soon thereafter, they started their business, Zuber and Company, with Shalom in charge of the business aspect, and Yenti applying her embroidery skills in making labels, slogans and special designs for the military and civilian customers.

They moved to Harold Street in Roxbury for two years and then to Walnut Avenue. In 1956, they purchased their home in Brookline, the home where Yenti still resides today. In 1999, Shalom died after having been homebound for ten years as a result of a stroke. They raised a beautiful family, well known in Boston for their involvement in the community, their *chessed* and charitable deeds.

The tablecloth that covers her dining room table is one of Yenti's masterful productions. She has also made crocheted runners for her immediate as well as extended family. Every new baby in the extended Zuber family receives a beautiful baby blanket. Yenti has sewn beautiful suits and dresses as well as curtains and drapes. She has crocheted more than one hundred afghans and baby blankets for distribution to seniors in residences and new mothers. Shawls and hats, her hands are never idle.

Huge bags of yarn are brought to her from the Brookline Young Israel for their Shut In Project. The March 27, 2009 issue of the *Jewish Advocate* of Boston featured an article entitled "Local Resident Knits the Community Together," a tribute to Yenti's active participation in the unique project initiated by Rabbi Gewirtz. One can just imagine the joy of the recipients, residents of nursing homes or homebound seniors, receiving items that provide physical warmth interlaced with human warmth.

The Zuber home is filled with photographs of children, grandchildren and great grandchildren. Ten of the grandchildren made aliyah and are very happy living in Israel, several of the young couples in Beitar.

"How were you able to locate all the wonderful photographs of your family?" I ask.

"In the ghetto, we hid things in a wine cellar," Yenti explains. "We had a gorgeous green velvet album. Scavengers broke in, stole the album and tossed the precious photos on the floor.

"In January 1945, neighbors that had been liberated found the photographs and gave them to a young man who had survived. He found our names on the survivors' list and mailed them to Sweden in regular envelopes with letters, a few each time. Other people also found photographs and we shared our pictures with one another."

Curious, I asked how she had endured readjustment.

"In the beginning, actually for a lengthy period of thirty years, I had horrible dreams. I was always running, running quickly. It was awful."

"I always spoke to the children about my childhood, about my family. Never about the Holocaust or concentration camp experiences, though.

"You know," she said, turning to me. "Shalom could not bear to listen to those memories. They filled him with incredible despair, hearing those tragic tales of woe. He never understood my deep need to talk about it."

"That was probably why you enjoyed spending so many summers in Bethlehem, New Hampshire, with all your *Landsleite*," I commented.

"Absolutely," said Yenti emphatically, in her pleasant, lilting voice. "We spent most of our days reminiscing about the past."

"I know," I said, "Shalom often mentioned that." And we laugh.

To this day Yenti takes a great interest in Holocaust literature, her bookcases bursting with material on that topic. "The world must never forget. Time marches on and the past seems like a terrifying dream, a nightmare with an air of unreality. We must keep the memory alive. We must honor the lives that were lost and constantly strengthen and rebuild our Jewish world." That is Yenti's philosophy on life. She has provided eyewitness testimony to the Spielberg Foundation, Yaffa Eliach of Brooklyn College, and the forthcoming Scandinavian documentary. She also has visited numerous Yeshivas to share her story.

Dynasty of Vishnitz

The Hager Family originated in Grosvardan, Poland with Rabbi Yisroel Hager. His son, Reb Menachem Mendel, lived in Oberviso, Romania. The area of Grosvardan became Hungary in 1940 when Hitler changed borders in Europe.

One grandson, Reb Mayer Hager, was married to Rotzelle Hager before the war began. Unfortunately they had no children, but they were still young, in their mid-thirties, and still hopeful. An uncle, Rabbi Chodorov, had immigrated and settled in New York.

When the situation in Hungary became serious, the offspring were advised to memorize the name and address of the uncle. When Rebbetzin Hager eventually arrived in Sweden from Bergen-Belsen, she contacted her American uncle to relate that she was alive. Her husband had likewise contacted this uncle and immediately came to Bergen-Belsen to find her, not aware that she had already left for Sweden. This Uncle Chodorov now contacted Rotzelle at Camp Lovo to notify her that her husband was alive. One can imagine the happiness of this couple to finally be reunited in Sweden. The Hagers became substitute parents for Yenti in Sweden, a continuation of the relationship of her parents, who had been active followers and supporters of Reb Mayer Hager's parents in Romania.

They immigrated to America and settled in Lincoln Place, in Crown Heights, Brooklyn. Rabbi Hager arranged to accompany my father to *yechidus*, a private audience, with the Rebbe Rayatz. Unfortunately these plans never materialized, as the Rebbe Rayatz died on the tenth day of Shvat in 1950.

When Yenti visited the Hager home in Crown Heights, she was astounded to see a huge, costly menorah, that looked like an exact replica of the one her father had owned. She was amazed to learn that this actually was the menorah of her childhood home. Rabbi Hager told her it had been a gift from her father. Mr. Ganz felt it was inappropriate that his menorah was more magnificent than the one of the Rabbi. During the war, this menorah was placed in a wooden crate in the ground under the floorboards of the bedroom of Rabbi Hager. After the war it was brought out from this hiding place by family members and today, that menorah is in Israel.

Epitaph

Many precious hours were spent discussing the material for this chapter. Yenti included minute details of her childhood in Sighet, the turbulent years of the Holocaust and the rebuilding of her life. Events that most people would have forgotten were included in her narrative. During a lengthy phone call, when I read this chapter to her, I was met with silence. Puzzled, I asked her, "Are you there?" Yenti responded in amazement, "I can't believe this is my story. It seems unreal, as if you were reading a Holocaust memoir."

When we traveled to Sweden in 2002 on our family trip, Yenti spent every night, until the early morning hours, reminiscing about the past. Although small in stature, she succeeded in enlarging the horizon of the younger generations.

I am deeply saddened that our dearly beloved Yenti is no longer with us. On October 13, 2010, a massive heart attack extinguished her life. The large number of people who attended her funeral was evidence of her role in the Boston Jewish community. A petite, quiet woman, always a lady, she will be remembered for her charitable deeds, her generous donations and her active participation in helping to make this world a better place.

Yenti displayed great interest and enthusiasm about the publication of this book, for she wanted the lessons of the past never to be forgotten. She strongly believed in the concerted effort to share, teach and publicize this period of history in order that the new generations should never be ignorant of the events that had transpired. The number of survivors, the witnesses, is rapidly decreasing and I feel very fortunate that I was able to conduct this important interview with Yenti. Her story is now in print and will always be remembered.

On January 13, 2011, Malka Yenti Meyer was born in Jerusalem, Israel. We hope this great-granddaughter of Yenti Zuber's will proudly bear her name and continue in the path of this righteous woman.

CHAPTER 3

She Walked in Beauty –
Sara Einhorn Zuber

She walked in beauty. Her life was not always wonderful; actually, she encountered countless challenges, but she chose to walk in beauty. She appreciated the "small things" and focused on the good. An excellent listener, she carefully steered the speaker away from gossip by introducing a new topic or providing another viewpoint that presented the positive qualities of individuals being discussed. Her family and home were the focal point of her life. Regardless of where she lived, no matter the circumstances, her personal appearance and the physical condition of her home were always immaculate. In truth, I learned from her that outward appearance impacts our inner well-being and orderly surrounding can aid in overcoming inner chaos and turmoil. An excellent homemaker, no one ever left her home hungry, unexpected visitors as well as invited guests. The tastes and smells of her kitchen were fondly remembered by all.

She enjoyed the carefree chirping of a bird on her windowsill. She picked flowers from her garden to give her home a cheery appearance. She welcomed the sparkle of glistening white snow and the changing colors of leaves in autumn. Every season had its beauty and she appreciated them all.

She gained her inner strength from prayers and psalms. She always appreciated and encouraged guests at the Shabbat or holiday table to participate in worthwhile discussions sharing Torah thoughts.

Had Sara known that I considered her my heroine, she would have been quite amused. She never considered her life particularly heroic or exceptional, but rather ordinary. Yet that is what made Sara special, that she accepted everything in her life and forged on, in the best way possible.

And so her life continued, with the normal ups and downs, joys mingled with trials and tribulations until...

I never forgot that last spring. After the demise of his wife, the Lubavitcher Rebbe initiated the Dollar Line, where he distributed blessings and a dollar for charity. My Sundays now alternated between hospital visits and the Dollar Line. During the week, I was forever in turmoil with an inner debate regarding my Sunday schedule. It wasn't right to inconvenience the Rebbe. After all, he had already given blessings for a speedy recovery, but I felt so totally helpless. The situation was very serious and I needed to do something.

My bedside manner leaves much to be desired. I freeze when confronted with illness – it scares me. I could tell her stories, even feed her, but I was terrified to assist her out of bed or massage her aching body. Somehow I needed that contact with the Rebbe, the reassurance and strength that his blessing provided. I know Sara appreciated those dollars, as she clutched them and carefully listened to the exact phrasing of the Rebbe's message.

The lines that spring were endlessly long. I would arrive home exhausted after four or five hours on the line, always painfully aware that my discomfort was insignificant in comparison to that endured by the Rebbe.

I met Sara the first time when my brother brought her home to present her as his future bride. There was a feeling of gaiety around her, a feeling of joy and happiness that permeated all of us. That is how she was throughout her life, radiating good will and finding pleasure in life. She adored my father and quickly became attached to my mother. It seemed as if she had always belonged to our family. She just fit in and instantaneously became a member of our household. To me, she was far more than a sister-in-law. She became a beloved older sister, friend, confidant and, after my mother's demise, a mother substitute as well.

Hardly the typical young bride-to-be, Sara was a Holocaust survivor, a graduate of the "School of Nightmares" and the horrors of Auschwitz. But she would not allow that horrendous period of her life to overshadow the happiness of the present. Indeed, that was her life's motto – to seek the good, to squeeze every drop of happiness out of each situation. Bitterness and anger, negative emotions, had no place in her life.

It wasn't that she blotted out the memories of that ugly past. It wasn't as if she never thought about it. She never could bear to see a movie that dealt with the Holocaust, not even a TV drama. She never wanted to read books dealing with that topic. But with her natural zest for life, her blessed enthusiasm, she was able to recall incidents from that time that showed caring and concern, faith in Hashem. Her anecdotes from that era were inspirational.

Though sad and tragic, they uplifted the listener, allowing the experience of faith and compassion to triumph over hate and evil and Nazi brutality.

She told stories of girls gathering at night to celebrate Chanukah, fashioning carefully saved odds and ends to bring forth light, pulling threads from their garments for wicks. She spoke of sharing a hardened piece of bread, carefully saved for one's own evening's sustenance, to help a weak friend who was near starvation. She spoke of the group of girls who helped an inmate hide her pregnancy and later assisted her in the secret birth, and then the subsequent circumcision performed with a sharp stone to ensure that the child would die as a Jew.

Through my tears, I would smile as I listened to the story of the fasting on Yom Kippur, which she jokingly commented was a matter of skipping the bowl of watery soup and saving the bread for the breaking of the fast. In the crowded barracks at night, the girls shared the remembered prayers, their whispered Yom Kippur service. Her stories dealt with courage and bravery, friendship and trust.

I was told something very surprising by my sister-in-law Yenti, Sara's childhood friend. They shared that special unifying bond of nightmare survival, for both had been inmates at Auschwitz.

Shortly after Sara's demise, Yenti told me that whenever she thought of her, it was not as she had looked the last time they met, or even the way she looked during the last few years of her life. It was not even the way she had looked during their early years of marriage when they lived in Boston, or the way she looked during the childhood years in Sighet, Marmarosh. The picture that flashed vividly and sharply in her memory was the way she looked when they were reunited unexpectedly in Auschwitz.

During that devastating period in the concentration camp, Sara carried herself in a regal manner and actually looked beautiful. She refused to let her surroundings affect her. Though she was dressed in the ugly, striped, shapeless prison garb that was so dehumanizing, she still managed to look attractive. Tearing a strip off the bottom of that hideous garment, she fashioned it into a belt. She would not allow herself to be defeated. She exuded a feeling of hope and optimism that spread out among everyone with whom she came in contact. That spirit of optimism was an essential part of her, the key to her existence. Throughout her life, even during those very difficult painful final weeks, she greeted visitors with a warm smile, always inspiring those around her with hope and courage.

That memorable day, when they were reunited in camp, Sara was walking across the concentration camp yard carrying a bucket and a mop. She walked briskly, erect and proud, as if en route to some interesting place. When asked where she was going, she responded that she was on her way to clean the latrines, undoubtedly one of the most unpleasant assignments. No, she added, she was not being punished, she had volunteered for this assignment. She jokingly elucidated that there was nothing really pressing on her schedule and that this task would provide her with a few extra rations of bread. Her cousins were weak and the extra bread would give them additional strength to live.

Upon her arrival in Sweden, with the help of Count Folke Bernadotte and the Swedish Red Cross, one of her first objectives was to organize the survivors to request that kosher food be served at the rehabilitation camp at Farnabruk. Her strong faith had never weakened during the sorrowful years, and the first opportunity she had to once again fully observe Torah and Mitzvos, this now became her major concern.

Her first encounter with "the illness" occurred soon after the birth of her youngest child, her only son. The adjustment to this predicament must have been very difficult, but Sara never complained. She embraced life with open arms and total joy. She found happiness in just being alive.

For more than three decades, she lived with the knowledge that "the illness" might recur, but she never dwelled on it. To her, life was to be lived, with warmth and friendship, with care and concern for others.

The last year of her life was a battle, but one she fought with every ounce of strength in her body. The steady stream of visitors was a testimony to her greatness. Everyone loved her and everyone rushed to prepare her favorite dish or fulfill any of her small requests. One day she expressed her wish to have some freshly prepared mashed potatoes. One of her neighbors left her bedside and shortly returned with the dish, but unfortunately, her appetite was very poor and she just had a few bites.

During the week of mourning, the house was constantly filled with people. The women discussed her interest in organizations, her involvement in community activities, in helping others. They spoke of her participation in charity fashion shows where she always stole the show with her natural ladylike grace and charming manner. They spoke of her great love for learning, her frequent attendance at lectures and numerous other Torah classes. During the horrendous war years, which abruptly severed her youth, she had never had an opportunity to study. But she had a keenly intelligent mind, truly loved words of Torah and found great pleasure in the stories of the Ba'al Shem Tov.

Beloved by all, she had the unique ability to make every one of her nieces and nephews, and every other relative, feel that they were her favorite. Yes, that was what made Sara special, her genuine interest in everyone, the love, care and affection that cemented every relationship.

It was in the beginning of summer that I had my last visit with her. When I asked her what I should bring back from Israel, she replied that she would be pleased with anything I brought her. I never envisioned that my last gift to her would be packets of earth from Israel, to be sprinkled on her grave.

The Sunday before my departure, I approached the Rebbe for a blessing. I was reluctant to face the real truth and I was devastated by her deterioration. I was brokenhearted that Sunday – watery eyed, blinking back tears as I walked through the aisles toward the Rebbe. And finally, there I was, right in front of him, and I could no longer stop the tears or choke back my anguished sobs. With great difficulty, I held out my hand and asked for a blessing for Sara bas Henia for a speedy recovery. I was truly amazed at the Rebbe's unexpected response. To my *great* surprise, in a loud clear voice he exclaimed, "*Lange, gute yahren,*" translated as "long, good years." How could this be possible? The situation appeared irreversible. I gained strength and comfort from the Rebbe's compassion and, blinded by tears, I stumbled as I clumsily proceeded to leave 770, Lubavitch Headquarters.

And then, something unbelievable happened. Someone gently grabbed my arm and said, "Go back to the Rebbe. He wants to see you." I realized that the entire line had stopped, and that the Rebbe was watching me, waiting for me to return. He smiled at me gently and asked me when I was leaving for my tours to Scandinavia. I had customarily asked the Rebbe for a blessing for these tours, but now, that had become of secondary importance, as my entire focus was on Sara. I gave him the exact date for the departure of the tour and the Rebbe happily gave me another dollar accompanied by a beautiful blessing. I continued on my way. I must have looked quite strange, tears still streaming down my cheeks, yet with a smile on my face.

That was the Rebbe. During a moment of total despair, he was able to renew hope. Life goes on and life is good.

I pondered the strange blessing, *Lange, gute yahren*, for shortly after that, Sara died. But in truth, the blessing was fulfilled. For, what does "long, good years" entail? In Sara's case, she filled her life with happy moments, gaining strength from the interaction with all her visitors, sharing in their joyous events. They were encouraged to speak about their activities, always minimizing discussions on her state of health. She considered every day of her life as a gift. She spoke of friends and relatives who had perished in the Holocaust, and considered herself fortunate, for she was a survivor. She cherished the thirty-five years of life that she had after the illness first appeared. It had given her the opportunity to see her children marry and watch her grandchildren's development. Those years were yet another gift. She imbued every moment of every day with meaning, with goodness. Hers was a life of quality, not necessarily quantity. "*Lange, gute yahren!*"

Sara's life is an inspiration to us all. I think of her often. At times of joyous celebrations, I miss her especially, for she was an integral part of family functions and gatherings. I know she is up there, watching us, praying and intervening for us to hasten the arrival of the Messiah.

CHAPTER 4

A Heroine with a Story – Magda Eggens

The well-dressed, attractive woman sits at the window of a train, a schedule clutched in her hand. In her eighties, yet still vibrant and mobile, Magda travels to fulfill her life's purpose, to inculcate children with knowledge about the evils of war and hatred. Her Swedish, despite having lived in Sweden for more than half a century, is still very accented. It identifies her as a foreigner, yet that does not impede her from lecturing. She has never learned to drive, and journeys everywhere alone, by public transportation, this courageous octogenarian, Magda Eggens, is indeed a heroine – a woman with a mission.

The young girl from Kisvarda, a small town in northeast Hungary, never imagined that she would live the major part of her life in Sweden. Magda Eggens had probably never even considered visiting that part of the world. During her first few years in Sweden, when she was employed as a factory worker, she never dreamed that one day she would write children's books. But sometimes reality is stranger than fiction, and Magda's life is a vivid illustration of the twists and turns of destiny.

"I grew up in a solid, traditional Jewish home, with loving parents, grandparents and a grandfather who even had a beard," Magda told me, explaining that the beard identified him as an Orthodox Jew. "We participated in Jewish holidays," she continued. "Tradition and culture played an integral role in my daily life." During Magda's teenage years, Nazism reared its ugly head and her life changed radically.

Living in Stockholm, an island of tranquility amidst the turmoil of Europe, I had not realized the gap between my unencumbered childhood and the turbulence Jews were experiencing in Europe until the huge influx of displaced persons arrived. Listening to Magda's story unleashed a torrent of tears, tears not shed during that tumultuous era, because living in a neutral country had shielded me from knowing. By choosing to interview Magda, I voluntarily exposed myself to this survivor's pain.

"When did you first recognize you were being persecuted?" I yearned to know. "Was it a gradual development or did it happen suddenly, like a thunderstorm?"

"It began with ugly remarks by classmates," Magda quietly began, "with insidious teasing and taunting. Teachers we had respected overlooked the bullying directed toward the Jews. Verbal abuse escalated into crowded ghettos, twisting narrow streets, feelings of uncertainty, constant fear of what the future would bring." Her voice rose and fell, pitched at times so low she could barely be heard.

Wrenched from her mother and younger sister, Yudit, in the infamous selection, Magda never set eyes on her parents or sister again. She remained with her sister Eva.

A sheltered existence is hardly adequate preparation for concentration camp. A vulnerable teenager, Magda suffered unbearably degrading, inhumane episodes, unable to be recounted by mere words. Every limb, her very being, was permeated with indescribable anguish.

"I chose to come to Sweden," Magda quietly stated, her eyes downcast. "I had nowhere else to go." I strained to listen to her voice, a mere whisper, but resisted asking Magda to repeat. Gripped by the survivor's pain, I clenched my teeth, to staunch the flow of tears. How did it feel, I wondered, to go alone to a country about which one possessed no prior knowledge, because there was no other option? Magda's pain became my pain and I trembled; the quintessential professional shivered at hearing the details of this woman's story.

There were no survivors in Magda's immediate family, and she had no desire to return to Hungary. Plagued by heinous memories from innocent childhood years before she was deported, when she had been betrayed by neighbors she had thought were her friends, she knew she would not be welcomed in her former, prewar country.

Given a safe haven in Sweden, Magda appreciated the kindness of the Swedes. She spent the first few weeks in a haze, sleeping and eating several meals a day, always small amounts of food. "It was a dreamlike existence," she said wistfully." I was actually afraid this heavenly situation would disappear." Slowly, slowly she found her way back to life.

"I was anxious to lead a normal existence again," Magda related, "so I accepted an assignment to travel to a small town, together with several other survivors, to work in a factory." Twelve random females were given train tickets and some pocket money, and sent on their way. "We traveled lightly," she joked, "a few belongings, some underwear, blouses and a night gown in a backpack." Their destination: Gislaved – a nondescript, ordinary town of working people dominated by a large factory of rubber production.

"My apartment on Abjornsgatan had two bedrooms, six beds per room for the twelve of us, plus a small hall and a bathroom," Magda said. "I worked all day putting soles on boots, seventy boots per day. My hands hurt." Peering at her fists, she opened her hands, perhaps examining them for hidden calluses.

Though her days were exhausting, there was a tremendous sense of peace and satisfaction in her living arrangements. Comforted by the key to her apartment buried in her pocket, Magda had regained control of her destiny.

She demanded little of life, after her nightmarish experiences. A table, two chairs and a radio furnished their small apartment, but the lone hot plate made food preparation very tedious. Only one item could be cooked at a time. Non-confrontational, she solved that dilemma by eating most of her meals at Ringbaren, a nearby cafeteria.

Life became predictable, somewhat monotonous, with long days of work and lonely evenings in the bare, cramped apartment. Everybody was polite; no one was unkind, yet there was a feeling of isolation and loneliness. The language barrier was exceedingly difficult, and the culture and people of Sweden were alien to her. After years of terror and hopelessness, freedom, sanctuary was incredibly uplifting, but life was challenging.

"My life after the war did not revert to the way it was before," Magda sadly confirmed. "My family was gone. I had no one. I had to begin over again, in a strange country, alone." She hugged herself, hands gripping elbows, as though illustrating that the war had rendered her totally self-reliant, with no one to depend on but herself. She could not resume her former life, her prewar existence in the bosom of her family, and was forced to begin anew. Life became stagnant, a colorless existence, barely tolerated. The small town had no synagogue, no Jewish presence whatsoever. This conspicuous absence accentuated the difficulty of adjustment.

Representatives from the Stockholm Jewish community would travel to speak to them on rare occasions, to encourage them, to distribute little gifts – a lipstick, a small purse. Sometimes the group made the long trek to Stockholm to attend a social event, to forge connections with other survivors. They were treated like pariahs by the Jewish youth of Stockholm, who did not extend themselves. The factory girls usually clustered in corners, forgotten, shunned and ignored. "I overheard boys commenting that the refugee girls were so beautiful," Magda recapitulated. "I longed to participate in the social dancing but no one approached me, not even to initiate conversation."

Magda had no special rapport with her roommates. The girls had never been formally introduced, just stuffed together haphazardly in the small apartment. Magda received invitations to join Swedish families for holidays, but felt like an outsider when she attended. She really was the Biblical "stranger in a strange land," unable to relate to the celebration or to even participate in the conversation. Within the holiday atmosphere of conviviality, she felt isolated, alone.

Miraculously, a young man from a building across the street took an interest in her. It began as a casual encounter at a local restaurant. He began teaching her Swedish, drawing simplistic pictures of common objects and labeling them. Thus, she developed her own personal vocabulary. He brought her special treats and the friendship flowered: neighborhood walks, a cup of coffee, everyday conversation. The simple outpouring of friendship brightened Magda's staid existence.

"Before the war I would never have mingled with people who were not Jewish," Magda retorted, her voice tinged with despair, resignation. "I certainly would never have married outside the faith. But living in a small town in Sweden, without a Jewish environment or support system..." she stopped, immersed in recollection and I silently filled in the gaps.

Unanchored, drowning in a swirling sea of loneliness, Magda grabbed the rescue tube with both hands. Grateful to have found a kind, caring man who noticed her, she seized the opportunity for a safe and happy future. He made her smile again, renewed her hope that had been extinguished, buried in concentration camp ashes. His family would have preferred that he marry a local girl, not someone from a strange country, someone they could not comprehend, someone to whom they could not relate. Magda was undoubtedly aware of the cool reception, but that did not disrupt her plans for marriage.

Her circumstances were hardly unique. There were many like her, young female survivors adrift in a sea of confusion, plagued by the loss of family and home, inflicted with memories of fear, hunger, deprivation and dehumanization, of the horrible life of the ghettos and concentration camps, of those difficult years that stripped them of the ability to notice the beauty of life. They were eager to embrace a normal life with husband and children and many made choices similar to Magda's. Today numerous Jewish children, offspring of female survivors, live scattered in small towns, brought up with virtually no knowledge of their Jewish religion and culture.

Magda and her husband worked hard, raising their two children in a small, lovely home in a suburb of Stockholm, in an area devoid of Jewish life.

Magda's son and daughter married Swedes; the grandchildren possess a rudimentary knowledge of their Jewish heritage from their grandmother, who invites them for holidays – a Pesach Seder, a Chanukah feast – celebrated with traditional foods. Magda regales them with background information about the holidays.

Her husband, a pillar of kindness and consideration, always facilitated Magda's maintaining some of her Jewish customs, encouraging her to light candles on Friday night, to usher in the Shabbat, and to examine the sky for three stars on Saturday night to determine its conclusion.

"My husband was a viable source of comfort during those years," Magda recalls. "I would frequently be plagued by recurring nightmares. The memories…" Her voice drops, and her hands drift towards her head, remembering the migraines. "My husband would gently awaken me and hold me. In a soft soothing voice he would tell me beautiful children's stories, substituting harmless stories for the horror, to wash away the ugly memories." Her face glows with love as she recalls those nights.

The tragedy continued. Her sister Eva returned to Hungary after the war and soon thereafter, the country came under Communist rule. "My sister Eva and I were separated for ten years," she sadly reported. "We had suffered so much together during the war, and then we were kept apart by the political changes. My sister married and had children and finally came to Sweden. My husband was marvelous. Without hesitation he opened his heart and invited my sister, her husband and their children to live with us in our small house." Magda smiles as she recalls those happy, though crowded, times and I wipe away an escaped tear that has drifted down my cheek.

Following the death of her husband, her children grown, Magda retired and began a whole new life reconstructing the threads of her past. She feels compelled to spread the message of the evils of war and racism and has become a prolific author of children's books. In addition to making youth aware of the ugly events of World War II through her books, Magda lectures, often visiting schools throughout Sweden, to share her personal war experiences, for history is destined to repeat itself if we don't pay heed.

Magda savors the multitude of letters from children who have been exposed to her ideas. She treasures their words, just as she hopes that they treasure hers. She is reaching out to these young people, molding them into wholesome individuals, in contrast to Hitler, who used his propaganda and writings to destroy naïve German youth. She strives to inculcate Swedish children with an awareness of the destruction committed by the Nazis, of the nightmarish events that resulted from allowing hatred to overshadow basic humanity.

I became aware of Magda's presence during a visit to the Jewish Museum in Stockholm on Helsingegatan, near the Odenplan subway station. The museum, dedicated to the history of Jewish life in Sweden, is filled with Jewish ritual objects, as well as photographs, posters and other artifacts. A section dedicated to the Holocaust prominently displays the dress of a Holocaust survivor, probably the first garment she sewed upon her arrival in Sweden, as well as several other items pertaining to survivors In the Museum of Jewish Heritage there likewise is a dress on display. The dress is representative of the return to life of a survivor – an important first step.

The bookshop really captured my attention! During my childhood in Sweden, the only books with Jewish content were the translations of the prayer book and Chumash, and a book with bible stories. It was gratifying to note several shelves of books of Jewish interest in the museum's bookstore, including four neatly arranged children's books by Magda Eggens with illustrated covers and titles referring to the Holocaust.

After leafing through the quartet of books, I was provided with Magda's phone number by Yvonne Jacobson, Director of the museum. I immediately contacted her and the interview was arranged. It was apparent that Magda's story would be important in developing an understanding of the history of World War II and its aftermath in Scandinavia. Receptive, Magda invited us to her home, where the interview was conducted in Swedish. Since I speak no Hungarian and Magda speaks neither Yiddish nor English, Swedish was our only common language.

Though Magda lives alone, she speaks proudly of her wonderful family; numerous photographs of husband, children and grandchildren adorn the walls. Very attractive as a young girl, Magda is still quite a good-looking woman. Her home, neat and tastefully furnished, is the home of a middle-class family, in a suburb of Stockholm.

Magda graciously welcomed us into her home. Lovely dishes were on the table and coffee was served. It was wintertime and her kitchen was suffused with the aroma of gingerbread cookies. Magda could have chosen to go gently into the good night, to live her golden years quietly and peacefully. Instead, she chooses to be actively involved, to impart the message that never again should evil be allowed to intrude and cause endless sorrow.

Having read extensively about the Holocaust and listened to numerous firsthand accounts, Magda's story was not unknown to me, but the simple retelling of her young life was incredibly moving. I thought I would infuse her with strength. Instead, I grew close to tears when translating her Swedish words into English for the interview taping. Her eyes filled with compassion, Magda had to pause to stroke my arm and comfort me. In retelling her story of childhood, I became an active participant. Expressing her words of anguish and pain penetrated my inner being and I was emotionally deeply affected. My voice shook, I choked back tears and a few times, I was so overcome with emotion that I had to momentarily stop, unable to continue.

"I was tortured by uncertainty," Magda stated, her face frozen, aloof. "I did not know the whereabouts of dear family members, and, against my better judgment, sought information from the SS Gestapo guards. They mocked me. They pointed toward the smokestacks. 'There are your parents,' they told me and laughed. I did not want to believe it, but I did not cry in front of them. I did not want to give them the satisfaction." She relays the incident coldly, psychologically removing herself from the scene.

Suffering intense hunger, Magda was not sure she would survive, and became enveloped by helplessness. Piles of dead bodies became a common sight. Death no longer shocked her, misery was her constant companion. This was her youth.

Magda shivers as she recalls the sleek, cold, steel shaver massaging her scalp, razing her locks, destroying her beauty. Tears cloud her vision but she can still see clumps of hair, a makeshift rug covering the floor. With fingers numbed by gusts of wind, she touches her smooth, unfamiliar scalp, foreign territory. She is constantly cold now, her head no longer protected by hair. Her ugly, bald head, though, is not as cold as her heart, shorn of hope.

The soldiers demanded that she undress while they stood by, gawking. Deathly embarrassed, her modesty compromised; never before had she undressed in the presence of any male, not even her father. Feebly, she tried to cover her body with her hands; she didn't know what else to do. "I was wearing a beautiful slip, a birthday gift. I did not want to take it off but they forced me. I tore the slip with my teeth, to destroy it." Her eyes glint with exultation as she relives gnashing the delicate silk slip, in a courageous stand against the omnipotent Nazis.

Magda's toileting needs, graphically described, were embarrassing because of the total lack of privacy. She lived in fear that she would not be able to perform on demand. Treated like animals, one was not permitted to relieve oneself when the need arose. Instead, the inmates had to exercise exemplary control and urinate only when the SS dispensed their permission. How cruel to deliberately thwart a human being from performing a basic bodily functions, to exert total regimen and control.

"The weather was always cold, freezing." Eyes bleak, the memories pour forth. "I still feel my teeth chattering, not just from the cold but from fear, a fear that defies description," Magda relates.

"Each prisoner was given a numbered metal plaque; my number was 11343. The numbered plate was a means of identification, in lieu of tattooing a number on the forearm." She glances at her arm in bewilderment, as though realizing she has no visible proof that she was ever there. "At night the prisoners slept not on beds, but on planks of wood, conditions so crowded that when one person turned over, the others also had to shift position." Dehumanizing, horrific, and here she was, just a young teenager.

In March 1945, toward the end of the war, the marches began. Germany was losing the war and wanted to remove any trace that there had ever been concentration camps. "We placed paper in our shoes," Magda recounted, "to protect our feet from the ice that blanketed the ground. Our shoes were so worn." She marched, her treasures concealed in a little cloth bag – a broken knife, a spoon, her numbered plate. She showed them to me, treasures carefully salvaged from the war, tangible evidence of the pain.

Brought to Sweden through the Swedish Red Cross, and the Folke Bernadotte mission, the survivors traveled on buses, which were then placed on ferries. Upon arriving in Malmo, Sweden, the displaced people were brought to a large stadium. Mattresses, arranged in neat rows, lined the floor, with disposable sheets of paper covering the mattresses. The survivors collapsed on the mattresses and slept, exhausted.

Many young girls arrived with advanced cases of tuberculosis and were transported to hospitals or sanitariums where they died – young girls, only sixteen or seventeen years old. Defined by hunger during this recuperation period, Magda could eat only a small amount of food at a time because that was all her emaciated body could handle. At first, the meals consisted of a thin cereal. She ate often. After a meal's conclusion, the survivors furtively lined their pockets with bread, crackers, sugar, and salt, frightened at the prospect that there might not be enough food next time. It took a while before they stopped hoarding, realizing that circumstances had changed permanently.

Magda, one of the fortunate ones who experienced Swedish hospitality, rose like a phoenix from the ashes of the concentration camp to publish nine books. Her eighth book is an allegory about a kitten that undergoes suffering and pain. The ninth book focuses on her prewar experiences, in contrast to her other books that addressed the difficulty of adjustment after the war. Perhaps Magda recognizes that she has adjusted adequately, and now feels empowered enough to recall the past.

Reopening healed scabs is painful. Magda could have chosen to forget, to repress the unpleasant memories deep down in her subconscious. Instead, she chooses to relive what is frequently referred to as the darkest period of Jewish history, in the hope of ushering in a better future to the world.

Today, Sweden has a ten percent immigrant population. It is predicted that by 2050, there will be a Muslim majority in Malmo. Magda lectures throughout Sweden to a very diverse group of students, much more heterogeneous than when she arrived in Sweden after the war. The foreign children, new immigrants, approach her following the presentation, their eyes filled with tears, as they lament their personal upheaval, their isolation, their outsider status. She hugs them and comforts them, encouraging them, reminding them that they will soon integrate, that they will adjust. For, after all, hasn't she gone through a similar journey? Hasn't she managed to rebuild?

CHAPTER 5

Rebuilding the World through Art – Lenke Rothman

We came to her home in Lidingo and she, herself, opened the door, no maid or butler in sight. Lenke is a world-famous artist with a career spanning sixty years, yet an unpretentious "real" person, petite, sensitive and very warm, with lovely, delicate hands that attest to her ability to create beautiful artistic works. An octogenarian with an aura of youthfulness about her, she must have been quite a beauty in her youth! Lenke is very feminine, flitting about her home like a butterfly.

Liberated from Bergen-Belsen concentration camp in 1945, Lenke arrived in Sweden after the war, a sixteen-year-old, her lungs riddled with tuberculosis. Her first six years there were spent in a hospital, in an iron lung, until 1951. During those years, she could move only her arms. A kind man in the hospital encouraged her to develop herself artistically, and she began to produce paintings, sculptures and collages. As a child, she had assisted her mother, a hairdresser.

During her childhood, Lenke had always enjoyed spending time in her mother's beauty shop. She was very helpful and with her quick mind and nimble fingers, she became a valued member of her mother's staff. Expertly, she placed rollers in the hair of the clients and applied clips to make waves. Selected to stay alive by Dr. Mengele because of her small, delicate hands and her manual dexterity, she was subsequently placed in a labor camp, where she was forced to do specialized fine work.Lenke had only recently moved into her apartment when we came to interview her. There were unopened boxes and many items in temporary locations. Lenke was well organized, however, and could easily access whatever she wanted to share with us. Though still in the process of unpacking, it was apparent that she enjoyed being surrounded by aesthetic beauty. Her eclectic collection of 300 paintings, collages, sculptures and objets d'art, testifies to her hobby of collecting. Lenke displayed a large book of reproductions of her artwork on the crowded coffee table.

She drew my attention to a photograph of a piece of driftwood and asked for my opinion. "It reminds me of a Torah," I told her, "rectangular, like a Torah scroll, and with the pointed top, like the crown of a Torah." Animated by my description, she demanded that I examine the driftwood more attentively. I complied, and saw some markings that I was unable to decipher without reading glasses.

"Look," Lenke said excitedly, handing me a magnifying glass. "I carved the initials of my six siblings into the wood." Now I clearly noticed the six Hebrew letters.

"This makes a great deal of sense," I replied. "It is as if your siblings are embedded in the Torah, that they are part of our Holy Scroll." Satisfied with that analysis, she nodded happily in affirmation. Suddenly I felt her looking at me intently, in a new way. No longer was I just a person interviewing her, but someone of interest.

"Chana," she said, "where do you live?"

"In Brooklyn, in New York," I answered. Lenke became very enthusiastic.

"I have relatives in Brooklyn," she continued, "in a very religious area. What neighborhood do you live in?"

"Crown Heights," I answered. She shook her head. "What are some other areas in Brooklyn?" As soon as I mentioned Williamsburg, she became flustered. "Yes," she said, "that's where my relatives live." Within moments she left the room and returned with a small, worn address book.

She flipped through the pages and found the phone numbers of her cousins with whom she had lost contact many years ago. It was at that moment that we bonded. Had we lived in the same place, at the same time, I think we might have been friends. Upon my return, with some detective work, I reconnected her with the relatives. When Lenke had visited New York, many years earlier, they had attempted to convince her to stay, but Sweden had become her place of rescue, her home.

Her youth lost in the concentration camp, the vivid memory of her mother and six siblings never totally leaves her. She was only a teenager when Doctor Mengele callously separated her from the rest of her family in his infamous selection, pointing her mother and six younger siblings in one direction while designating her toward life. She never saw them again after that. The number eight assumes exponential importance in her life, constantly reminding her of the gnawing absence of her six siblings and parents. A ring of eight stones in a jewelry store evokes powerful memories of her family; compelled, driven, she purchases the ring.

Watching a duck swimming happily in the water alongside her six ducklings, again her delicate equilibrium is shattered. Within a rock formation, she visualizes the figure of a mother holding out her hands to a child; she is that child, yearning to run toward her mother. Six boards near a building engulf her with memories from the past. The camp experiences may have faded but the memory of her siblings and parents constantly haunt her.

While in the camp, Lenke was afraid to close her eyes at night; gripped with fear, she was afraid she would never be able to open them again. A sensitive daughter, she wanted to prevent the suffering of her poor father. What would happen if he returned to realize he was the only survivor? The horror! In actuality, of course, she never saw or heard from him again.

Numerous references to Jewish existence are sharply embedded in her mind: the chanting of her father's Torah study, melodies sung by her mother, inspirational Chassidic tales told by her father. The buried past keeps emerging, capriciously kindled by the present. Yom Kippur prayers, her father ceremoniously swinging a chicken over her head, a symbolic removal of her sins, earmarking her for life. He blesses her, his hand lightly caressing her head. The pressure of his hand on her innocent head protects her but cannot assuage his destiny.

Proprietor of an umbrella shop, her father created beautiful hand-made umbrellas, the Singer sewing machine humming as he sewed the silk material. His real love was Torah learning and teaching. She sees a workshop full of broken umbrellas that he repairs skillfully, meant to shield from the rain. Her father could not shield himself from death.

Years later, during one of her numerous surgeries, her body helpless on the operating table, she hears the sound of the sewing machine being dragged from their home, the noise it makes as it grates against the uneven cobblestones in the street. It is the knife cutting into bone that mimics the sound, the pain obliterated by the anesthetic.

Her deep, unwavering faith in Judaism helped her survive. As a young child, she was told of the imminent arrival of the Messiah. This message was present in every task she completed. Wherever she went, on errands for her mother, especially to fetch water, she would pass through the courtyard of the synagogue, and put down the pails to rest her aching arms. She wanted to greet him, and then race back to her family to announce his arrival. Told that *Mashiach* would come when times were truly difficult, she believed that the war years would be suitable for him to make an appearance. I could clearly visualize her touching, vivid description and feel myself accompanying her with the same anticipation and longing.

A small flame flickers in her bare room in Bergen, ushering in the Jewish New Year 5745. Different episodes illustrate one common theme: optimism piercing through darkness, energy shattering isolation, Lenke's spirit prevailing over adversity.

Art is a way of communicating and Lenke's persona is clearly revealed through her artistic endeavors. With her own unique style and technique, using a variety of materials, including ink, chalk and tempera, her productivity is incredible. Her entire life has been dedicated to bringing beauty into the world, perhaps an unconscious response to obliterate the ugliness of the war years.

Her collages are a window into her essence. Her dear friend Jan Lundvik remarked, "Lenke always found things. A rock on the beach, a twig in the woods, odd buttons in the flea market; discarded items were given new life when placed in a collage." *Was this symbolic of her life*? I wondered. Subconsciously, was there a connection with her own life, arriving in Sweden barely alive, helpless, with a serious case of tuberculosis? In her collages there are symbols of sewing machines and umbrellas reminiscent of her father. Broken clocks may indicate the loss of teenage years in the camp, of time, equivalent to life, severely interrupted or destroyed.

An indomitable spirit, Lenke loves life. Her sad and destructive experiences have never diminished her zest and appreciation for beauty. One day she find a stalkless blossom of a chrysanthemum on the street, slightly crushed by the wheels of a car. She picks it up, brings it home, places it in a dish, and watches, with happiness, as it rejuvenates, spreading out, and offering its wonderful aroma. She enjoys its beauty and revels in having infused it with new life, a celebration of existence and beauty.

A "shopaholic," she incessantly purchases items attempting to fill a void that cannot be filled. She collects pieces of material and stitches the remnants together. Perhaps the pieces of cloth represent fragmented parts of her life; joining them will impose order, bringing wholeness, completion. Is this an attempt at mending that which the Nazis tore asunder? I am puzzled. Cloth shields us and protects us. Fragmented cloth exposes us, defenseless, revealing the ugly truth.

Certain incidents Lenke has experienced caused emotional torment so powerful, it paralyzed her. In the late summer of 1944, merely fifteen years of age, she witnesses a terrible episode in the camp. Late at night, she has gone from the barrack to the bathrooms, and is walking back to her bed when she witnesses an SS Nazi guard brutally beating an old woman. Blood gushing from the woman's open wounds, the Nazi guard orders her dog to attack the woman. Lenke hides to remain unnoticed, not to become the next victim, but she is devastated at her inability to help. The ugly scene, imprinted on Lenke's soul, terrifies her, rendering her speechless. She remembers feeling powerless, unable to help the woman. Cowardly, she slinks away to save herself, lacking the courage to help the woman. She surrenders her power of speech, the trait that distinguishes man from animal. The incident inspires the image of lips sewn together, voice paralyzed, unable to utter a single word because words cannot express these deep feelings; they can only be expressed through tears.

Lenke's views on language are interesting and I can relate to them. She criticizes people for paying less attention to the content of a second-language speaker's words than to the technicalities of the language. Overly concerned with correcting the pronunciation, syntax or structure, people frequently miss what the person is communicating: the depth of feeling in what is being said often is quite lost. Lenke's experiences mirrored mine as a newcomer to the United States, a period of frustration.

Highly intelligent, Lenke reveals herself also through her writing. She feels betrayed when outsiders, people who have not been residents in camps, attempt to describe the experiences of the Holocaust. She does not think it possible for them to comprehend the feelings of survivors. Her language was restored in Sweden as her life was renewed.

With great sadness, Lenke empathizes with the death of Primo Levy, a distinguished chemist in Italy before the war. Unable to resume his profession and return to normal life after surviving the atrocities, he became an author, a spokesperson for the survivors. Forty years after the war, he committed suicide. Lenke, too, is unable to resume her past life seamlessly, constantly gripped by the memories that threaten to overtake her.

Lenke describes a touching relationship with Nelly Sachs, the Nobel Prize recipient of literature in Stockholm. Invited to Sweden by Selma Lagerlof, the first Swedish Nobel Prize winner for Literature, Nelly Sachs was rescued from Germany, along with her mother. Memories are awakened upon meeting Lenke, and the two develop a deep relationship. Nelly Sachs dedicates a poem to Lenke in response to a picture she painted. "I feel a special bond to Lenke; I remember being like her as a child, quiet and serious. Her thoughts, her ideas impress me deeply. Her story could have been mine."

People write to recreate their lives, to transform their lives into art. Graduates of concentration camps were not merely robbed of a few years of their lives; the experience changed them completely, rendering them forever scarred, irrevocably damaged. An inmate, upon leaving the concentration camp, was radically different from the naïve individual who had initially entered. Had both these individuals met in the street, they probably would have had nothing in common. Frightened of one another, they might have even been reluctant to communicate. Yet, one body, possessing such varied experiences, had to integrate the constant conflict. Both individuals had to co-exist harmoniously afterward. Lenke Rothman, one of many survivors, is plagued by the impossibility of reconciling the past and the present.

"Language," Lenke insists, "is not sufficient to express painful thoughts." It is evident that the legacy of her beloved father's teachings of Chassidic philosophy and his approach to life are deeply embedded in her. The teachings of Kabbalah introduce the concept of removing the *klipah*, the outer shell that covers the fruit, slowly removing one layer after another, like the skin of an onion, to expose the innermost kernel, life's purpose. She longs to peel back the bark of a tree to reveal what is underneath, to finally be free. The intrusion of memory creates confusion, an incoherent, indecipherable code.

Her autobiography *Rain*, fascinating and well written, represents her search for the deep meaning of *life*, an attempt to uncover the eternal secret, a quest addressing questions that have no answers. *Rain*, written in diary form, is replete with copious references of her concentration camp recollections. Memories crowd her mind and, throughout the rest of her life, color everything she sees and does – memories that burst forth uncontrollably.

Lenke's situation can perhaps best be described as a dichotomy, She wants to forget, but is unable to. Memories resurface, uninvited, a constant struggle between past and present, like a thread that weaves experiences into a composite. She describes Bergen, a Norwegian city she visits after recuperating from her lengthy illness. She recalls families being separated at the selection, Dr. Mengele deciding the fate of individuals by merely pointing his finger, protectively enclosed in a glove. She witnessed families torn asunder, fear in their eyes as they turned to retain a last view of their loved ones, before they were taken away.

The cover of her book features a reproduction of one of her famous paintings, entitled "Rain" – tempra on canvas – from 1963. Raindrops are scattered over a page of Hebrew letters, randomly placed in horizontal and vertical rows, making no sense, unreadable. Lenke's language, infested with raindrops, with salty tears of sadness, her jumbled memories are illustrated by these randomly scattered letters. Language, she insists, is not sufficient to express painful thoughts; the intrusion of memories creates confusion, an incoherent, indecipherable code.

Her book is replete with keen observations of daily life around her. Peering from the window of her hotel room, she sees chimneys, and the harmless smoke evokes reminders of the concentration camp. She notices and records everyday scenes – of a woman shopping, touching and examining the fruit, of men relaxing on a park bench.

Her travels through Norway, the land of tunnels, mirror my experiences, yet our views differ. I anticipate the light at the end of the tunnel, reveling in the return to magnificent scenery; Lenke views these tunnels as roads to death. She describes a fjord cruise, the still waters of the fjords with the mirror images. We both appreciate the magnificent formation of the mountains, the abundance of fauna and the well-kept, small houses, mirrored perfectly in the still, clear water.

"Your vibrant laughter, so vivacious, it's like a young child's," someone tells her. She steps back and analyzes; she has become remarkably proficient at analyzing, a regular scientist with regard to her own life. She makes an interesting observation about laughter, and realizes that childlike laughter is the only type of laughter that she can remember – carefree laughter expressed as a young child – for after the war, she forgot how to laugh. She was incapable of laughing as an adult, as the joy in life had been taken from her during the Holocaust years.

She recalls frightening incidents from the camp; gaping at a woman as she is severely beaten, listening to her praying, teeth rattling with fear. After the war, the cruel Nazi female guard resettles in Sweden and describes her new life there, employed as a caretaker of children. She claims to have considerable experience working with children, never admitting that her activities mainly consisted of terrorizing helpless people, both young and old, in a concentration camp.

Yet Lenke courageously prevails over the sadness, preferring to surround herself with beauty. Collecting and preserving odds and ends – from a flea market, a park, a beach, or a street; an interesting-looking stone, a piece of driftwood, buttons – she gathers them and transforms them into beautiful collages. Determined to transform the ugliness of her experiences into something meaningful, she has made it her life's quest to recycle ordinary odds and ends into objects of aesthetic pleasure.. She looks for beauty, and chooses to share it with the world.

Lenke is revealed through her writing. I wish I had read her book before interviewing her. Nevertheless, we had a wonderful and productive meeting. She presented her book to me and wrote a personal inscription: "To Chana, with very good wishes for the year 2007 until 120 [years]. January 14, 2007."

I have contacted Lenke via email, and sent her several letters praising *Rain*, lamenting that the book was available only in Swedish, and therefore accessible to a very limited audience. People everywhere in the world, I am certain, would benefit from perusing her stories. I send her greetings for Passover and Rosh Hashanah and she always responds with appreciation.

Her artwork is a testimonial to her resistance to destructive forces, to her desire to surround herself with beauty, to make life meaningful and hopeful. In 1994, she contacted Per Kaks, Director of the Swedish National Museum of Ethnography, regarding a memorial for Raoul Wallenberg. The memorial, "Tracks," contains an actual plaster cast of the railroad track from Auschwitz, cast in bronze. Placed strategically between these tracks, a forlorn bright, little, red ball gives an indication of life amidst the death wagons. Thus she created a vivid and authentic monument to Raoul Wallenberg, the savior of thousands of Hungarian Jews.

She was commissioned to construct a memorial honoring Raoul Wallenberg, which was completed in January 1998 and placed in the Parliament in Stockholm. The triangular-shaped glass monument in a corner of the room contains small stones transported from the Swedish safety houses in Hungary; an authentic replica of his appointment book; a section of the dispatch dated July 18, 1944, the date of his appointment; an official report with his signature and a pair of candlesticks. Candlesticks are reminiscent of Jewish ceremonies: the lighting of the Chanukah menorah to recall the miracle, and the Shabbat candles for times of joy and peace. Sandblasted into the protective glass is the statement, "To Remember the Outstanding Deed."

Lenke, a survivor, used the experiences of her life to create beauty. A meticulous observer, she truly knew how to transform the ordinary into aesthetics, to rebuild and redesign her world through art.

Epitaph

I was very saddened to receive the news that Lenke Rothman had passed away on November 27, 2008. She died peacefully after a somewhat lengthy illness. Lenke was very organized regarding her funeral arrangements, ascertaining that all details meticulously adhere to Orthodox tradition. A white outfit hung forlornly in her closet. She had prepared it with a note attached, instructing that this be her burial outfit. She was laid to rest in a simple pine coffin, at her request. A small, intimate crowd attended the funeral – no flowers or music. She faced death heroically, the way she always faced life.

She composed her own obituary. "It is painful," she wrote, "that in the midst of life, I must leave all those dear to me, all good friends. There was so much I wanted to accomplish, but there was not enough time. Perhaps eternity will present new possibilities. I now leave to you the Lamp of Life, to bring forth a better world with more time than was given to me. Lenke, November 2008."

In the funeral chapel, the only artistic work evident is a tapestry of her painting "Rain," encapsulating her philosophy on life. Customarily, in Sweden, a Jewish obituary features a Magen David. However, at Lenke's request, the word "*Chai*" was featured, representing her intense focus on *life*.

CHAPTER 6

A Hero with a Song – Ben Olander

Ben is a *mentch*. This Yiddish word "mentch," adapted into the American language, is an accolade that eludes translation. This all-inclusive term refers to someone who possesses the best mankind has to offer: honesty, decency, dependability – someone who can be totally trusted. A multifaceted, extremely talented individual, Ben conducts himself as a mentch in every area of his life.

"He has a grandfatherly look," Dassy comments as she scrutinizes the photograph on the inside cover of his book, *Gladjehuset: The House of Happiness*, a definitive history of his company, Butterick. "He appears kind and patient, compassionate, with a glint of humor in his eyes. I think he enjoys a great joke, likes to laugh. And those big, round glasses, they are really cool." Her final comment is accompanied by soft giggling. "Well," she remarks, a big smile brightening her face, "Bubby, how am I doing?"

I am amazed by my granddaughter's precociousness. I remark, "That was impressive. Ben is well known in many fields, yet he is down-to-earth, low-key, and always makes you feel comfortable in his presence. I am always delighted when he sends me email. I value them so much, I save and reread them."

"Bubby, you are so lucky," exclaims Dassy. "How did you find all these interesting people to interview?"

"That's a great question," I respond. "It began with a list of people I wanted to meet, many of them admirers of Wallenberg"

"I know," interrupts Dassy, "Jewish geography. Everybody knew somebody, right?" And we both laugh.

Ben is a successful businessman, third generation of his family, in the one-hundred-year-old Butterick's branch in Stockholm. It is his business philosophy that I particularly admire. His concept of business is reduced to a simplistic formula of two people who exchange goods or services with both being satisfied by the outcome. Ben's succinct description: "Think of what you have, seek out those who require what you possess and then strike a deal that benefits both." When I told him about my Scandinavian tours, I admitted that I was more concerned with the satisfaction of my customers than with the financial gain, and we both laughed.

I was particularly impressed that Ben complied with his parents' wishes not to pursue a career in music and actualize his teenage dream. He planned to accept a position in the diplomatic corps when his father had a heart attack. Concerned about the future of the business, Ben promised his father to remain at the helm until his father's health improved. Unfortunately, his father died, but Ben kept his word and fulfilled his role masterfully, with pride and love, addressing the financial growth of the company as well as expansion into new areas. Ben is always a mentsch in his business dealings, conducting himself with integrity and honesty.

We arrived at his newly decorated, cozy apartment in Kungsholmen in Stockholm, near the famous City Hall, Riksdagshuset, to interview him for the Scandinavian documentary. His presence filled the sparsely furnished home that had been acquired just days before. Greeted with great warmth and friendship, we immediately felt "at home." Had I known of Ben's fame in the world of business, I might have been somewhat intimidated. Had I known that he was famous in the world of music, a songwriter and composer, I might have felt awed. Had I known about his published book and stories, I might have been duly impressed. But I knew just one aspect of Ben: his love of his grandmother and his admiration for Raoul Wallenberg.

"My first memory dates back to an incident that happened in the schoolyard when I was seven years old," relates Ben. Forehead furrowed, he speaks wistfully, "A classmate was being attacked, brutalized by a group of schoolyard bullies. I was upset and asked my teacher about it. She was uncomfortable and dismissed it saying, 'This is a subject we will discuss in the higher grades. Wait until then and don't worry about it.'"

Dissatisfied with her explanation, Ben approached his mother, identifying the boy by name. "My mother was unaware of the circumstances and had no answer. Then I decided to discuss the situation with my grandmother, the favorite person of my childhood." He paused. A faint smile appeared on his face, an automatic response, triggered by the memory of his grandmother.

"A progressive lady, she relished the puff of a good cigar. She listened to me intently, paying close attention, validating my concern. After I completed the narrative she became very incensed. She removed the cigar from her mouth, sat me down, and told me about racism. She explained that the little boy was Jewish and that the children were victimizing him only because he was Jewish. She spoke about the ugliness of racial hatred and how the Swedes had been instrumental in helping the Danish Jews resettle in Sweden after the Danes had participated in their escape across the Sound. She also told me that a considerable number of Jews were employed in the family business and that many of their associates were of Jewish descent."

Love of humanity and respect for all races and religions are part of Ben's inherent genetic make-up, an inheritance from his grandparents. Ben's grandparents had relocated from Copenhagen to Gothenburg, where they resided during the turbulent period when Danish Jews were rescued and smuggled to Sweden in fishing boats. Their home instantly became a haven, an oasis that provided housing, food, jobs and whatever assistance was needed for the Jewish Danish refugees.

"My grandparents were resistance fighters during the war," said Ben. "They housed Jewish refugees in their home, and hired a Hungarian woman to work in their house. She must have been a refugee. She always looked very sad." Ben's voice cracks and he forces himself to continue. "I am sensitive. I noticed these things, even as a child.

I asked her why she was sad and she shared with me the intimate details about the kindness of Raoul Wallenberg." Ben Olander was only a child when he heard, from the mouth of a survivor, the story of the Swedish diplomat who during his six-month stay in Budapest had saved approximately 60,000 Jews by issuing his special Schutz-Pass, the life-saving document mentioned earlier. Deeply impressed by Raoul Wallenberg's refusal to capitulate to the status quo, from that moment, Raoul Wallenberg became his hero.

Ben believes in the message of Raoul Wallenberg, frequently quoting him. "We have the option of choosing, of deciding the course of our lives. When we act," Ben continues, "we can achieve what might initially have appeared to be impossible. Raoul Wallenberg exemplified what an individual can accomplish if he unhesitatingly plunges into situations that initially seem overwhelming, because he is propelled by a strong belief in the mission." Ben is an authentic, no-ersatz person.

His music is an expression of his innermost self and represents the qualities of a mentsch: decency, integrity, loyalty, compassion. His meteoric rise in the music world is unprecedented. At age forty-nine, when most musicians have already reached their peak, he began his music career. What is inspiring is what his attitude was. He fulfilled his filial obligations and accepted the position as CEO in Butterick's with aplomb, never displaying resentment or disappointment that he could not actualize his dream of becoming a musician. With great loyalty, with total dedication and devotion, he used his creative abilities and energy to continuously expand the business.

He had always mingled with creative, artistic people in the entertainment world. Encouraged by his friends, he began to set aside time to compose music to his own lyrics. Within the first two years, he composed seven popular songs which were included on the Swedish Top List. His music is uncomplicated, reflective, lyrical easy listening, belonging to the genre of popular or folk music. It is atypical in that it does not address love, but features topics that inspire or evoke a smile. Mild satire interlaced with humor, his songs are insightful, focusing on values of life, a love of humanity and the danger of passivity.

The themes of his songs are friendship and nature: the beauty of spring, the lightness of summer, the falling of raindrops and the brilliant colors of fall. This renowned folk artist offers insights into life and builds qualities of character. I enjoy Ben's music because it is very pleasing and makes you feel good. The songs that convey messages come across clearly, the importance of fighting tyranny, and being courageous. I wish I could attend one of his concerts.

During our interview session, we noticed Ben's guitar. "I never go anywhere without it," he stated, and we asked him to provide us with a sampling of his music. Our private performance was very exciting. His voice is warm and vibrant. When we left, he gave us a CD of his music and a copy of his special PowerPoint presentation.

A hero, Ben has chosen to dedicate his life toward making the world a better place. He has composed a PowerPoint presentation consisting of beautiful pictures, accompanied by his own original music and lyrics, dedicated to the life of Raoul Wallenberg. He sets aside time from his important business concerns to travel throughout Sweden, the United States and Israel to present his program, gratis, to reinforce the message of hope for a better world – a world suffused with peace and harmony. He has shared his program with Yeshivas, secular schools and numerous other groups and organizations.

Photography is another one of his passions. He has mailed me countless photographs from his travels and from the Swedish countryside. Familiar scenes from Israel or New York are wonderful, for there is an added dimension when viewing them through Ben's eyes. After his recent trip to Israel, Ben shared his enthusiasm with me. He visited the usual tourist sights: toured Masada, went swimming in the Dead Sea and spent some time at a kibbutz. Impressed with the accomplishments of a country that is a mere sixty years old, he appreciated the scenic beauty and historical monuments. Ben's most powerful impressions were the Tunnel Tour and the Kotel on Friday night.

A mentsch conducts himself with high moral standards at all times – *that* is Ben and I am proud to be his friend. He is well known in the business world, a renowned folk artist, a persuasive balladeer with his Wallenberg message and an interesting writer and storyteller, and yet still finds time to keep in touch with ordinary folks like me. Also a devoted husband to Toni and a loving father, he values family and friendship. Unlike many entertainers, Ben is in a category by himself.

A descendant of the Vikings, their blood flowing through his veins, their courage and love of adventure is part of Ben's essence. Unafraid of public opinion, he has become the spokesperson for Israel in a Swedish society that today is unfortunately presenting a one-sided negative view. Sweden's steadily growing Muslim population has impacted on Swedish society, and the media's approach to Israel is negative. Ben vociferously expresses his belief and refuses to be intimidated by possible consequences.

Angry at the Swedish Press and CNN, he comments, "Jews have no problem living with Arabs, but Arabs have a problem living with Jews." He wonders why Egypt did not open its borders to the Gaza population. He writes to his friend, "Why have you never sent me mail regarding actions of Hamas versus civilians, not even one piece of correspondence? The world turned its back on Israel, forcing them to take action. Jews are protecting themselves after having been attacked for seven years by Palestinian rockets. That is self-protection, not military action." He quotes Per Wastberg: "Evil receives nourishment from passivity." Ben's theme is "No Hesitation" – stand up against tyranny, stand tall and straight. Tenaciously hold on to your belief. Don't be afraid to be a single voice. Ben proves, with the philosophy of his mentor Raoul Wallenberg and the presentation of his message, that a single voice can have a powerful effect.

The legacy of Raoul Wallenberg burns brightly within Ben. I have met many successful businessmen, I have encountered authors and performers within the entertainment world, yet Ben is unique. His creativity permeates every area of his life. But that is not what endears him to me. Ben is a true friend to our people. Our challenges are his challenges. Our concerns are his concerns. He will not stand by to let us be victimized in any place or in any situation. Ben incorporates that spark of humanity that burned brightly within Raoul Wallenberg. He is the gleam of hope within our world today. There should be no place for bigotry in our world.

In a recent email, in June 2009, Ben describes his great happiness at having acquired a partner "to assist me in rearranging my Wallenberg program. As previously mentioned, I am disappointed that I was not included in the Forum of Living History (a Swedish government project focused on The Holocaust). The reason for my having been excluded is probably linked to my approach of centering on the heroism of Wallenberg, who, even to this day, is still an uncomfortable open wound for many Swedes.

"I sometimes feel that the Holocaust is viewed as a Jewish problem according to many non-Jews. I have been told that those that are non-Jews should not occupy themselves with that subject, but should leave it for Jews, survivors and their offspring; I deem that attitude horrific! In my opinion, Jews should be least involved in this subject because it is *essential* that the attitude of everyone else must be transformed radically."

His latest project involves bringing students to tour Auschwitz in the spring, to further their understanding of the Holocaust. This project will be financed by Ben, himself, from his personal performances.

We need friends like Ben. May he continue to experience success in all areas of his life, and may his quest for building a better world – a world filled with fairness and kindness – be crowned with success. Ben Olander's songs featuring Raoul Wallenberg promote Holocaust awareness and encourage audiences to truly believe that through courage and fortitude, each individual can change the world.

CHAPTER 7

A Private Matter

This was one of the strangest experiences I have ever encountered. It began as a private matter; the privacy remained and nothing was ever revealed. All the facts in the story are accurate, as far as I know because I was involved. The only other person that could have verified this was Rabbi J. J. Hecht, but he is no longer alive.

As in most cases, there were two opposing sides, but what was unusual here was that I sympathized with both. My heart was equally broken for both women, the unfortunate birth mother who never could meet her only child, and the adoptive mother who must forever keep the secret, always living in fear lest the truth be revealed. No names were ever mentioned, no photographs displayed and no actual meetings took place.

Had the events happened ten years later, this story would never have occurred. At that time, in the late 1940s, children born out of wedlock were considered an embarrassment. Even in Sweden, a very liberal country, illegitimacy was viewed with scorn. Being a single mother in the United States in the early 1950s would have been overwhelming. Liv would encounter disapproval upon returning home expecting a baby. Remaining on her own in the States was not a feasible option. It was with great reluctance and much heartache that Liv gave up the rights to her daughter.

My heart broke for Liv, who only wanted to meet her daughter, to be certain if the decision to give her up had been a good choice. Meeting her in person would have fulfilled the dream of her life, but even a photo and a report of her daughter would have meant the world to her. Adoptions at that time were sealed. All doors were closed for Liv with no possibility of obtaining any information.

Yet I also felt the anguish of the adoptive mother, with her worrying that this could cause problems for the daughter in terms of finding a suitable mate, and now always living with uncertainty, with the fear that somehow the facts could be revealed. This matter did, however, remain private as far as I know and seems likely it will forever remain a secret. Had Dr. Mengele never conducted his disgraceful, atrocious experiments on young Jewish girls, leaving them unable to bear children, this adoption would not even have taken place. The story as far as I know was never resolved.

Liv came to the States as an au pair to improve her English. Refining her language skills, Liv felt, would enhance her future. The naïve blonde, from a small town in Sweden, was honest and trusting. Young and inexperienced, the teen was flattered by the attention of her handsome, successful employer. Enchanted with her beauty, he took advantage of her and before long Liv found herself in an unenviable situation.

"You will have to leave," he informed her. "I don't want my wife to ever discover your pregnancy." Although the employer had betrayed his wife, he did have the decency to provide the unfortunate young woman with sufficient funds for living expenses. His desire to keep his marriage intact did not diminish his responsibility for what he had caused.

Too embarrassed to face her family or friends in Karlstad, she remained in the United States, where she gave birth to a healthy, beautiful girl. Her family was never told about the pregnancy or the child; thus, without options, Liv gave the child up for adoption and returned home.

Every incident is part of a chain. A past event transforms the future, sometimes with excruciating consequences. One fall day, my phone rang. Immediately I recognized the distinct voice of Rabbi J. J. Hecht, an active community leader in Flatbush, in Lubavitch circles and in the Jewish world at large. "Chana," he said," please come to my office as soon as possible. I am confronting a highly sensitive situation and your input would be invaluable."

Curious and excited, I hurried to his office on Eastern Parkway near Kingston Avenue in Brooklyn. "Here," he said handing me an envelope with a familiar Swedish stamp. "Please read this and then give me your opinion. Your personal understanding of the Swedish psyche is essential."

I was deeply touched by this letter and affected by the pain and anguish of the distraught mother. Reluctantly she had given the child up for adoption – a decision she has regretted since. She had been irrevocably harmed by her misadventure and, though she became a successful psychologist, she had never married. Her long-ago employer had shattered her life, and the crushing episode might have resulted in Liv's mistrust of men and avoidance of relationships. Extremely distraught, she gave up the child with great sorrow.

Liv longed to contact this child, her only offspring. Twice she came to America but was unsuccessful in the attempt to locate her daughter. She carefully saved her money and subsequently hired a private investigator. The search had led her to Rabbi Hecht's door, and this letter, sent through the investigator, was an appeal to the Rabbi, beseeching him to assist Liv in completing her search. Perhaps the investigator sought Rabbi Hecht's input because, as a member of the clergy, he might be able to open channels limited to laymen.

Carefully replacing the letter into the envelope, I looked up, my eyes tear-stained, chin quivering.

"What should I do?" Rabbi Hecht asked. "What do you think?"

"My heart breaks for this woman," I quietly replied. "Swedes are decent and honest. I want to help her. Her daughter, at this point, is eighteen or nineteen years old. Liv just wants to know that her child is alright. I doubt that she has any ulterior motives.

"I will be the go-between," I urged Rabbi Hecht. "She has gone through so much agony already. Let her communicate with somebody who speaks her language, somebody who sympathizes with her plight." After much deliberation, it was decided that I would contact Liv to discuss the matter.

My heart refused to rest in my determination to facilitate a reunion between the mother and daughter. I only wished that innocent lives would not be crushed by the juggernaut. Life was so complicated sometimes; a simple dalliance could reverberate eternally. The situation was unspeakably tragic and I wanted with my whole heart to help Liv.

In the midst of Rabbi Hecht's dialing, I requested that he replace the receiver. What would I say? How would I begin? I was feeling tense and anxious.

After collecting my thoughts, there was a second attempt. I introduced myself in Swedish and as soon as I mentioned the name of Rabbi Hecht, I could hear her sharp intake of breath.

Tremulously, in a whispery voice she responded, "Yes?" Hesitantly, she continued, "Thank you for calling. This means the world to me. For many years I have tried to make this contact." Tense, heavy silence.

"I'm calling regarding the search for your daughter," I responded, almost gasping at the figurative drowning in a sister's quagmire of distress. "Tell me exactly what you want."

"Please." The voice was low, apologetic, and almost desperate. "I don't want to invade my child's life or cause any difficulty. I don't want to impose my identity on her. She does not have to be told I am her birth mother. I just want to know that she is healthy and happy. All my life I have regretted the decision to give up my daughter for adoption," continued Liv in her soft, gentle voice. "I was so young. And I was afraid. In those days, things were different. Often I think that I should have been brave and kept her."

The staccato statements flung like darts. It took me a few seconds to digest the contents.

"I understand," I told Liv reassuringly. "Let's figure out a plan."

Several options were explored, but we finally agreed on trying this one: "Let's arrange an 'impromptu' meeting at a restaurant," I suggested. "I'm a tour guide for Scandinavia," I continued. "I will tell the adoptive mother to concoct a scenario about her being interested in traveling to Scandinavia. She will meet me and bring her daughter along for company. You will pose as a personal acquaintance and local guide in Stockholm."

"Thank you so much for helping me." Liv's overwhelming gratitude seeped into me. Clenching clammy hands into fists, I prayed that the arrangements would go smoothly. They didn't.

Again I visited the office of Rabbi Hecht. Since this was a private matter, he would not provide me with any information about the adoptive parents; after all, he was a clergyman, sworn to confidentiality. He dialed their number, introduced me briefly and handed me the phone. The parents, concentration camp survivors, had been unable to have children as a result of Dr. Mengele's experiments. After adopting Liv's baby, they had gone to live in Europe for a year, to distance themselves from gossip and questions No one knew that the little girl was adopted; it was a well-kept secret.

"My daughter does not know that she is adopted," the adoptive mother whimpered. "I don't want any difficulties to ensue that might impede her opportunity for marriage," plaintively attempting to justify her position. She sounded absolutely terrified.

"How about allowing me to meet your daughter alone," I suggested, as a compromise. "Then I could send the birth mother a personal description. That would probably satisfy her." Anxiously, the woman attempted to end the phone conversation. Her carefully constructed world was crumbling. Her discomfort was clearly evident.

Who was to blame for failure to comply? The woman had gone through so much at Mengele's hands, her female identity ripped asunder. Heartbreaking and pitiful that a woman who longed to bear children could not, while a teen who did not want to bear a child had been inflicted with an unwanted pregnancy!

I could not judge this poor woman. She would probably never have considered adoption under normal circumstances. The evil Dr. Mengele's tampering had ruined countless lives. The repercussions were still swirling.

Torn apart, I felt sorry for Liv and equally sympathetic toward the adoptive mother. Could this dilemma be reconciled? King Solomon had been faced with two mothers and one child, each mother claiming the child as her own. Confronting a young unsuspecting teenager with this dilemma could shatter her world. I wondered if too much information could result in psychologically splitting her world?

"Would you just give me a picture to send her," I pleaded. "A photo would satisfy the mother in Sweden – that and a brief report of her character and schooling."

"Leave me alone," she implored, her voice barely audible. "Leave my family alone. Go away."

Adamant that no contact be made, the adoptive mother would not give an inch. Absolutely no capitulation. No compromise. She was distraught, filled with fear and panic. Her carefully constructed life, rebuilt with great care, was no longer on solid ground. She was unsteady, caught in quicksand.

"I hope all will be well," I sadly sighed. "Just be aware that the birth mother might hire lawyers and initiate a forced relationship. If you are helpful now, it might be more palatable."

The story ended here, at least as far as I was aware. The birth mother was denied the opportunity to meet her daughter, even to see a photograph or receive information about her life. The adoptive parents will always live with the secret, always fearful that the truth will emerge. The ripple effect of the Holocaust continues. Survivors, somewhat whole in body, continue to carry deep scars within. Distrusting and secretive, their pain is eternal. May there be healing.

CHAPTER **8**

Life's Game of Chess - Marianne Ahrne

"**G**od tells the Jewish people, 'You will be a stranger in a strange land.'"
It all began in the reading room of the Swedish Consulate at Dag
Hammarskjold Plaza in Manhattan. An interminable wait for my Swedish
passport, I was absent-mindedly browsing through random books when
a title, *Katarina Horowitz Drommar*, caught my eye. This was strange, an
anomaly, to find a Jewish surname in a Swedish book.

A romantic novel, *The Dreams of Katarina Horowitz* describes a heroine
confronted by several challenges. Hardly an unusual theme, what separates
its contents from the ordinary was that this heroine wrote a *kvittel*, a kab-
balistic request for intercession, and brought it to a *Rebbe*.

Who is this Swede, I wondered, so familiar with Jewish Chassidic prac-
tices? Inherently proactive, I penned a letter to the author, addressed it to
the publisher, and was surprised to receive a swift response. However, it was
more than a decade, ten consecutive winters and long summers, before a
meeting with Marianne materialized.

We simply kept missing each other. When I traveled from the States
to Sweden, Marianne also traveled, deserting her native land for the foreign
climes of France, India and Africa.

Finally, in 2007, a meeting was arranged for Marrianne's interview.
Suzannah and Nachum eagerly looked forward to meeting this complex
writer. "Your anticipation is infectious," they remarked. "We can't wait to
meet her!"

Marianne lived in Sodermalm, the area very familiar to me from my
childhood. Her home had recently been featured in a major Swedish publication. A beautiful, vivacious woman with lush, dark hair framing her face

and magnificent bluish-green intelligent eyes, Marianne welcomed us into her home. We peered wide-eyed at the floor-to-ceiling bookcases that lined the room, confirming Marianne's appreciation for the written word.

Interspersed among her collection was an entire shelf of Judaica – Chassidic tales, Kabbalah and Eli Wiesel – demonstrating her eclectic taste in literature. A copious collection of travelogues indicated her proclivity for exploring foreign territories. A woman of many hobbies, a camel saddle from Niger and several trophies demonstrated her skill as an equestrian. Provocative masks and objets d'art, collections from her travels, added to the interesting decor.

Could Marianne's restlessness be attributed to unconscious feelings of displacement? Hardly Nordic in appearance, she undoubtedly felt different from the homogenous blonde inhabitants that populated the city. An accomplished author and talented film director, Marianne had published prolifically – a total of nine books – and also contributed some forty reels to the field of film. Yet, despite her intelligence and artistic success, she may have felt disconnected from her surroundings. She appeared exotic, a strange bird with her dark plumage.

"I grew up in a small town in Sweden, and was raised by my grandparents and uncle," she began the saga. At the age of three, her life was drastically altered. Her mother relocated to Stockholm and left Marianne in the care of her parents. Eventually she married and her new husband flatly refused to permit Marianne to live with them.

The infrequent visits, a scant two or three times throughout the year, exacerbated the relinquishing of her motherhood status. Marianne knew almost nothing about her father. Her grandparents possessed a slight, inaccurate knowledge of the man and Marianne never asked any questions.

Academically successful, Marianne retreated into the world of books. Comforting the hole in her heart with the company of dogs and horses, she developed her skill as an equestrian, competing in shows and winning trophies. She worked during vacations and spent her earnings on maintaining her horse.

I was intrigued with Marianne's discussion about *The Dandelion Children*, an autobiographical TV series about her early years of growing up with minimal direction or supervision. Marianne elucidated the symbolism of wildflowers flourishing in the cracks of sidewalks, seeds sprouting through concrete. Laughingly, she admitted, "My mother often referred to me as her *dandelion child*." Vaguely familiar with the term, I never fully grasped its underlying meaning until devouring one of Marianne's other books, *Father Unknown*.

In her personal dedication, Marianne inscribed, "To Chana – when we finally met. From Marianne 11/1/07." I received six books authored by

Marianne, but *Father Unknown* was the most emotionally gripping. An autobiography, it portrayed the poignant yearning of a daughter for her father, a man virtually unknown to her, an elusive stranger.

In this deeply emotional memoir, Marianne recalls the immense challenges in forging a relationship. Father and daughter from two diametrically polarized worlds, Marianne's attempt to bridge the gap is fraught with problems.

At the age of seventeen, she bravely finalizes her plans to meet her father. His unusual name makes it relatively easy for Marianne to embark on her quest. She uses a three-day weekend to journey secretly to Stockholm, with no definite plans and limited funds, undertaking this project in solitude.

Burdened by her mission, she reveals her itinerary to no one. She has never seen her father, not even a glimpse in a photograph. The only information she possesses is a name and address scrawled on a paper, carefully folded in her pocket. I imagine her forcing herself to appear calm, trying not to draw undue attention to her predicament, probably nervously fingering the precious information.

Her desire to meet him is strong. I feel her anxiety, like a flame threatening to engulf her ordinary life. Product of a small-town upbringing, Marianne is intrigued by the crowds of people in Stockholm, the massive cars, the large number of bikes and the huge buildings that comprise Sweden's bustling capital. The traffic, the crowds, the noise – quite a contrast to her bucolic hometown.

She stands at an intersection, stopping, staring. She takes the streetcar to Engelbrektsplan, switching to a train to one of the northern suburbs. Approaching strangers to seek directions must have been exceedingly disconcerting.

Finally reaching her destination, she gazes at the beautiful villa perched on a hill, a stark contrast to the apartment of her grandparents. She notes the name on the door and pushes the bell. Her heart throbs in anticipation, pumping furiously. She listens to the musical chimes and…no response.

The preparation, the planning, the ultimate letdown when there is no answer. She rings the bell several times, waiting for nothing.

A neighbor offers to drive her back to town. "Were you looking for the architect?" he queries. "He and his family are away on vacation."

Excited to finally be conversing with someone acquainted with her father, Marianne bursts out with a question. "Is he friendly?"

The neighbor shrugs. "Not really. He will address you civilly and then thrust a knife between your shoulder blades." Uncomfortable after realizing Marianne's relationship to him, he apologizes for the disparaging comment. Sheepishly attempting to salvage the situation, the former colleague graciously mutters, "He is very intelligent, a brilliant man." He repeats the phrase again, obviously impressed with her father's intellect and knowledge. But Marianne is slowly becoming disillusioned with the romantic version of her father.

In October, Marianne takes advantage of another three-day vacation weekend with a second attempt to connect with her father. This time she is more self-assured. Intuitively, she knows her grandparents will disapprove, but the passion to connect with her father cannot be ignored. She prepares by phoning ahead as soon as she reaches Stockholm. A man answers and Marianne introduces herself as his daughter.

Stony silence. Then, "I'm sorry. Could you repeat your name?" Marianne's father, Karel, politely requests that she repeat her simple statement of introduction, so astonished is he by the unexpected revelation.

She repeats the information. After a brief pause, pregnant with discomfort, Karel demands to know the purpose of the phone call.

"I would very much like to meet you, if possible." she admits. "Of course, I don't want to disturb you."

For years, the daughter has been longing to see her father, and he barely reciprocates, or even acknowledges, the depth of her feelings. Her entire existence is defined by inner turmoil, yet this male stranger appears just slightly interested in the relationship.

When Karel became aware that she was only visiting for a few days, he decided to grab the opportunity to see her then. His wife and children were away and since he did not want them to know about the existence of Marianne, he suggests a meeting that day, at four o'clock, in his home. Adept at budgeting, Marianne rarely indulged in frivolous spending. Her meager pocket money barely covered the upkeep of her horse. But she longed to look attractive for the occasion and had purchased a beautiful olive green dress accented with a dazzlingly white collar.

"I never spent money on clothes," she said, "but I wanted my father's approval. I would never have recognized him if I had stumbled across him by chance," she reflects. "I noticed an unbelievable similarity of our ears when I first saw him."

The beautiful home is equipped with a study and an office accessorized with architectural tools. The home has tasteful furnishings, paintings, a variety of works of art, and an abundance of books. Marianne is delighted by the presence of his black poodle. Maybe a sign of common interest? He welcomes her into his home. After decades of living in Sweden, his voice still retains the tinge of a Slavic accent.

Their initial encounter, formal but not cold, consists of a brief handshake. He is a Middle-European intellectual, polite and kind, well-versed in European literature, fluent in twelve languages.

The walls of his library, devoid of any personal attachments, practically burst with books: a total of twelve thousand volumes, including the complete works of several classic and modern writers, like Hanna Arendt and other Jewish authors. Marianne's intense thirst for knowledge often triggers nausea when in the presence of an abundance of books. Panicked, she hopes all will be well; she can't ruin the visit by vomiting Intoxicated by the world of books surrounding her, she swallows and does not flaw his pristine home.

Karel revels in his daughter's unspoken admiration. Awed by the depth of his knowledge, Marianne longs to enter into his universe of literature and art. The scholarly, erudite Czech native, graduate of a classical European education, and Marianne – self-educated, academically proficient, raised in a middle-class family in a nondescript town with a small town library, a few government buildings and a museum – are world's apart.

Ripe for the molding, the father wishes to remake his daughter in his image. An ardent intellectual, he criticizes and belittles her taste in everything. Despite all this she still felt, they'd spend a pleasant afternoon in interesting conversation. As Marianne prepares to leave, however, the father astonishes her by saying, "I am nearly bankrupt."

Marianne looks at him in great surprise, standing there in his tastefully decorated home, the likeness of which she had never seen before. In truth, though, she had heard of the Kreugercrash.

"I offered him two-hundred kronor that I had been saving for my summer vacation in England," Marianne admitted. "I will be happy to give it to you," I told him. Her father appeared startled and shaking his head stated that he only wanted to clarify the situation.

Marianne thought her father was wonderful. In her childish innocence, she felt pleased that her father trusted her and choose to share his concerns with her. I muttered angrily, "Doesn't she realize that he wanted to make sure she never would attempt to seek financial assistance." Naive, her heart brimming with love, only later did Marianne grasp the intent underlying his words.

Her father devalues her personality, her creativity, her sensitivity. I think, *How tragic that such a pivotal figure in her life is not able to appreciate her glorious selflessness, her willingness to endure sacrifice, just to meet him.*

Marianne sent her father a gift, a slim book of Ferlin's poetry, to share her taste with him. I was deeply saddened when the gift was returned unopened, with an accompanying note harshly pronouncing that the poetry was worthless drivel, that Marianne should not have squandered her money.

Their relationship mirrors the original encounter between her parents. Karel had left his wife and two children in Czechoslovakia when he immigrated to Sweden in 1939. Alone, without family or friends, he became involved with Marianne's mother, a cartographer in his office. Impressed by his brilliance, she soon became pregnant and Marianne was born. Karel gave her mother a one-time sum of money, seven thousand kronor, simultaneously warning her that there was to be no contact, as his wife and children had recently arrived in Sweden. She obeyed his instructions, never attempting to introduce his daughter to him. Consequently, there was very little contact between them.

Karel's mother, born Jewish, married a military man and was forced to "convert," much to the sorrow of her family. Though educated in a monastery school, Karel retained his inherent Jewish genetics. Karel was not interested in the military world of his father, much preferring the world of the mind, characteristic of his innate Jewishness.

Eventually his father deserted his mother. In a poignant scene, dramatically rendered, the mother kindles the candles on Friday night after her husband leaves, healing that which has been broken. Marianne's grandmother dies in Auschwitz, together with other Holocaust victims, even though she had "converted." When Marianne eventually travels to visit her father's family, they relate this to her.

Gripped by the dramatic ending, Marianne has always been fascinated by her father's family history. She arranges to meet his Jewish relatives and is instantly accepted. She feels comfortable in their presence, a sense of kinship. During her late teens, she begins to learn about her heritage, about Judaism, eagerly selecting books of Kaballah and Chassidic tales. The puzzle solved, I had discovered the source of the eclectic literature, and the exotic look.

"I have to thank Hitler for my existence," Marianne remarked, her outrageous statement punctuated by brief outbursts of laughter. "Had Hitler never existed, my father would never have moved to Sweden. He would not have temporarily separated from his wife and children, would never have had a relationship with my mother, and I would never have been born. I owe Hitler my life!"

During the Nazi era, Europe became Hitler's chess board. Six million Jews were moved around, forced to leave family, home, community and country in his scheme of resettlement, a euphemism for deportation to ghettos and concentration camps. The map of Europe was changed with the altering of borders. Countries were occupied and stripped of their independence. The unfortunate Jews were like the pieces on a chessboard, in constant movement, desperately hoping to remain alive – whether like the castle, moving vertically and horizontally, like the bishop in long diagonal strides, like the pawn in small forward steps or like the horse in an irregular pattern, they were constantly in motion, never knowing where the road would end.

The ripple effects of Nazism are clearly evident in this book. Hitler's evil agenda uprooted the lives of countless individuals, irrevocably damaging the Jewish world by separating families and wreaking havoc on the most basic building block of society, the home.

I wish Hitler had never existed, but I cherish having met Marianne, an indirect gift of the Nazi era. Today Marianne is a member of the Stockholm Jewish community. A fringe member of the Great Synagogue, she is a spokesperson for Israel, attempting to counterbalance the negativity of the Swedish press. Hitler never planned this, but Marianne's life has turned out to be a blessing. Her writings and films have affected the lives of many people. May Marianne's life continue to be productive, and may she continue to be a source of blessing, a credit to the Jewish people.

Toward the end of the saga, Marianne approaches a Rabbi to discuss her deep inner desire to convert to Judaism. The Rabbi listens attentively to her request and responds impulsively. "You are already one of us. We will just arrange the technicalities."

At her father's funeral, Marianne ponders the family members who perished in the Holocaust, most of all, her father's mother. "When the time comes," she concludes, "I want to be buried in a Jewish cemetery."

Her father was buried in a non-Jewish cemetery. That is where she was when she actually made this statement. With this, her book ends and the idea of conversion solidifies.

CHAPTER 9

Casual Encounters

On the journey through life, there sometimes is a brief encounter, just a moment in time, like a snapshot on a long reel of film representing the totality of *life*. Though short in duration, the impact might be deep and meaningful, forever remaining in one's thoughts. The following two portraits, each different, each unique, were of great significance on my Scandinavian journeys.

The Stockholm Guide

An enthusiastic guide, Gunilla, loved Stockholm with a passion. Her perky demeanor and pleasant speaking voice rendered her the guide of choice. When I arrange tours and contact the guide association in each city, I always hope that the guide will be effective for that is of major importance in a sightseeing tour. Saturated with charm and surprisingly articulate in English, my tourists were privileged to be entertained by this notable Nordic representative.

"May I have your business card," I inquired enthusiastically. "I would like to contact you for future tours."

"With great pleasure," Gunilla responded happily, placing a card in my outstretched palm. "I enjoyed meeting your group. They seemed genuinely interested and asked a lot of questions."

Glancing at the card briefly, I paused in great surprise as I noted something unusual. "Why is the name 'Rosenberg' printed there?" I remarked, "and then you crossed it out and substituted the handwritten name 'La Costa'?"

"Oh," Gunilla laughed. "I am in the process of ordering new cards. That's my married name," she added, pointing to La Costa. "Rosenberg was my maiden name."

"That's a very Jewish name," I commented in wonder. "Are you Jewish?"

"No!" Gunilla protested, shaking her head vigorously. She appeared quite surprised. "Why do you ask? I have never been asked this question before."

"Because Rosenberg is quite a common Jewish name," I said.

"You know," answered Gunilla, suddenly in a very serious tone, "my father came to Sweden from Austria in 1938. He was a dentist, and had studied dentistry in Austria. He never speaks of his childhood, nor his family or home. He never discusses his youth."

"In 1938..." I reflected, shaking my head. "It's very possible that he fled, as Nazism was on the rise. And his reluctance to share his past...I wonder." My voice drifted off and we parted ways. A few weeks later we met again with my second group.

As the tour drew to a close, Gunilla approached me, suggesting that we pause for a cup of coffee. It was apparent that she wanted a private conversation.

"You know," Gunilla began, "after our conversation, well, I couldn't just put it aside. It sounded like a mystery. I sat down with my father for a serious talk about his background. Rather formal, usually unemotional, he became very angry and refused to talk. He actually was hostile.

"'There is nothing to talk about,' he told me. 'Do not bring up this topic again. This has nothing to do with you.'"

"What does your mother say about all this?" I inquired. "Have you ever broached the subject with her?"

"My mother died when I was just nine years old, but I really think you are correct," Gunilla admitted. "There are no photographs of my father's family. It is as if they never existed."

I nodded in quiet agreement, acknowledging the information silently. "I would like to know something about Judaism, though," Gunilla said meditatively. "I might be partially or even completely Jewish."

I suggested a visit to the Great Synagogue on Wahrendorffsgatan and possibly a meeting with the Rabbi. I also supplied Gunilla with a list of books.

The following summer Gunilla was in Spain, so we contacted another guide for our tours. We drifted apart and the episode was eventually forgotten.

One summer day, five years later, I visited Riksdagshuset, the Swedish Parliament Building, to view it alone for possible consideration for future tours. This magnificent edifice, located near the Royal Palace, is filled with meeting rooms with impressive furnishings. Suddenly I heard running footsteps, heels clicking on the stone floor. The noise grew louder and I turned to see who was there. It was a pleasant surprise to encounter Gunilla, now an official guide in this building. "I recognized you from the back," she said breathlessly, and I am really happy to see you." This had become her year-round job, she explained, while during the tourist season she still conducted city tours.

Gunilla encouraged me to bring tours to Riksdagshuset, where she would personally provide the guiding. It was a very pleasant reunion. We spoke briefly about our present involvements, then Gunilla told of her visit to the synagogue. Though she had found the experience interesting, her father remained cold and indifferent, totally unreceptive when she attempted to discuss the adventure with him. Gunilla actually felt that he would prefer not to discuss this topic.

Her Catholic husband and six-year-old son caused her interest to evaporate eventually. Gunilla wanted no future upheaval and preferred a continued smooth existence, unencumbered by contradictions.

Hitler's nefarious reign, like atomic fallout, destroyed countless future generations. Many lost souls float around Scandinavia, still confused, uncomfortable or unaware regarding their Jewish heritage.

On The Plane

"Excuse me, but do you have a kosher snack?" I asked the flight attendant.

"Let me check," was the offhand response. The stewardess returned empty-handed a few moments later. "Sorry," she said, "not on these short inter-Scandinavian flights."

Disappointed, I settled into my seat, welcoming a much-deserved rest after having just concluded a hectic two-week tour. Closing my eyes, I attempted to take a nap.

I felt a brief tap on my shoulder. "I hope you don't mind my asking, but what is 'kosher'?" The question came from my seatmate, a middle-aged, nondescript woman – mousy-brown hair, casual attire – hardly the typical polished Scandinavian.

Having no interest in a lengthy conversation, yet not wanting to appear rude, I curtly replied, "Jewish people eat only kosher food. They don't mix milk and meat, only eat fish with fins and scales, and slaughter meat in a particular manner. In addition, all processed foods have to be checked and certified by a Rabbi."

"I guess that means you are Jewish." The woman became animated. "I think I am Jewish. I never met a Jew before in my life. I would like to know more about Judaism."

Perplexed, I wondered what had precipitated the questioning. Why suddenly at this stage in her life? Why had she never attempted to research the topic previously?

As if reading my mind, the woman continued. "Permit me to introduce myself. I just got carried away when you mentioned kosher. My name is Carla and I live in Falun. My mother died six months ago. When her illness became debilitating, she made me promise not to cremate her. She told me that her family and relatives had been gassed by Hitler. She even asked to be buried in a Jewish cemetery."

Now wide awake, I peered at her intently. "And before that, she never spoke about her background?"

Carla shook her head. "She was a war orphan. The family housekeeper brought her from Bremen, Germany in 1938. Her parents were supposed to follow, but could not procure a visa. Fortunately, the housekeeper, a widow of a Swedish man, had a Swedish passport. After my mother was left without any family, the housekeeper adopted her. Only at the end of her life did my mother reveal her Jewish lineage."

She paused, recollecting the unexpected revelation. She had always known her grandparents had died in the war and her mother had been orphaned, but the Jewish ingredient had been kept hidden. "My mother never discussed the early years, prior to her arrival in Sweden. During my mother's childhood, the family celebrated Jewish holidays, a fact she revealed to me only during the final days of her illness." "But when she left with the housekeeper," Carla continued, "her mother warned her never to reveal her Jewish heritage. She explained that it could be dangerous and cause bad things to happen. The secret had to be kept if she wanted a good life."

The housekeeper never spoke of the past and Carla's mother accepted the silence, assuming that tragic moments would trigger poorly healed wounds.

Listening intently, I absorbed all the details. "Carla, you are a real Jew," I exclaimed. "If your mother was Jewish, you are Jewish as well."

Flushed, Carla mumbled, "Strange! All my classmates knew details about their families but I had no history on my mother's side, no relatives, no shared stories. Tell me," she urged, her eyes glistening, "How can I find out more about my heritage? Eskilstuna has no Jewish presence, no house of worship, no Rabbi."

Her youth had been spent in Falun, a place with no visible Jewish presence.

"Go to Stockholm," I urged, "either to my father's synagogue in Sodermalm or the Great Synagogue. Maybe you should visit the Jewish Museum," I suggested.

As the plane descended, concluding the one-hour flight, we exchanged addresses and phone numbers. Soon after my return, I mailed a package of books to Carla about Jewish history and Holidays. Letters were exchanged, but time marches on and the relationship faded.

Carla's teenage daughters found it somewhat amusing and quaint to be Jewish, while Carla's husband remained uninterested. Not surprising, since Swedes generally are disconnected from religion. Clean air, sports, nature, healthy living fills their lives.

In many small towns in Sweden, throughout Scandinavia, one finds offspring of survivors with no knowledge or awareness of their Jewish heritage. Hitler destroyed the lives of six million, but the tearing of families, the scattering of survivors, the continued loss is interminable.

CHAPTER 10

Mir Leben Eybig - Transcending the Camps - Bertil Neuman

Bertil Neuman, highly talented in many fields, and his wife, Kikki, evoke pleasant childhood memories. I fondly recall Kikki's parents, the Sharlins, members of my father's congregation Adas Yisroel on Sankt Paulsgatan. Petite and vivacious, Kikki flits about like a songbird, spreading happiness with her smile and infectious laughter. She wears her hair casually, reminiscent of schooldays – short, soft curls, a halo framing her face. A great hostess, she makes you feel wonderfully at home during your visit.

Summer lunch at the Neumans' is always a special treat. Kikki prepares stromming, a Swedish small fish in the herring family – two small fillets with spinach in the center, fried on both sides – with a side dish of tiny, new potatoes, an incredible meal. The delicious luncheon, the warm, friendly conversation, reminiscing of days gone by, memories of my parents – I relish the splendid afternoon.

It was early evening when we came to their home for the interview on the island of Kungsholmen, a fashionable residential area near Stockholm's City Hall, the dauntingly ornate building with the symbolic three crowns on a staple. Their aesthetically pleasing home, replete with antiques and objets d'art, is a tribute to Bertil, an avid and knowledgeable connoisseur. They derive pleasure in surrounding themselves with beautiful items. On one of her visits, Kikki presented me with an antique glass plate, as glass is symbolic of Scandinavia.

A highly successful businessman, Bertil was nicknamed Mr. Marketing in 1940, I presume by a business magazine or his colleagues, but in any case, among the business people in Sweden. He founded "Neuman and Nydahl," the first Swedish consulting firm, and has lectured extensively, not only throughout Sweden, but in Europe as well. In addition, he is actively involved in Jewish life in Stockholm and serves on the board of directors in many major organizations. He is also involved with the publication of Judisk Kronika, a major Jewish Swedish publication.

In 1989, Bertil published his first book, and since then, he has published three additional books. His first book, *Something Disappeared Along the Way*, focuses on the family history of the early Jewish settlers in Sweden, who arrived in the 1920s. His family came from Lithuania and settled in southern Sweden, in Lund, a university town.

Despite intense materialistic deprivation, his ancestors, spiritually rich in heritage and culture, banded together to form a cohesive, supportive community. Bertil's book addresses the changes of Jewish life in Sweden throughout the years. He addresses the rate of assimilation, due considerably to Sweden's tolerance and acceptance of Jews. With his somewhat negative outlook, he believes that by the year 2050, Jewish culture and heritage will have declined at an alarming rate. He paints a very dismal picture of the future of Jewish life in Sweden.

Bertil presented his book to me with a poignant inscription: "With wishes that my book will enrich the memories of your childhood in Sweden. Warmly, Bertil Neuman."

Bertil and Kikki, both Swedish born, are descendants of these early settlers. Captivated by the detailed description of Bertil's grandparents' and parents' lives in Sweden, I was intrigued by these Viking Jews, a previously unexplored phenomenon, an area in which I had lacked knowledge.

With the passage of time, Bertil records, European Jews changed their affiliation, deserting the Orthodox synagogue to attend the Conservative synagogue on Wahrendorffsgatan. They gradually discarded the laws of *kashruth* starting with dining at non-kosher establishments. This was followed by the mixing of meat and milk in the country home and introduction of non-kosher food, which was gradually allowed into the city home as well.

"It seemed hypocritical," said Kikki shaking her head, "to invite guests for a Shabbat dinner in a non-kosher house, so we discontinued those dinners. However, a Pesach Seder or Chanukah gathering was still celebrated. Participating in Jewish life, they had one foot out the door, with the outlook that in the future, there would be further movement away from traditional Judaism. Of course, this erosion of Jewish life paved the way to intermarriage.

"I refute his projection," I declared in a firm voice. "Chabad Houses have been established in many of the major cities in Sweden: in Stockholm, Gothenberg and Malmo. Their aim is to bring assimilated Jewish people back to their roots, to encourage them to explore their heritage and culture, and they have encountered much success. In my opinion, there are positive changes in the Scandinavian Jewish world."

Bertil's provocative book, *To Laugh or To Cry: Humor in the Concentration Camp*, seems a blatant oxymoron. Could there possibly be humor in a concentration camp – in a situation so appalling, it would seem to leave room only for pessimism? Viktor Frankl, a graduate of Auschwitz, now a professor of psychology and psychiatry, wrote about the importance of humor in the concentration camp. "Humor," he insists, "is a weapon for the soul, nourishing and imbuing it, a life-giving source." Life must have meaning, Frankl added, if one is to avoid succumbing to despair. One finds meaning in life only if one can consider a future, a normal life, a return to a life filled with meaning.

Viktor Frankl and another inmate made a conscious decision while in Auschwitz: to share a humorous story daily in the hope that this would propel them to contemplate a future, to focus on the light at the end of the tunnel. "One must mentally remove oneself from the painful present," Frankl preached, "by shaping and creating an inner world." The Nazis could try to crush, frighten and torture people, but they could not pollute the inner world of the Jewish prisoners. The camp inmates created a sanctuary, emotionally removing themselves from the sordid horror that threatened to engulf them.

Religion became instrumental in assuring that people retain a positive outlook on life. Those people who maintained their faith, according to Bertil, were in less danger of succumbing to pessimism.

"Neither time nor place exist." Bertil Neuman quotes from the timely diary of Philip McAnnalis, circa 1943 in Auschwitz. "Imagination, humor and love of nature can overcome bodily enslavement and the harshness of incarceration behind barbed wire enclosure."

Essentially, he seems to be asserting that laughter overcomes fear and depression. We know that laughter, even in the field of medicine, is an effective means of promoting good health. Humor strengthens human worth and dignity.

Concentration camp inmates composed poetry and songs, which imbued them with the strength to face the future. Themes of remaining alive until the end of the war were sung as prisoners trudged through the snow, holes in shoes, toes frostbitten, on the horrible Nazi death marches.

Humor has always played a significant role in Jewish life. The famous expressions, *Lach fun tzoras* (Laugh away the difficulties) and *Tracht gut vet zein gut* (Be positive in your thinking and all will turn out well) help to promote positive thinking. A positive attitude strengthens people, enriches them with hope, with the strength to continue, even in the most dismal conditions.

Bertil Neuman interviewed one hundred survivors to obtain anecdotes. These vignettes, humorous slices culled from despair, provide insight into the fortitude of the concentration camp inmates.

The SS officers, immaculately clad in spotless uniforms and shiny boots, accessorized with pointy guns and swirling batons, intimidated the Jewish brethren. Recalling humorous tales while facing the onslaught of these vicious guards would infuse the inmates with inner strength.

Imagine recalling this anecdote when facing the icy brutality of a Nazi officer. An SS guard had a glass eye. So proud was he that the glass eye had been impeccably shaped that he arrogantly accosted a poor Jew. "Tomorrow, you will die," he threatened. "However, I will allow you to gamble. One of my eyes is glass. If you can guess which one is glass, you may remain alive."

The Jewish man looked at him intently and then exclaimed, "Your left eye!"

Astounded, certain that no would be able to detect which eye was the manufactured one, the SS officer exclaimed. "How were you able to guess correctly?"

Without missing a beat the Jew replied, "The left eye has a human look. It is compassionate and warm."

The capacity to laugh at oneself is indeed a blessing.

In another good story related by Bertil, Jacob sits on a bench reading *Der Sturmer*, a vile Nazi paper, saturated with inflammatory propaganda. His friend David passes by, annoyed. "How could you read such racist drivel!" he screams, incendiary words pummeling Jacob.

"You don't understand," Jacob calmly retorts. "Jewish papers depress me, the tragic happenings, the persecution and dangers that Jews are facing. The Nazi paper empowers me, makes me believe that Jews are powerful, that they will take over the world, that they are famous, wealthy, competent. I feel uplifted!"

Two stories featuring Joseph Goebbels, the Minister of Propaganda, are included in Bertil's repertoire. Upon visiting a school to inculcate the youth with Nazi ideology, Goebbels prompts the children to suggest exciting slogans. The typical "Zieg Hitler," "Heil Hitler" and "Deutschland Uber Alles" are offered. Dissatisfied, Goebbels requests something new, original and bewitchingly powerful. Inspired, a youngster calls out, "Our people should live forever." Pleased, Goebbels asked the child to repeat his words again, loudly. The boy complies.

"Well done," Goebbels praises him. "What is your name, my child?"

"Moishele Goldberg," the previously unnamed student tells him.

The following story, about the cups, is very amusing in my opinion. Apparently, toward the end of the war, as Hitler's powers were waning, Goebbels became a bit concerned with Hitler's cruelty toward the Jews, thus he sought to justify their existence by demonstrating their business acuity.

On a shopping excursion to purchase cups that are specifically constructed for left-handed people, Hitler and Goebbels enter a German establishment. Red-faced, the shopkeeper apologizes that he has none in stock. However, upon entering a Jewish-owned store, the Jewish storekeeper gleefully produces the necessary items. "Fortunately, I have some in stock," he explains, "and I can obtain more if needed."

"This, indeed, is evidence of the brilliance of the Jews," Goebbels remarks triumphantly. Unimpressed, Hitler retorts that the Jewish proprietor was just lucky. He simply happened to have left-handed cups in stock.

An abundance of humor addressed the importance of paper in Germany, a country that prided itself on maintaining meticulous records. Transports of Jews were accurately documented, like inventoried merchandise, and German record keeping became the subject of gallows humor. In addition, toileting became a social scene where news, messages and information was exchanged. A physical necessity, once unmentionable, evolved into an interactive, social experience.

One day, Fritz Grunbaum, an inmate at Buchenwald and cabaret performer, finds himself in the bathroom without any toilet paper. He requests some from the SS guard but is told that there is a dearth of the paper product.

"If you can't afford toilet paper," Fritz remarks, "you should not be operating concentration camps!"

Pondering this joke might alleviate, even counteract the incessant misery of being faced with a humiliating, dehumanizing situation.

Another chuckle: An SS officer aboard a train knocks on the bathroom door requesting papers. The answer from inside is a relieved, "Yes, thank you. I definitely could use some."

Numerous anecdotes were exchanged regarding identification papers, whose absence often resulted in a beating or worse. Shmuel's friend Yankel visited St. Petersburg without authorized permission, a crime that could cause fatal consequences. The two men were out strolling when they saw police approaching from afar.

Yankel was advised to stay rooted and later return to the apartment where they would meet. Shmuel, in the interim, ran away, pursued by the police. After a long chase, the breathless police finally caught up with Shmuel. About to handcuff him, Shmuel calmly produced the proper identification papers. "Why were you fleeing," the astonished officers asked, "if you had identification papers?"

"I'm not running away from you," Shmuel replied. "I'm following doctor's orders, to run half an hour daily for health reasons."

"But why didn't you stop when you saw the police chasing you?" the police officer interrogated.

"Oh, I thought you were using the same doctor."

Conditions in the concentration camps were simply unbearable – the crowding, the cold, the fear and brutality – but worst of all was the hunger, a gnawing hunger from the moment one awakened until the moment before falling into bed totally spent. The wish for a magnifying glass to make the morsel of bread masquerade as an entire slice became a source of laughter.

Women clustered to savor recipes, imagining tastes and smells of tantalizing foods. These precious recipes were stashed among meager belongings, scraps of paper, copied with great difficulty, as writing materials were not readily available. The recipes became a hope for the future, a beacon of light heralding an era when, once again, meals would be prepared for holiday gatherings. Recipes signified home, a normal life.

One woman cried bitterly during a recipe exchange because her life in the barracks, when contrasted with all she had lost, became overwhelming. This sadness reverted to laughter after an inmate commented that she cried because that fabulous cake had burnt from being left too long in the oven.

Jokes circulated about prayers for bread. One young child was told to thank Hitler and God for the bread. When the child innocently asked what he should say after Hitler's death, the answer was that then one should *really* thank God.

Allotments of three hundred and fifty grams of food daily made the hunger for bread unbearable. Yet, the Orthodox Jews, even in this horrendous situation, refused to eat bread on Pesach. This shining example of resistance, of refusing to compromise one's beliefs, proved that while the body could suffer, the soul would remain unscathed.

When words were inadequate to express emotions, when language could not transcribe a message, music and art became the vehicle for transmitting deep feelings. "The Scream" by Edvard Munch, in the Munch Museum in Oslo, Norway, envelops the viewer in a nightmarish situation. The anguish and pain of the noiseless scream reverberates more sharply than mere words. Picasso's "Guernica," a masterful statement about the evil of war, mesmerizes – each detail contemplated as the masterpiece unfolds.

Music, the notes on an instrument or the wordless melody, brings forth emotions of strength and hope, of ecstasy. Art and music, languages of the soul, are the deepest non-verbal means of communication. The song *"Mir Leben Eybig" We Will Live Forever* was composed in a concentration camp. Perhaps the inmate was contemplating Jewish survival through the ages, the enslavement in Egypt, the Babylonian exile, the Inquisition and the Crusades intermingled with pogroms and blood libels. A pivotal stanza shrieks: *Es brennt a velt, mir leben eybig on a groshen gelt* – the world is in flames, the world is burning and we continue to live without a single coin. The song climaxes on a triumphant note: Our lives will continue, we will persevere and we will overcome the unbearable times. The melody, filled with hope, is positive, life-affirming, powerful.

I remember singing that song with great gusto, and when the survivors in Sweden heard my childish, young voice blending in with their emotion-laden voices, they were overjoyed. Just released from the pit of hell, soot still clinging to their fingernails, they had assumed Hitler had been successful in vanquishing all the Jewish youth. To discover a child who spoke Yiddish instilled them with hope for the future, for rebuilding the Jewish nation.

Cleanliness is next to Godliness, the Nazis promulgated. Their spotless uniforms, highly polished boots, rakish cap, tilted at just the right angle, gave an air of elegance in the most horrendous of circumstances. Appearance was all that mattered to them. Superficial, pristine beauty camouflaged the blackness of evil, augmenting it with its contrast.

Cabarets flourished in Thereisenstadt – musical performances, complete with costumes, dance and makeshift orchestras staffed with Jewish inmates. This "model" concentration camp, which staged innocuous conditions to give an intentionally deceptive false impression to the outside world, was the site for Nazi propaganda films. It was the only camp that permitted visits from Red Cross representatives and foreign officials.

The crafty, resourceful Germans concocted a vernacular of euphemisms to express their factory-of-death agenda. Harmless phrases such as "resettlement," "final solution" and "selection" cloaked the horror of their activities in a veneer of respectability. Bars of classical music greeted fatigued travelers as they descended the cattle cars, finishing their arduous journey at the final destination, the concentration camp.

Inmates focused on existence not for mere survival, but to embellish their lives with meaning, with feelings of love and friendship. They exchanged handmade birthday cards, sketches of homes and nature scenes and miniature tea sets or other innovative presents, such as rings and brooches fashioned from wire obtained during forced factory labor. Those chosen for work, selected for their manual dexterity, would surreptitiously smuggle thin wires into the barracks, subsequently fashioning them into presents. Prisoners would attempt to celebrate birthdays and holidays. They clung to a shredded human dignity and looked toward the future.

I treasure the gift of flowers created by a survivor in Sweden and presented to my mother in appreciation of her kindness and help. The bouquet of red and pink flowers, accented with green stems and leaves meticulously created of beaded wires, is a special memento. Similar items were frequently presented as gifts for birthdays or simply to gladden someone's heart.

Brutal scenes of camp life, recorded in drawings, served as historical documents to remember, to repair and to prepare for a better future. The world needs to be reminded of the horror, to give meaning to those who perished.

Countless stories illustrate the human touch that was prevalent in the camps. Threads, ingeniously extracted from blankets, were placed in a sliver of margarine saved from the rations to become a short-lived Shabbos candle, and for a brief moment the women could utter a blessing and recall the sanctity of the day. A Passover Seder, celebrated without matzo, also had no bread or any required symbolic items. Bitter herbs were not needed, as the bitterness of the situation permeated the entire seder.

Inmates heroically refused their portions of bread on Pesach, though it was one of the only foods they were allotted. Nazis deviously calculated when Pesach appeared on the calendar, cruelly offering the Jews extra rations of bread then. A sharing of paragraphs of the Haggadah, a retelling of the story of freedom and the joyous singing of the familiar tunes made this holiday a meaningful event. Recalling the special foods, the tastes and smells, added to the atmosphere. Chanukah menorahs were fashioned from discarded potato pieces. Rosh Hashanah and Yom Kippur consisted of sharing memorized passages from prayers, punctuated with additional stories and nostalgic memories.

Mistreated and starved, surrounded by fear and death, the camp inmates resisted the destruction of their moral fiber by cultivating inner dignity and humanity. The physical bodies were infested with disease, emaciated from malnutrition, marked and scarred from beatings, shriveled, but the souls remained pure, untouched.

CHAPTER 11

Boras, a Town of Survivors –
Litzman Family

The town of Boras, Sweden and that of Monsey, New York are worlds apart. Among the more than three hundred guests present at the wedding at Ateres Charne in Monsey, only a handful were aware of the existence of Boras. The second and third generation Litzman family members were perhaps familiar with the name, but in no way could they fathom the challenges of growing up in a town void of Jewish history.

The look-alike brothers, Mordechai and Tuvia, with their full, blackish gray beards, black suits and black hats, typical of Chabad Chassidim, would never have been recognized by their childhood friends. Were they to meet, the Boras inhabitants would probably regard them as aliens from another planet, though their sister, Yaffa – mother of the *chossan* – tall and slim, elegant in her stylish chocolate colored gown, youthful in appearance, would easily be recognized. They would admire her "upsweep" hairdo, never imagining that she was wearing a *sheitel*.

Boras, population 63,500, located in southwestern Sweden, near Lund and Gothenburg, was founded in 1622 by King Gustaf II Adolph. The coat of arms of this city consists of two sheep-shearing scissors, indicative of the numerous smiths who lived here. Why, I wondered, did the Forty-fivers decide to settle here? Although this is a very old town, one of the oldest in Sweden, this place has no Jewish history. No Jews ever lived here, so there was no synagogue, no cemetery, no mikvah, no Hebrew school. Puzzled, I shook my head.

"Let me explain," offered Mordechai Litzman, a son of survivors, who spent his childhood in Boras. "When the Holocaust survivors came to Sweden, they were settled in rehabilitation camps."

"Yes," I interrupted. "Sweden opened its doors and established one hundred and fifty rehabilitation centers. Some were exclusively for women or for men, and a few were mixed. My brother Mendel was very involved in arranging social activities so they could meet and socialize."

"Exactly," continued Mordechai. "And after short courtships they married. Generally, the marriages were between people who came from the same region and spoke the same language."

"I know," I said. "My father, Rabbi Zuber, often officiated at these weddings. And he worked endlessly on freeing *agunot* so they could remarry."

The survivors wanted to embrace *life* fully. "That meant marriage and children," stated Mordechai. "They were so alone in a strange country, a strange language, and with no home."

"But Boras?" I exclaimed. "Why settle in a town without a Jewish presence!"

"Boras had several large textile factories and a record number of Swedish mail-order firms that translated into jobs for unskilled workers. The survivors, brutally uprooted, lacked skills and language. In Boras, they could earn a living. Two hundred and fifty families, about six hundred people, eventually settled here – less than one per cent of the population," Mordechai added.

The Litzman family history is the story of the rebuilding of a Jewish family. Victimized by the Holocaust, the father, Shlomo Yehuda – 'Lars' in Sweden – lost his wife and three daughters in the Shoah. He came from Bonyhad, near Pesh in southern Hungary, where only two percent out of thousands of Jewish males in that area survived. He arrived in Sweden in poor health and expected to live for only one year. He recuperated in a sanatorium in Gotland, transferred to Wasa Sjukhus in Gothenburg and was released in August of 1945.

He married Rifka Leya Barbro, and they settled in Falun, where Mordechai was born. Two more children were born in Gnosjo; then, in 1960, they settled in Boras and raised their three children there. Mordechai's father lived until 1969. Most community members left within a few years and today, a very small number – just a handful – are left. "I am sure many offspring intermarried," I said solemnly, "and they no longer know of their Jewish heritage." We shook our heads sorrowfully.

Mordechai – known as Folke at that time – joined our household as a frequent Shabbat guest in 1967, soon after his arrival to the United States to study at Columbia University. A member of Bnei Akiva in Boras, he visited the branch in Manhattan, and laughs when he recalls the general reaction: "A Jew from Sweden!" – that was definitely a surprise.

Being lonely, Folke was pleased when Bnei Akiva arranged Shabbos meals for him with a family from Argentina, assuming that all foreigners would relate well with each other. His hosts suggested a visit to Crown Heights, an international gathering place for Jews. Upon his arrival, he was referred to me, the Scandinavian outpost. Eventually Folke became Mordechai, transferred to Yeshiva University and, in 1969, was introduced to Malka, a Bostonian Stern College student.

"I was delighted when you brought her to our home, to ask for our opinion," I recalled. Mordechai laughs heartily. "Yes, and I remember your response: 'You are really lucky to have found this wonderful young woman.'" They both finished school and married in New York in 1970.

Mordechai's sister Yaffa – Ingrid at that time – went to Kibbutz Lavi for Hachshara for one year after graduating gymnasium in Boras. Inspired by the Bnei Akiva movement, she wanted to make aliyah. She attended Bar Ilan University in Israel, but upon graduating, she returned briefly to Boras. In 1971, Mordechai had become a Lubavitcher Chassid. At the suggestion of The Lubavitcher Rebbe and Mordechai, Yaffa came to America. The blessing of the Rebbe was powerful. Within her first week here, she met her future husband, Zalman Zager, and obtained a position as a teacher at Sarah Schenirer High School.

I recall Yaffa's visit to our bungalow that summer. My young children were terrorized by a large dog we encountered on our Shabbat walk, but Yaffa handled the situation masterfully. Strongly admonishing the children to stand still, and not run, she addressed the dog in a firm, commanding voice. "Go away! Go back where you came from! Leave right now!" She raised her arm dramatically, pointing. The children were impressed. The dog looked at Yaffa and seemed to shrivel. His tail hung limply down and he looked dejected, beaten, as he slowly walked away.

Tuvia, known as Lille Bror, Karl Johann, I did not know nearly as well as the other two siblings. Mordechai and Yaffa settled in Monsey, New York, but Tuvia has been living in Israel since he was eighteen years old, except for a five-year period when he returned to Sweden to be with his newly widowed mother and attend the University of Stockholm. Bnei Akiva was his anchor to Jewish life in his childhood in Boras. At the age of fourteen, he joined at the suggestion of his sister, Yaffa.

"The winter and summer camps became the highlights of my life at that time," Tuvia recalled. "I never identified or attached myself to the non-Jews at school. I knew I wasn't like them, even though I didn't wear a yarmulke outside and I never put on Tefillin after my Bar Mitzvah. After only three days in the Bnei Akiva camp, I began to put on Tefillin daily and continued that practice after my return home. Bnei Akiva made me aware of my Jewishness; my Jewish pride was developed." At fifteen, Tuvia became a counselor in the camp. Each time, the camp was located in another Scandinavian country, a wonderful opportunity for the scattered Jewish youth to gather and forge friendships. Indeed, several marriages resulted from these encounters.

Tuvia spent one year in Kibbutz Lavi in Hachshara, like Yaffa. Then he volunteered in the Israeli army for fifteen months, perhaps one of the first Bnei Akiva members to accomplish this. He returned to Sweden when his father passed away and became *Rosh* of Bnei Akiva of Scandinavia while completing his university studies in Stockholm. In 1972, he came to America for Yaffa's wedding. He remained and studied at Hadar Hatorah, a branch of Lubavitch. At a private audience with the Lubavitcher Rebbe in 1972, he was urged to return to Sweden and organize an energetic, strong Bnei Akiva. Then he could leave for Israel, or America. The Rebbe stressed that it is important "not to forget the six million Jews in America." Tuvia returned to Sweden, completed his studies and, in 1973, returned to Israel, where he married the daughter of Lubavitcher Russian immigrants and settled in Kiryat Malachi.

"It was very difficult to live a Jewish life in Boras," stated Yaffa. "My father always told us that Boras was a temporary place. Sweden was like a railroad station; a wonderful country to visit, but not suitable for permanent residence if one wished to remain an Orthodox Jew. He never wanted to buy a house or car, for he had no feeling of permanence. My parents were too tired to move, but they told us we should leave, marry Orthodox mates and settle in secure Jewish communities."

Yaffa feels a great debt of gratitude to Sweden for offering a refuge for her parents, for saving them. "I will never say anything negative about Sweden and don't like to hear bad things about Sweden." Yaffa has positive childhood memories, even though her father always reminded her, "You can't be like the other girls."

"I had good friends in school," Yaffa continues, "but I was always on guard. The education was good with great teachers. I was a diligent student. As a teenager, life became more complicated. I became reserved and was uncomfortable mixing freely. One had to always be careful not to become assimilated. Only one other family had a strictly kosher home, so we never could eat anywhere else. Our parents always stressed our Jewishness."

Tuvia spoke of being different, of being placed in the hallway during religious instruction. As a five-year-old, he was reprimanded for refusing to sing the daily hymns.

Boras was unique in that before the survivors came there had been no Jewish presence there. Thus they now had a community of Jews who all were concentration camp survivors – a very unusual situation. In all other communities there was a mixture of the established Jewish community and the newcomers.

A social worker from Gothenburg, Mirjam Sterner Carlberg, wrote a doctoral thesis about the phenomenon of Boras called *Gemenskap ock over-levnad* (Community and survival). Yaffa expressed this as an unusual life experience of the second generation, the offspring of Holocaust survivors. "We had no angst or fears. We were comfortable with our existence. The entire Jewish community of Boras consisted of survivors, so there was no stigma attached, no cast system. Everyone had parents who had been in concentration camps, so that just seemed natural."

"It was definitely different in Stockholm or Malmo," continued Tuvia. "In big cities there were two distinct, separate groups: the indigenous Jews and the survivors. And often they did not mix very well." He paused, and then said reflectively, "I just realized that in my youth, I never attended or heard of a Jewish wedding."

"What do you mean?" I asked, quite incredulous. "There were no people getting married?"

"No," stated Tuvia, "all the Jews in Boras were in the same age group and had married right after the war. And no one had grandparents except for one family. Everyone was of the same generation. I never attended or heard of a bris either, since all the children were born when we were very young. There were Bar Mitzvahs to celebrate, though; many around the time I celebrated mine.

"What are your fondest memories of childhood?" I asked the Litzman siblings.

"Nature," responded Yaffa immediately. "We went biking with our mother along the west coast of Sweden, near Skagerakk. We loved the area around Smogen and Halmstad, especially during our summer vacations. We would take the train to Varburg and during the two-and-a-half-hour wait between trains, we would leave our belongings on the platform and go hiking. Can you imagine that nobody ever touched our belongings – and there it was in public view." We laugh, for that was indicative of life in Sweden, love of nature and the honesty and decency of the people.

"I am grateful to Sweden," concluded Yaffa, "but I have no desire or interest to return. When I came back after five years in Israel, I felt like a stranger. After age sixteen, Israel became The Place. On my visit to Sweden, I biked everywhere and said goodbye to the lakes, the woods, the beautiful Swedish landscape. But it was a final goodbye."

In speaking about his return, twenty years after he I had left, Mordechai recalled, "When I went to Gothenburg to visit my father's grave, I could not believe that I had ever lived there. It was so totally non-Jewish. You know," he said, "the water in the lakes in the woods was blackish, from the pine trees. The Jewish community of our days was like a rock thrown into these still waters. Momentarily there were ripples, some movement, but then it reverts back to stillness. That was Boras. It reverted back to its original status. Most survivors left, perhaps to Gothenburg, but today the community is basically gone."

"Did your mother miss Boras?" I asked. Barbro Litzman immigrated to Monsey in 1979 after her retirement. She must have been very lonely those last few years with her children away and her husband gone. "She missed the beauty of Swedish nature," responded Yaffa. "Can you imagine – when she prepared to come at age sixty-two, she asked if she should bring her bike! She loved the biking and hiking, picking mushrooms and berries. And yes, those final years alone in Sweden were difficult, but she never wanted to be a burden on us. She really enjoyed being surrounded by family in Monsey, though. And we were happy she had ten years with us."

If you ask the Litzman siblings for the magic formula that enabled the parents to raise their children to grow up in a small town in Sweden and remain strictly Orthodox, raising their children to follow in the same footsteps, they will unanimously agree: "It was the home." Kosher meat had to be brought from Malmo, a considerable distance and large expense. *Taharas Hamishpocha*, observance of the Laws of Family Purity, was not especially difficult during the summer; however, in the winter, Barbro joined a Polar Club, immersing in the ice-cold water, sometimes even breaking the ice to make a space to enter. The children always thought she enjoyed this winter sport, never imagining that this was essential for the observance of that commandment.

The three siblings were enthusiastically commenting on the basis for Jewish survival: a strong Jewish home built like a fortress. "Our father prayed three times a day." "And he brought us to services every Shabbat." "We always celebrated *Shabbat* and all the Jewish holidays." "And, of course, Bnei Akiva played a very significant role." Bnei Akiva's role in strengthening Jewish values and pride was clearly evident in the Litzman family.

On the first of February, 2009, at the Monsey wedding of Yaffa's son Nachum to Esther, I could feel Mrs. Litzman's presence. I visualize her sweet, kind face, the soft smile, her eyes glistening with pride as she proudly views her offspring – the children, grandchildren and great-grandchildren – a group numbering well over a hundred. I enjoyed speaking Swedish, our common mother tongue, chatting and reminiscing, with the three siblings in one place, for this was an unusual opportunity, a perfect time to recall the wonder of Boras. The Jewish identity implanted by their parents in this insignificant town in Sweden is now blossoming in full bloom: in Monsey, New York and in Israel.

CHAPTER 12

Doctor Abe from Malmo

L ocated on the southern tip, in the province of Skane, Malmo is the third-largest city in Sweden. At one time this region belonged to Denmark, but after the Treaty of Roskilde in 1658, it became part of Sweden. One of the earliest industrial towns in Sweden, Malmo's location contributed to its rapid expansion. The modern harbor with the Kochum shipyard was established in 1840. The railway line that opened in the mid-eighteen hundreds played a major role in the city's growth. The city's proximity to the University of Lund, one of the oldest and most prestigious universities in Sweden, was another important factor that contributed to its growth.

On July 1, 2000, the Oresund Bridge and Tunnel opened, which facilitated connections between Copenhagen and Malmo, two important cities. A busy access, trains cross this ten-mile-long structure every twenty minutes, with the tunnel accessible to all types of vehicles. Prior to that, the hydrofoil connected these two cities.

Jews were not permitted to live in Malmo until 1860, and in 1872 the entire Jewish population consisted of seventy-one men, fifty-five women – fifty-two married, two widowed and one single – and seventy-three children, according to the recorded Jewish history of Malmo. They all settled in the eastern area of the Old Town near Humlegatan and Gronegatan and established a section called Jerusalem. There was great poverty among these immigrants from Poland, Russia and the Baltic States. In the fall of 1872 they established a cemetery on Foreningsgatan and in 1903, on that same street, they built a magnificent Oriental-style synagogue with horseshoe arches, a stylized Lotus flower motif and a Turkish dome.

The Jewish residents of Malmo will never forget the arrival of the Danish Jews in 1943. Yom Kippur Services were held at the Philadelphia Church, and for this unusual situation, the Christian symbols were covered with white cloths. With the arrival of nearly the entire community of Danish Jews, it was impossible to accommodate everyone in the synagogue. The escapees expressed their deep gratitude to the Almighty and their fellow citizens – these emotions intermingled with despair and anxiety – in an unforgettable service conducted by Cantor Gordon of Helsingborg.

In 1945 the White Buses arrived in Malmo with 12,000 Jews, pitiful survivors from the Holocaust. This resulted in a population explosion in this city with an increase from 500 Swedish Jews to 1,500 as a result of the new immigrants. The Malmo cemetery contains more than a hundred graves of Holocaust victims who perished shortly after their arrival. An impressive memorial was erected by the sculptor Willy Gordon, who also sculpted the memorial in the courtyard of the Great Synagogue in Stockholm. In 1969, after the Communist revolution, three thousand Polish Jews arrived in Sweden and one thousand of these immigrants settled in Malmo. In 1990, several hundred more Jews arrived, from the Soviet Union, and further increased its population.

In 1991 Harry Rubenstein, one of the founding members of this community, established an eyewitness organization to spread information about the Holocaust in the schools. About one thousand of the community's survivors are members of the organization as well, and many participate as volunteer speakers to develop an awareness of the horrors and dangers of racism. Twenty speakers have presented 2500 programs in schools and special gatherings thus far and continue to be active in this worthwhile project. Harry Rubinstein also published a book, *Eyewitness Accounts*, filled with memories of survivors written in their own words, and is the father of Rabbi Meyer Rubinstein, now living in Kibbutz Lavi.

In 2003, in cooperation with the Malmo Museums, a beautiful book was created as a tribute to the centennial one celebration of the establishment of the synagogue. The title, *A Stone from the Temple Fell on Foreningsgatan*, was inspired by a legend from the Midrash, which states that when the Temple in Jerusalem was destroyed, the Almighty spread the stones all over the world and in each place where a stone fell, a synagogue was established. That is why each synagogue is referred to as a 'miniature Temple'.

The large influx of Muslims began about twenty-five years ago. Their influence in Malmo is constantly expanding. Presently, one quarter of the population of this city is Muslim and it is predicted that by 2049, there will be a Muslim majority. The population is polarized. There is a large rate of unemployment, and there has been a considerable increase in crime within the last ten to fifteen years. A local Muslim politician expressed that "Malmo is the best Islamic state in Sweden." Malmo today has the highest proportion of individuals of non-Scandinavian extraction. It is considered unsafe to wear a *yarmulke* in public. Many Jews are now in the process of leaving this city because being Jewish in Malmo is becoming more and more uncomfortable. The Jewish community of Malmo in 2010 has now been reduced to 700 members.

There have been several unpleasant incidents at pro-Israel demonstrations and members of Jewish sport teams have met with hostile encounters. The latest incident occurred in 2009 when clashes erupted at the arrival of an Israeli tennis team for the Davis Cup tennis match. Activists hurled rocks and firecrackers at police vans as the riot police attempted to break through the barricades and remove the protestors.

In 1945 Chana Sosnoweasz was brought to Malmo from Bergen-Belsen concentration camp on the White Buses. She arrived ill and weak, suffering from tuberculosis, an illness prevalent among the survivors. She recuperated slowly, but remained somewhat sickly. Unfortunately, in 1950, just before the Salk vaccine was invented, she contracted polio. Even after that setback, with her strong will to live, she found employment at a millinery shop and was highly respected for her creativity and talent.

In 1953, Chana married Yehuda, a survivor from Warsaw, Poland, her home country. During the war Yehuda had been interned in a labor camp in Auschwitz. He escaped and eventually became a soldier in the Red Army in Uzbekistan, the Soviet Union. In 1947, he was discharged from the army and returned to Poland. He had heard rumors about Sweden, that it was a place with great opportunities for survivors. A large number of Polish Jews, who had been rescued with the White Buses, sent letters to their brethren praising their new country of residence in glowing terms. With great difficulty, after a long and hazardous journey, Yehuda arrived in Malmo as an illegal refugee seeking political asylum.

In 1953, when Yehuda and Chana were married, the community consisted of a majority of Holocaust survivors, young families with young children. This was, indeed, a living tribute to the indomitable spirit of the Jewish people, to have faith in the future, to have hope, and thus rebuild families and establish homes. They were lonely, without parents, siblings and extended families, yet they were the conquerors. Hitler had caused physical destruction of enormous proportions, but the soul and spirit of the Jewish people, he could not obliterate. The survivors searched for people who spoke their language, who came from their country of origin; lonely and anxious, they searched for companionship and after short courtships, they bravely started a new life.

Yehuda and Chana were hoping to build a family. He was thirty-one and she was twenty-seven, a good age for marriage and having children. He became a welder and later on, a salesman for children's clothing. Chana, though not in the very best of health, continued as a stylist of hats in the millinery store. They were happy, filled with hopes and dreams. One year passed, then another and another. Their prayers for a child were unanswered. Around them, the families were growing steadily. Ten years passed, that crucial year when, according to Jewish law, a husband can divorce his wife for not having produced any offspring. But Yehuda loved Chana and life went on. Then, miraculously, in the thirteenth year of marriage a son was born. Words cannot suffice to describe the joy of this couple. Abe was given a festive bris and the small family was filled with thankfulness that their prayers had been answered.

Abe grew up in a home filled with love and joy and Jewish values. His parents, totally dedicated to their child, were always interested in his welfare. One topic was avoided – they never discussed the war or their camp experiences. Abe grew up knowing very little about his parents' childhoods and early years.

Their home was kept strictly kosher, and Yehuda prayed three times a day at the synagogue. As soon as Abe was able to walk, he attended the services with his father. Abe attended Talmud Torah once a week, like the other Jewish children in the city. In addition, his father taught him at home. A private tutor prepared him for his Bar Mitzvah, with Tanach studies included. His Bar Mitzvah was celebrated at the Malmo Community Center with lavish food and joyous music.

In grammar school he was often the only Jewish child in his class. He had many friends and socialized with the Swedish children, who fully accepted him. Abe felt different, however. He was younger than the offspring of the majority of survivors since he had been born years later than they were. It was difficult to have older parents. He could not eat at the homes of his friends since his family ate only kosher food. He could not eat lunch at school for the same reason, and always went home on his lunch hour.

Fortunately, there was an active Bnei Akiva in Malmo, which provided him with social opportunities and Jewish knowledge. In the summer camp and the winter camp, he developed love for Israel and pride in his Jewish heritage. Friendships were formed with Jewish children from all the Scandinavian countries, long-lasting, warm friendships.

Abe was a good student and received much encouragement from his doting parents. He attended the University in Lund for three years and completed his studies in the Malmo division in another three years. His parents were very proud when he received his MD in Oncology and Radiotherapy.

He had always enjoyed a close relationship with his mother and when she died, his life changed. Abe was then twenty-seven years old and now he no longer felt the need to remain in that part of the country. Stockholm, with its large Jewish community, beckoned to the young man

In 1997 Abe moved to Stockholm for Residency at the prestigious "Karolinska Institutet" (Karolinska University Hospital), which awards the Nobel Prize in Medicine. It was a fantastic opportunity to relocate to Stockholm; yet his feelings were mixed, as he was leaving his aging father alone in Malmo. In 1999, he spent the summer at the University of Michigan for a summer course in statistics. In 2000, his father died and now Abe was all alone. His parents had come to Sweden as lone survivors and Abraham was an only child. There were two cousins on his father's side who lived in America, relatives with whom the father had always maintained a close relationship, as they had grown up together; however, they were old and far away.

On my summer tour in the year 2000, I met Abe at the Shabbat services at my father's synagogue, Adas Yisroel. I noticed him immediately from the upstairs women's balcony, a well-built, handsome young man, visibly different from the middle-aged and elderly congregants. During the social hour of Kiddush, I introduced myself to him and we quickly developed a warm friendship. In 2001, Abraham visited America for three weeks, meeting his cousins in Connecticut and New Jersey. He spent Shabbat with us in the Five Towns on Long Island and in the synagogue, he was immediately noticed by the women. After all, an eligible, good-looking Jewish doctor who speaks perfect English – that created quite a stir.

Settling in America was definitely very tempting, for the opportunities to find a suitable mate here would be quite easy. The situation in Stockholm was difficult because there was a very small selection of possibilities – not just in Stockholm, but in all the Scandinavian countries. And since the numbers were minute, they were all too familiar with each other, like brothers and sisters. The possibility of relocating, however, was too overwhelming. Abe would have to acquire American certification, which would necessitate at least a year of studies and then the exams. Who would support him in the interim? And going back to school again, that was not of interest to Abe. Reluctantly, he returned to Sweden, fully aware of the situation confronting him. I am sure he was worried about the future, of finding a suitable mate.

Rabbi Horden had been sent from Israel to strengthen Jewish life in Stockholm. He organized classes and lectures and *Shabbatonim* for the youth of the city. Abe noticed an attractive young woman at these classes, a newcomer to this group. Born in Sweden, Shirley had lived in Belgium and England the major part of her life. Now she was in Stockholm completing her studies. Eventually they were introduced by mutual friends. Gradually, the relationship developed and blossomed. They dated from 2003 until 2004, when they were married in a beautiful, memorable wedding. In 2005, their daughter Ruth was born, and in 2009 their son Yaakov was welcomed into the family.

In 2007, at their home for a Friday night dinner, I was overjoyed to see Abe's happiness with his new family, a beautiful wife and adorable daughter. The table was set with costly Royal Copenhagen china, the famous pattern of blue flowers on white background, *Musselmalet* in Danish. Abe had inherited this service for twelve from his dear mother, who had lovingly purchased the settings, one by one, piece by piece, within a period of fifteen years. The small family had traveled to Copenhagen several times on holidays to add to their collection. On Shabbat and holidays in his childhood, these dishes had always been used and now, they were enhancing his own home. Shirley had served *varmrokt lox*, a Swedish specialty and a kosher variation of Swedish meatballs. The atmosphere was wonderful with the beautiful singing of old familiar melodies and words of Torah. I could sense the presence of his departed parents, the immense pleasure at the continuation of Jewish life.

Abe and Shirley frequently have guests for Shabbat and holidays. They are involved members of the community and attend lectures and classes. Abe, an active member of the synagogue, always attends services. Theirs is a strictly observant Jewish home filled with the values of Torah and good deeds. Perhaps some day they will relocate to Israel like many of the young couples in Sweden today. It is heartwarming to encounter this wonderful family, rebuilding a Jewish future from the ashes of the Shoah. May they continue to contribute to the reawakening of our Jewish world.

CHAPTER 13

A Heroine with a Camera and a Pen – Lena Einhorn's Saga

While gathering information about the forgotten hero Gilel Storch, I discovered Lena Einhorn's biography, *Trading in Lives*, a page-turner that captivates the reader like a mystery novel, a tribute to Gilel Storch, real-life hero. Lena skillfully portrays the stateless Latvian businessman who managed to arrange negotiations with Himmler to release Jewish women from concentration camps by employing bravery and verve sprinkled with a dose of old-fashioned chutzpa. Subsequently, the book became a vehicle for a brilliant documentary entitled *Stateless, Arrogant and Lunatic*.

Lena makes history come alive. Her book is filled with information of historical significance, well researched, yet enjoyable to read. I was touched by the account of her own parents' personal meeting with Gilel Storch. He generously provided them with funds to rent their first apartment – remarkable since they were total strangers. He truly cared about the difficulties of all survivors.

A versatile, accomplished individual, Lena Einhorn had experienced great success in many fields. A doctor involved in medical films, she left the medical field and has become famous in Sweden as a filmmaker, having written and directed more than twenty documentaries and films. She has received countless awards including Best Script, Best Director, Best Documentary and Best Screenplay in Europe, Israel, the United States and China. A renowned author, Lena received the National Book Award. She recently started a musical band that just had its first gig in Stockholm Pride. Her accomplishments attest to her talent and productivity.

I asked Lena, "In what area are you most interested?" Her response: "I enjoy all of them equally."

Her interview was the first one on our schedule, and I looked forward to meeting this highly eclectic woman, a daughter of Polish Holocaust survivors, with great enthusiasm. Her apartment, located in a building amidst a row of similar-looking ones, is near a park in the center of Stockholm. Her home was filled with books, journals and papers, a busy place indicative of an active, involved person. She was dressed in casual attire, rather ordinary looking, serious, low-key and down to earth. My carefully constructed questions encouraged open-ended responses. Lena described her childhood and close involvement with a tight-knit group of offspring of Polish survivors, children of her own background. *Her childhood was vastly different from mine*, I thought. *She was fortunate to have a strong peer group of like individuals.*

"Did you ever feel truly Swedish?" I queried, wondering if Lena's views would mirror my own. Lena replied that she had always felt different, forever aware she was not a "real" Swede. With great enthusiasm, I noted a kindred spirit reflecting my personal confusion a generation earlier. It amazed me that Swedish-born Lena, a generation later, should feel separate, apart from the mainstream. Was that her cultural heritage? It was clearly evident in *Nina's Journey*, Lena's biography of her mother, that in anti-Semitic prewar Poland, the Jewish population maintained a distinct distance from the Poles. The youth walked on their own streets, in their own groups, always apart. Was that the reason for her family's strong ties with Polish Jews in Sweden, for the formation of such a close-knit group? Lena's family celebrated Jewish holidays, were members of the Jewish Community and had strong positive feelings toward their Jewish heritage. Although not observant in their practice, they never disassociated from their roots or assimilated. *Very meaningful, indeed*, I thought.

"Swedish society was very homogenous," Lena declared, in an attempt to explain her feelings.

Americans cannot fathom the life of a Jew in Scandinavia because the United States encompasses countless nationalities and races. Diversity is the way of life and everyone is different. Brimming with excitement, I felt a kinship to Lena, that we both had felt so identically displaced. I am excited about this, for that is a situation typical of those of us who have experienced being a small minority

Peering about the room, I noticed a colorful bug under a small side table. "This is a *Guldbagge* Award," Lena explained, in response to my question. This award was a prestigious recognition of her recently produced film *Nina's Journey*, based on her biography of her mother, published in 2005. The colorful bug resembled a child's toy and seemed quite content under the lamp table. Lena smiled at my surprise when told of the significance of this award, given to the winner of the Swedish National Film Award for Best Film 2005 – a most unobtrusive spot for the equivalent of an Oscar.

The book, based on lengthy discussions with her mother during her final illness, became very popular in Sweden. It provides the reader with an understanding of the trials and tribulations of life during World War II and is a powerful portrayal of a daughter's love for her mother. Lena's respect and admiration for her mother is very touching. The description of life in the ghetto focuses on everyday challenges: crowded conditions, concerns about the future, financial worries, lack of many amenities and food deprivation. Adversity is contrasted with the closeness of family and warmth of the community.

The love for education, exemplified by her tackling the difficulties of paying tuition for Nina with a very tight budget, is indicative of the deep commitment of parent to child, evident in the relationship of Nina and her mother. Classes were held in secret, in constantly changing locations, in very cold, uncomfortable settings, with limited supplies; however, Nina's strong desire to continue her schooling was never hampered. That same appreciation for education continues throughout later generations. Nina and her mother visited America before the war and she could have remained there, avoiding the tragedy that befell the Jews of Poland, but Nina's deep feelings for her hometown, Lodz, drew her back with great force and discouraged her from remaining. In minute details, the mother recalls her prewar existence, the teenage years of horror in the ghetto.

I was deeply affected by a scene that occurs toward the end of the book: After her mother's demise, Lena finds, in a plastic bag in the closet, a hand-sewn teenage bra, lovingly made by Nina's mother for her young daughter, one of the only items of a personal nature that remained.

Lena's parents, Nina and Jerzy Einhorn, studied medicine in Poland after the war at Lodz University from June 1945 until July 1946. Two friends with identical agendas, they traveled to Copenhagen during the summer of 1946 as part of their medical training because there was a lack of laboratory equipment in postwar Poland. While there, they heard about a pogrom in Kielce, Poland, on July 4, 1946, where forty-two Jews were slaughtered. "Don't return," they were advised by family members. Since remaining in Denmark became impossible, they courageously escaped to Sweden.

After many trials and tribulations, the young couple arrived in Sweden in 1948, to a completely alien world, penniless, unfamiliar with the language and without family or friends. They felt privileged to be allowed as non-matriculating students at Uppsala University, a task that was overwhelming. *I can just imagine the incredible frustration to be in a large lecture hall barely understanding the professor*, I thought, as I recalled my own experience as a new student in an American high school. They must have had incredible determination and fortitude to engage in medical studies. Imagine using a Polish-Swedish dictionary to attempt to comprehend a complex lecture. The study of medicine is difficult under normal circumstances and this was an extraordinary situation. Nina was the stronger and more courageous one and it was due to her perseverance, and persistence that they both received medical degrees. Her husband was at times overwhelmed but Nina's encouragement gave him strength.

Eventually they married, completed their medical studies and raised two children, Lena and Stefan. The youngsters, influenced by their physician parents, followed in their footsteps and also took the Hippocratic Oath.

Nina completed her studies in Uppsala University in 1949 and received her medical degree from Karolinska Institutet, the University Hospital in Stockholm. In 1986 she became Head of Oncological Gynecology at Radiumhemmet, where her husband became the CEO. She published three hundred scientific articles and gained fame in her research in ovarian, cervical and uterine cancer. A remarkable woman, she was a superb wife and mother in addition to her important contributions in the field of medicine. She died in 2002 from breast cancer.

Jerzy Einhorn, Lena's father, was simultaneously a medical doctor, a researcher and a politician. Born in Poland, his autobiography, *Utvald att leva* (Chosen to live), is a wonderful account of his life, including the experiences in the Czestochowa Ghetto and the Palcery Concentration Camp. He recounts the obstacles encountered upon the arrival in Sweden with the status of medical student, with no means of earning a living. Jerzy Einhorn writes: "Fifty years of distancing myself from the war experiences was essential. Only then did I have the stamina to reminisce and recall the happenings of my life."

Utvald att leva is a wonderful depiction of life in the Polish shtetl before and during the war. Jerzy grew up in a home filled with Jewish tradition and always remained a proud Jew – not religiously observant, but his people and heritage were of uppermost importance to him. He also describes his student years and the rebuilding of life in Sweden. The difficulties involved in receiving Swedish citizenship during the Cold War era are dramatically related. It reminded me of my father's excitement when he was granted citizenship, the sigh of relief he must have felt. It was a celebration, like a holiday, I recalled.

Swedish citizenship was deeply valued by Jerzy Einhorn, for, now, he finally felt rooted, at home. Jerzy Einhorn died of Leukemia in 2000. Ironic that these two individuals who devoted their lives to cancer research both succumbed, in the end, to that dreaded disease.

Active in communal life, they were important fundraisers for Israel. From 1991 until 1994, Jerzy served as MP for the Christian Democratic Party in Sweden. Their contributions to the betterment of the world are presented in a book entitled *There are People We Are Talking About*, published by Bonniers in 1998.

Stefan Einhorn, Lena's brother, followed in the footsteps of the family. An oncologist at Radiumhemmet, he subsequently left the field of medicine and has become an author of acclaim, jokingly referred to, by no less than *Dagens Nyheter*, the largest Swedish newspaper, as the Swedish Doctor Phil. He writes that kindness is not equivalent to being wimpy or spineless, but the single most important factor in achieving success and satisfaction in life.

Lena is involved in the aftermath of World War II, her heritage as a child of survivors. Her parents instilled in her great pride for her heritage and many of her documentaries attest to this fact.

The Einhorn family played an extensive and significant role in Sweden. There, they were granted an opportunity to rebuild their lives and help make this world a better place. Sweden instilled the survivors with hope, providing them with a safe place in which to live and a chance to develop their talents.

My father, Rabbi Y. Y. Zuber.
Stockholm, 1944.

My sister-in-law Yenti with Shalom. Boston, 1960s. Photo:
Chana Zuber.

My brother Mendel and sister-in-law Sara at their engagement.
Stockholm, 1946.

At the home of Magda Eggens, author of children's books. Stockholm suburbs, 2006.

With Lenke Rothman, world-famous artist, surrounded by her creations at her home in Lidingo; 2006.

Ben Olander, businessman and composer, dedicated admirer of Raoul Wallenberg. Stockholm, 2007.

With Sterna, my daughter, in the forefront, and Marianne Ahrne, famous writer and filmmaker, at extreme right. We met in Manhattan on her visit, 2009.

Bertil and Kikki Neuman, dear friends from my childhood. Bertil wrote about the importance of humor in the concentration camps. Stockholm, 2006.

Left to right: Yaffa, Mordechai and Tuvia Litzman, the Boras siblings, at a rare reunion in Monsey, NY, 2007. Photo: Mordechai Litzman.

Lena Einhorn, daughter of survivors, well known in film, writing and music. Stockholm, 2007.

Section 3

RESCUES AND RESCUERS

CHAPTER 1

Gilleleje

Gilleleje is a small, charming town at the northernmost tip of the island of Sjælland, Denmark. Because of its location, just ten nautical miles across the Sound, Oresund, to Malmo, a southern port in Sweden, a large percentage of the rescue of Jews in 1943 took place here.

Historically, Gilleleje had always been a popular resort town, equipped with fine hotels and spas for recreation and recuperation where wealthy Danes enjoyed a stay during the brief summer season. Main Street winds through the small town, filled with assorted shops and a sprinkling of coffee houses and restaurants. The buildings are basically low, private, modest homes with well-kept, small gardens. Years ago, fishermen lived here and one still sees a variety of boats docked at the marina. Quiet and peaceful, this is a town where everyone knows his neighbors.

The drive from Copenhagen, Denmark's capital, where more than one-fifth of the total population resides, is about three hours along the scenic highway Strandvejen. There is an optional shorter route, but it cannot compare to the drive along the Danish Riviera. Luxurious vacation homes in various architectural styles are located conveniently along the water, with private beach facilities. Some have roofs in the shape of an inverted-V, while others have a modernized version of the old thatched roof. The road winds past public beaches, clean and well-kept, though not world famous or attracting foreign tourists, for the summers are short and with few beach days. On sunny days, few and far between, Danes take a day off from work and grab the opportunity to relax. The beautiful blondes, with their toned bodies, expose their skin toward the luxurious rays of the sun.

The left side of the road contains winterized homes as well as convales-cent homes, none higher than three stories. Danes appreciate their homes, which is obvious from the clean, starched curtains and the sparkling, shiny windows. The gardens have beautiful flowers, artistically arranged amidst small apple and cherry trees. Some Danish farms have livestock – cows and horses, chickens and pigs.

Denmark has no mountains or forests. The country produces cheese and other dairy products as well as grains and vegetables in abundance. Karen Blixen, pen name Isak Dinesen, author of *Out of Africa*, lived on Strandvejen, less than an hour from Copenhagen. Her home, Rungstedlund, near the hamlet of Rungsted, was converted into a museum displaying Danish life sixty years ago. The road passes by the Louisiana Art Museum, which houses modern art and also has wonderful sculptures in the lush gardens that surround it.

During the first two years of Nazi occupation, the King rode his horse through the city of Copenhagen daily. When asked why he had no body-guards, he replied, as mentioned previously, that the Danish citizens were his chief protectors. His attitude, his fairness and humane ways, encouraged and inspired the Danes to rise to the occasion.

The Danish underground arranged to transport Jews out of Copenhagen from the small fishing villages. The rescue began on Rosh Hashanah of 1943, when the announcement was made regarding the impending round up on October 1. By Yom Kippur, 98 percent of the Jews had been safely evacuated and relocated to Sweden.

The scenic highway is dotted with small fishing villages of modest homes inhabited by ordinary, working-class Danes. The entire population of many of these villages volunteered to rescue their fellow citizens, the Jews. Ordinary Danes also mobilized, alongside the members of the Resistance Movement. Speed and secrecy were imperative. Supreme coordination en-abled the rescue operation to proceed smoothly. Neighbors were contacted. Almost everyone responded by opening their doors for temporary refuge of departing Jews. Drivers used assorted vehicles to drive the refugees up north to the fishing villages. Nondescript cars and vans were used. Hospitals packed refugees into ambulances camouflaged as ill patients. They would hide in a hospital, even a morgue, awaiting further instructions.

Funerals were staged with hearses transporting fleeing Jews, additional ones in escorted cars. Trucks that usually transported goods were also used.

Contacts were made with the local inhabitants who lived in the fishing villages. There were rescue operations from Dragor and Amager to Malmo by a group known as "Two Women." Lyngby, just North of Copenhagen, had a large resistance group. Bisbebjerg Hospital in Copenhagen, a base for resistance activities, was endorsed by the hospital staff, doctors, nurses, orderlies and ambulance drivers. Even the staff at the morgue cooperated by temporarily housing the refugees as well as escorting them up north.

Denmark was occupied. Nazi soldiers lounged everywhere, patrolling waterways, flashing searchlights on small vessels. People had to appear relaxed, not tense, so as not to arouse suspicion. In the dark of the night, the Jews stealthily walked to the waters of Oresund where the vessels were waiting. When the moon was full, they had to exercise more caution. Wordlessly, they boarded, as indicated by hand motions from the Resistance team.

Space was at a premium. The captains were paid for their participation, but no one was refused passage because of lack of funds. Members of the Jewish Community helped those in need and the Resistance also cooperated. It was indeed a miracle that more than ninety percent of the population was escorted to safety. Of the total number of Jews, 7,200, nearly twenty percent or 2,000 were rescued from Gilleleje.

On Strandvejen, near Snekkersten, on the right side of the road, a large memorial stone commemorates the captain of a ship who had been apprehended and subsequently sacrificed his life. Rescue operations were dangerous because of the Germans and possible betrayal by non-members. Yet the majority of the Danes, peace loving and respectful of life and humanity, participated in the rescue.

Fishing boats sailed from the Danish northern cities of Humbleback, Espergade and Elsinore – called Helsingor in Danish, the twin city of Helsingborg in Sweden. These small fishing villages on the coast are located in an area where the nautical distance to Sweden is the shortest. One can travel by train from Copenhagen, and continue across the water with another train on a ferry to Helsingborg. It is an exciting ferry crossing, to suddenly be on the water in a railroad car, tracks leading on to the ship, and exiting the train to watch the movement of the ferry from the railing. During that era, crossings from Elsinore/Helsingor were infrequent, as this area was heavily patrolled by the Gestapo. A thick presence in the town, they inspected train travelers and the large number of commercial vehicles that crossed on the ferries. Gilleleje, a fishing town at the highest northern tip of Sjælland, became the most frequently used route.

Gilleleje became an additional feature on my Danish tour, retracing the heroic 1943 operation after my dear friend Ib Bamberger described the inauguration of the memorial statue erected in May of 1997. Ib had been rescued with his family and described the journey in his essay, "God's Handboat," published in the *Theological and Halachik Reflections on the Holocaust.* When his brother Bjorn arranged an evening of tribute to thank the Danes on the fiftieth anniversary of the rescue, and presented a shofar to the Danish Consul in New York, in memory of the rescue having been on Rosh Hashanah, I was invited to join. Rabbi Bamberger frequently visited Denmark and Iceland and shared local news.

In 1998, I added the dramatic tour from Copenhagen to Gilleleje, passing the small villages that had been instrumental in the Danish escape. "Try to imagine the vehicles on the first leg of their journey," I would state in a soft, whispery voice, as we drove up the winding road. "Imagine the fear, the secrecy, not knowing the exact destination, not even knowing the driver. Placing the safety of your family in the hands of strangers – that must have been overwhelming."

The tour members would sit on the edge of their seats, deep in thought. Many tourists, Holocaust survivors or children of survivors, were overcome by the contrast of the Danish experience with the rest of Europe.

"Behind every tree, all along the route to the water," I would say, "were members of the Resistance group, acting as lookouts. Bushes were cleared to make a path to avoid excess sounds. The refugees had to move cautiously, quietly so as not to be detected." Then I would present Ib's dramatic description of his own rescue as a young boy and the entire bus tour of people would listen breathlessly, absorbing every detail.

I would slowly unfold the transcript of Ib's story and carefully begin to read. No matter how many times I repeated the saga, it was always very emotional.

"Certain moments define a person's life," he writes, describing the drive from Copenhagen in a strange car with an unfamiliar driver. Their destination was a crowded barn where almost two hundred fellow Jews were gathered. "We stayed at the farm on Tuesday and Wednesday," he writes, "waiting for the fishing boats that would take us across the Sound. The moon was too bright and that augmented the danger. On Thursday, the two hundred people boarded trucks and were taken to the beach. "Behind every tree, behind every wall and house, a member of the Danish underground was standing, ready to defend the human cargo."

They were taken in small rowboats to large fishing boats, waiting further out in the Sound. And then…"in the worst possible situation, the engine would not start. After a nerve-wracking hour, the engine miraculously was reactivated. It felt as if the hand of the Almighty actually carried the boat to safety. Not a sound was heard, but the prayers on everybody's lips must have reached the highest places. These sincere words of desperate people must have crashed through the gates of Heaven." After two hours of travel, the ships were in Swedish waters and a torpedo boat picked them up.

"In May 1945, upon their return," Ib records, "Great, indeed, was our surprise…My mother had set the table, the candlesticks, the plates, the flatware; the silver cups had all been prepared to usher in the new year. After twenty-two months, the table was still set exactly the same way as when we had left."

And then, the dramatic final paragraph: "I do not know why the Jews of Denmark were saved. Many reasons had been advanced. This much, however, is sure: I felt the hand of God on that memorable night when we were taken from slavery to freedom, from darkness to light and from death to life."

Approximately 6000 Jews were saved and 464 were brought to Thereisenstadt, where they experienced preferential treatment at the hands of the Scandinavian Red Cross. All returned except for fifty-seven who died of natural causes – old age and sickness from pre-existing conditions, not necessarily camp related. Two children born in the camp are still alive today.

When the Germans combed the country for Jews, they found a few elderly and sick members who had opted not to flee. These few were brought to Thereisenstadt, where they suffered far less than in the other camps, for the Scandinavian Red Cross supplied their citizens with food packages and supplies. Fewer than sixty people died.

Was the Jewish rescue a very clever strategy to rid the country of Jews? After all, Denmark became Judenrein cleanly and efficiently. The homecoming indicated a very different plan, however, clearly showing their humanity. When survivors returned to Kielce, Poland, they were greeted with open hatred. "We thought you had died," some gloated, while others said, menacingly, "Why did you return?" Poles were living in their homes, using their linen and tablecloths, enjoying their furnishings, paintings and carpets. They had confiscated their businesses and now organized pogroms to kill the survivors, though the actual war had been over. What a difference!

We traveled to Gillaleje by train and walked to Pyramiden, the local museum, to film for the Scandinavian documentary. The summer was drawing to a close and the schedule had already changed. Staff was available, but the place was closed for visitors. Fortunately my knowledge of the language, and the professional appearance of the video crew, allowed us to gain entry. They filmed the wonderful displays of life at the turn of the century: the shoe store, hat shop, fashionable clothing store and grocery shop, the stuffed local birds, as well as the collection of common toys and household items.

Of immense interest was the display of the schedule of the fishing boats used in the rescue. The glass case contained official documents with dates, names of ships, names of captains and number of passengers. Maps of the routes and photographs made the rescue seem more real. Everything was written in Danish, as foreign visitors rarely come. I translated the Nazi posters that threatened punishment for helping Jews and rewards for disclosing their hiding places.

Behind Pyramiden, in the large surrounding grounds, facing the Sound, are two impressive monuments associated with the rescue. In May 1997, the six-foot-tall statue of a Chassid in traditional garb – long, flowing caftan – and holding a beautifully carved Shofar, reminiscent of the eventful night in 1943 when the announcement was made to flee the city on Rosh Hashanah, was unveiled here. The dramatic statue, silhouetted against the Sound, with the Swedish skyline clearly visible, is the work of George Weil, known for his creative jewelry designed in London. Yuli Ofer, an affluent Israeli business-man, donated the statue and presented a replica as well, which was placed in Haifa. The shofar is symbolic of the Great Shofar that will be blown to an-nounce the Messiah's arrival, the end of *Galut* and the dawning of a new era.

Suzannah and Nachum avidly photographed the scene from various angles. I had to cultivate patience, to develop the understanding that pho-tography involves careful study and contemplation. When clouds appeared on the horizon, the drama was intensified and there was another shooting session.

Near the statue stands a fishing boat – not a model, but an actual fish-ing boat used in the rescue, which adds to the authenticity of the scene. A flap was cut out of the side of the ship to provide spectators with an inside view. The display depicts a man and woman, dressed in holiday clothing, seated, with luggage nearby. Glass shields the opening. Their clothing sub-stantiates that the rescue occurred on Rosh Hashanah.

While viewing the monument and boat, I noticed a group of students listening to a lecture from their guide. I also saw an elderly man closely ob-serving and listening to my detailed explanation of the rescue to Suzannah and Nachum. I thought he could provide additional information to fill in the gaps with his own personal knowledge, but when I addressed him, he became uncomfortable and moved away.

I followed him and asked if he could please share his memories, for I felt it would enhance the project, but he shook his head and turned away. Once more I attempted to engage him in dialogue, but he looked at me intently and from this look, I realized that he had been involved. Placing his fingers on his lips, after all these years, he still valued the oath of silence of the Resistance Fighter. With a sorrowful look, he let me know that he had much to share, but his pleading eyes made me aware that his privacy must be respected.

Suzannah, usually easygoing and soft spoken, insisted that I locate an old fisherman for an interview. This interview would be essential and Suzannah positively knew I could do it, despite my protests to the contrary. We strolled through the town toward the harbor, and in an open garage that had been converted to a workshop, we saw a fisherman busily organizing his

fishing gear, rods and nets. I paused to speak to him and he responded in a
friendly manner, typical of the Danes. He told me where an elderly fisherman resided and we followed his directions.

Walking past numerous anchored boats, turning at the first street on
the right, as directed, to the small white house in back of the red dwelling
facing the harbor, we located the home of the old fisherman. As we neared
the home, Suzannah suggested that I walk ahead, introduce myself and then
bring them in. I knocked on the door to the small, modest home and within
moments, I was invited in by the friendly, smiling, elderly woman. She welcomed me like an old friend. I explained the purpose of the visit and then
beckoned to Suzannah and Nachum to join me. It was obviously the home
of a fisherman, with photographs of ships proudly displayed on walls and
models of ships on shelves.

The tall, gaunt fisherman welcomed us with great excitement. He had
been a teenager when he had assisted in the rescue missions. His parents had
been supportive, but had requested that he be cautious. A few times, it had
been necessary for him to stay several days in Hoganas, the Swedish destination, because being seen too frequently on boat crossings could arouse unnecessary attention.

Upon hearing that Suzannah and Nachum came from California, the
elderly couple grew animated. They felt like celebrities, honored to wine and
dine people from Hollywood. The gaunt fisherman had been comfortably
seated in a huge arm chair, somewhat slumped over. Now he straightened
out into his full lanky form. The wife was all smiles, glancing furtively in
the mirror, hurriedly fixing her hair, removing her apron and smoothing
her clothes. They were very gracious and made us feel welcome, as if we
were doing them the favor instead of us seeking their hospitality. Wonderful
Copenhagen, country of fairy tales. Where in the United States would total
strangers be invited into the home of defenseless seniors?

With great joy, he pointed to the photographs of ships he had sailed
and ships he had owned. I am not knowledgeable about ships, but Nachum
moved closer to scrutinize the different vessels and models, some in bottles.
He also inquired about interesting medals on display. The fisherman spoke
of the war, bringing back memories from the past. His eyes sparkled and he
shook his head sadly as he recalled the fear and uncertainty of the Jews as
they had boarded the ship. He was ashamed that the Germans could be filled
with hate and cause fellow citizens to flee for their lives, that they could be so
evil. A peace-loving man, typical of the Danes, he disliked war.

Would this scene have been repeated in an average small town in the
United States, I wonder. This was not a Jewish community, just an ordinary
small village in Denmark. I was and am impressed with their display of

friendliness. To open a door and allow total strangers to come in? Their enthusiasm increased after our presentation of the purpose of our visit.

His wife watched with great happiness as her dear husband shed years off his life. "He looks like my handsome, young husband," she told us gratefully. "Before you came, he looked sad and tired. Now he looks invigorated, like my young sailor." We had brought the couple moments of joy as they relived the past.

Friendship was kindled; the atmosphere in the tidy, little house was pleasant. We were invited for dinner, but I explained that we only ate kosher food. We departed with hugs and handshakes and were invited for a return visit. It had been an interesting afternoon, interviewing this gracious couple.

We continued to the Church of Gilleleje, an important part of the rescue. The church was surrounded by a well-kept cemetery. "On Wednesday, October 6," I related, "five hundred refugees were scattered in the small homes awaiting passage. One hundred hid in the loft of the church." Nachum focused his camera on the high steeple of the church, the attic area, where the Jews were hidden.

"The resistance members had brought bedding and supplies to make the stay as comfortable as possible," I continued, in a somber, expressive voice. "A local young girl had become involved with a German soldier and informed him of the activities. She was promised five kronor for each person caught. In those days, that was a large sum of money for a poor country girl. German troops entered the church and marched the poor people out. One man managed to escape."

I pointed toward the bell tower. "He stood there an entire night. He saw the unfortunate Jews being led away by the Gestapo. Frightened, he thought he would be noticed." While I was speaking, Nachum and Suzannah glanced up at the small area of the clock tower, with just enough room for the bell to swing back and forth in regular rhythm. With the open walls, and the heavy, large bell continuously moving back and forth every half hour, this was, indeed, a precarious situation. When the bell was swinging, it actually brushed the sides of the small bell tower.

"I can't imagine the fear," commented Suzannah, shivering slightly, as the air was getting chilly. "What happened to him? Was he saved?" As she was speaking she began adjusting her camera.

"They found him in the morning," I answered. "He was nearly frozen to death, but he was rescued. The girl was a great embarrassment to the entire town. The money she received did not compensate for her betrayal of the good Danes."

We returned to the train station and purchased tickets for the trip to Copenhagen. The train was almost empty and when the station for

Helsingor was announced, I told them to exit. "You must visit the castle," I said. "It is a very famous place." Kronborg Castle, in Elsinor, well known from Shakespeare's play *Hamlet, Prince of Denmark*, looked like a fairy tale castle, with its seven turrets. "Can't you just feel Hamlet running around here searching for Ophelia?" I said, wistfully.

"To be or not to be," stated Nachum; "that was the focus of the rescuers in Denmark."

"How was it that Denmark was different?" tour members would ask in admiration. In response, I would state that there never was any anti-Semitism in Denmark, there were no discriminatory laws and the people in general tend to be easygoing and peaceful. Denmark does not have any poverty, because there are numerous programs of social welfare. Traveling back to Copenhagen, I noticed a middle-aged Dane sitting quietly in our section. I asked him if he remembered the war years. "Yes, but I was a very young boy," he replied.

"Why do you think the Danes saved the Jews?" I asked.

"They were our fellow citizens. They were good people. They had to be saved," he said emphatically. "There was no question about it. This is not a debatable issue. It was the right thing to do. If human beings cannot be concerned about the welfare of their neighbors, then they simply are not human. If we want to live in a civilized world, we have to respond to the plight of fellow human beings. Otherwise, we would be like the wild animals in the jungle. Isn't that what life is all about?"

To him, as to the majority of Danes, this rescue operation was not something extraordinary, just a fact of life. Denmark will always be remembered as a glimmer of hope in a world lost in the darkness of hatred and cruelty. Simple words, uttered matter-of-factly, but beautiful music to our ears – a melodious harmony of friendship contrasting the horrors of the *Shoah*.

CHAPTER 2

Germany - Wannsee and Ravensbruck

"**C**hanele," says Suzannah exuberantly, "How would you like to come to the Film Festival in Potsdam?"

Suzannah's documentary on matchmaking had been accepted at the upcoming film festival, a significant triumph in Suzannah's fledgling career. I had never attended a film festival and it sounded exciting.

"You'll be my guest," Suzannah enthusiastically continued. "I really would like you to participate in the question and answer session after the show." I had been interviewed for the documentary and appeared in several sections. The follow-up sessions were always interesting, for the discussions included the role of the Jewish woman, in addition to dating and marriage.

Though traveling had always played a significant role in my life, Germany had been one place I had adamantly refused to visit. And then I remembered Ravensbruck. My reservations began to slowly dissipate. From Berlin it would be easy to travel to Ravensbruck, and that would be a very important place to film for the Scandinavian documentary, for that is where it all began.

Globians Film Festival, August 11-19, 2007

And thus, in August of 2007, I left for Berlin, where I would join Suzannah and Nachum at the Hotel Savigny at Brandenburgische Strasse.

I was filled with misgivings upon arriving at the Tegel Airport in Berlin, but within moments, like ice in the midst of bright, warm sunshine, my mood totally changed. Two young representatives, sent by the director of the Globians Film Festival, Joachim Polter, met me with a huge "Welcome" sign and escorted me to the hotel where Nachum and Suzannah were waiting. Within a short period of time, we were at the International Documentary Film Festival. It was very exciting mingling with producers and directors. And I had an official badge. There were documentaries on the schedule from two o'clock in the afternoon until midnight, every day of the festival. And there were interesting follow-up discussions after some of the events.

Excitement and tension was growing as we awaited the presentation of *Match and Marry*, scheduled to take place on Monday at 8:30 PM.

How would they react, I wondered. Would they laugh? Would there be unpleasant remarks? Would there perhaps be a polite, veiled cover-up of disrespect?

The room darkened, the film began and there was total silence. Everything about this documentary was authentically Jewish, including the setting of Crown Heights and Boro Park, and the music. The film ended amidst thunderous applause with countless questions from the interested audience. At the conclusion of the film, the three of us separated and had follow-up meetings with interested members from the audience.

Young people gathered around me in the lobby to continue the discussion. It was obvious that the German youth of today appear to be a new breed. It gave me a great deal of hope. Perhaps a lesson has been learned. Hopefully "Never Again" will be the theme of our future.

Wannsee

The House of the Wannsee Conference was the first destination on my agenda after the film festival, for if one wants to start at the beginning, that would be the logical starting point. We ambled to the nearby station at Konstanzer Strasse and then switched at Charlottenburg for the train to Wannsee.

The magnificent edifice, once owned by an affluent businessman, had been used as a conference center and guest house for the Nazis during the turbulent war years, from 1941 until 1945. The entire area of Wannsee was breathtakingly beautiful, featuring palatial homes and lush gardens, obviously a playground for the rich and famous. Many wealthy Jews owned homes there, summer residences for the Berliners. Max Lieberman, a world-famous artist, owned a villa that he referred to as his "Lakeside Palace."

During the forties he was forced to sell the property to the Nazi *Reichspost*. Max Lieberman died before the onset of the WWII but his wife, Martha, could not believe the German Nazi government would confiscate her beloved home. In 1943 she committed suicide, a viable option over deportation to Thereisenstadt according to her. The atmosphere of Wannsee, so serene and peaceful, was saturated with the beauty of nature, the architectural masterpieces indicative of "the good life," the comforts and pleasures of the world of wealth.

Inconceivable that in the midst of these pristine surroundings, in the magnificent villa with windows overlooking incredible scenery, a group of fifteen high-ranking representatives of the SS, the NSDAP and other ministries would meet for a brief forty-minute session on January 20, 1942 to discuss the "Final Solution." They met midday at an elegant buffet luncheon, with magnificent table settings and polite waitresses in perfectly starched, immaculate uniforms, while they resolved to use Cyclon B to gas the Jews; they rendered this the most efficient, expedient and economic means of eradicating the Jews of Europe. Cyclon B was manufactured in Germany, which was another added incentive. Superbly organized, their evil plans included locating ghettos near railroad stations to facilitate the forced removal of victims to concentration camps for extermination. The minutest details were considered for smooth operation.

In the midst of God's aesthetic nature, those evil minds formulated a plan for deportation and mass murder of European Jewry. Waves of nausea engulfed me, leaving me queasy. "It seems so utterly insane," I gasped, my stomach heaving, "that people could be so corrupt, could behave so barbarically."

The contrast is unbelievable between the elegance of the Wannsee Conference Center, with its highly polished parquet floors, large windows that invited sunlight and costly antique furniture – sturdy, solid, glistening conference tables with matching chairs – and the sinister plot of mass destruction that was conceived here. These surroundings were suited for intelligent, cultured individuals, not for beastly nefarious sub-humans.

The Wannsee Conference Center exemplifies the Nazi movement during World War II. Today, the villa is a memorial and and educational site, with an extensive exhibit depicting the history of the persecution of the Jews that begins in 1933, and continues with the ghettos, deportation and then the ultimate conclusion, the attempted extermination of European Jewry at the concentration camps. Another exhibit focuses exclusively on the January 20 conference.

A visit to Wannsee is an unforgettable, tragic remembrance of humanity's debasement.

Ravensbruck

Ravensbruck was a concentration camp often mentioned by the Swedish survivors. Count Folke Bernadotte, nephew of King Gustav V of Sweden, President of the Red Cross, was involved in prisoner exchange, focusing primarily on Scandinavian political prisoners. He extended his rescue with the White Buses to include women, which is how inmates from Ravensbruck were transported to Sweden.

It was not difficult to travel to Ravensbruck from Berlin. The hourly train went from central Berlin to Furstenburg, then we continued on foot, two kilometers, until we reached the camp.

"To us, this is a remembrance of the unfortunate camp victims who had to undergo the long marches," I commented sadly.

"Yes," Suzannah agreed. "We are walking at a comfortable pace, in summer weather. Imagine embarking on this during the cold winter."

"With threadbare shoes," Nachum added, "hungry and weak."

They proceeded in silence, steeped in their own thoughts, inadequate images barely piercing the threshold of pain their Jewish brethren had forcibly experienced. The group paused at the memorial sculpture that portrayed a group of women.

"This reminds me of the Vigeland sculptures in Frogner Park in Oslo," I sighed, glancing at the sculpture of three women carrying a makeshift stretcher on which lay a dead child. One woman stood erect, looking ahead; her partner was bent, dejected and the third woman in the group stared at the child's lifeless form. Analytically, the sculpture represented resistance, the ability to retain one's humanity and compassion in the face of savagery.

Upon arriving at Ravensbruck, we split up. Nachum and Suzannah walked off in search of interesting spots to photograph, determining the best angle and assorted pertinent details, while I wandered over to the Wall of Nations – formerly the Camp Wall – embossed with names of the twenty countries from which prisoners came who had been incarcerated and murdered.

I delighted in the beautiful bed of roses nearby until I noticed a small, unobtrusive sign. Horrified, I began to shudder as I quietly read, "This rose bed is on the site of the original crematorium." Realizing that I was standing at a mass grave, I burst into tears, trembling at the camouflage, the German intent to mask death with the perfume of roses that flourished on the fertilized ashes of the crematorium victims.

The center of the camp contained a large, empty area where the distressed and bewildered prisoners were forced to stand at rapt attention until everyone was accounted for, the cruel daily roll call – 'appel'. I painfully imagined the wet, muddy puddles, the prisoners that would line up for hours, especially if someone was missing.

On this sunny day, the area appeared nondescript, a vacant, harmless field. Faint outlines on the ground indicated where bunkers had once stood. It was peaceful, calm: the Memorial Museum, a place survivors would never recognize.

When I shared my visit with Yenti, she responded, "I never want to visit a concentration camp. It would upset me too deeply, to witness how my suffering became trivialized. The horrors, the nightmares, the disturbed sleep… everything has been altered. They might be called "memorials," but they are void of substance. The evil, the death – victims' cries rent the air!" She lifted her hands dramatically. "The memories are buried everywhere, but the visitor is greeted by a museum, carefully arranged exhibits in glass cases. Suffering cannot be contained in a glass case," she concluded, her gaze scornful. "It is so unreal, the ugliness and bestiality totally hidden."

The construction of Ravensbruck began in 1938 with inmates from the Sachsenhausen Camp supplying the labor. Ravensbruck has the distinction of being the only large concentration camp in Germany designed for women. In the spring of 1939 a group of one thousand female prisoners were brought from the Lichtenburg Concentration Camp.

In 1942 a youth concentration camp was established there as well. The camp grew exponentially, with more barracks added. In 1944, after the physical space had been exhausted, a huge tent was added. From 1939 until the end of the war in 1945, there were 132,000 women and children who resided there, with an additional thousand teenage girls.

The Siemens and Halske Company erected twenty factory buildings where the inmates were forced to work. In addition, there was a textile factory with eight sheds for SS use, and an industrial yard with additional SS workshops. Chana peered through the dusty windows and could make out old, rusted sewing machines, remnants of a bygone era.

Additional satellite work camps were constructed throughout Germany, more than seventy under the auspices of Ravensbruck. Female prisoners became slave laborers for these work camps, a large portion participated in the armament industry. When the unfortunate inmates had been literally worked to death and were no longer productive, they were disposed of in gas chambers and crematoriums. Special bunkers were set aside for prisoners – small, ugly cells – and others for specifically selected prostitutes.

On the surface, everything appeared peaceful, a pleasant memorial park. An attractive lake, birds chirping among the foliage. The inmates could never enjoy the view. Huge walls surrounded the camp to isolate this factory of destruction. Why does this view intrigue visitors rather than presenting them with the bleak truth, the sordid, ugly chapter of unspeakable cruelty and shame?

We regrouped and began to leave the camp when we noticed the large, well-constructed administration building that had formerly served as SS headquarters.

That particular building housed the female SS guards. The unbelievable stark contrast between their quarters and the inhuman conditions in the barracks was shocking. We paused to examine the exhibits in the building, exploring the history of the camp. There were numerous oversized photographs throughout the building of the female SS guards.

"Look at those faces," I exclaimed, "that cold visage, that unfeeling expression." Ice-cold, virtually sickened by those portraits, mesmerized, I continued staring sorrowfully at these inhuman women.

"Their eyes," Suzannah gasped; "they could kill you with their eye, eviscerate without shedding a tear, devoid of human emotion."

"How could they have lived in comfort," wondered Nachum, "while nearby, countless women were exposed, subjected to the most degrading existence? I wonder if they ever thought of this discrepancy...or were they completely unfeeling, without a conscience?"

We stood silently, deep in thought. "The world must not be allowed to forget," I exclaimed in a strong voice. "I cannot believe a camp of this ilk could exist among such physically beautiful surroundings. I cannot believe that the neighboring population, in this health resort area, really had no knowledge of the existence of this death camp!"

On our return, I surreptitiously glanced at my fellow passengers on the train, the majority of whom were middle-aged, too young to have been active in the Nazi party in World War II. Are they still Jew-haters? I wondered. What about their parents and grandparents? Were they Nazi sympathizers? Unable to contain myself, I began to converse with the nearby travelers in German, my least favorite language. "What do you know about Ravensbruck?" I asked. Almost everyone knew of the existence of the concentration camp and several had visited the place.

"We are ashamed of the conduct of the past generation," they stated. "It will be our responsibility to restore the damaged reputation of our country." One man commented, "I look at the elderly people in my community and find it incomprehensible that they attached themselves to that monstrous, cruel leader, the personification of *evil*." They appear embarrassed and sorrowful, eyes bewildered or downcast, heads shaking in disbelief. They are acknowledging the black chapter of German history.

CHAPTER 3

The White Buses –
Count Folke Bernadotte

There are always two sides to every story – actually, three: yours, mine and the real truth. This idea applies to every event, past or present, the main basis for the multitude of conflicting news reports and varied interpretations of historical events.

Count Folke Bernadotte, grandson of King Oscar II of Sweden, was involved in the exchange of German and British war prisoners. Deeply concerned with the plight of Scandinavians in German prison camps, he arranged to alleviate their difficulties by supplying Red Cross food packages. The Danish Jews in Thereisenstadt were fortunate to receive these packages as well.

His negotiations with Himmler inspired Gilel Storch to attempt his rescue mission of Jewish camp inmates. Count Folke Bernadotte, vice president of the Red Cross of Sweden, was instrumental in rescuing tens of thousands of inmates in the concentration camps. His rescues are well known and many grateful survivors are able to provide personal accounts of their experiences. Yet numerous historians and politicians have published accounts that minimize the greatness of this historic event.

On January 18, 1945, the Death March from Auschwitz with 66,000 inmates resulted in the death of 15,000. Time was of the essence. On April 11, 1945, Buchenwald was liberated and on April 15, Bergen-Belsen was liberated.

Exact figures of the rescues vary. According to the Ravensbruck Information Booklet, 7,500 inmates were brought to Sweden and Switzerland shortly before the end of the war. In 1995, secret files of Folke Bernadotte were opened after the required fifty-year wait, including his pocket almanacs

208

of 1944 and 1945. The numbers changed. Seven thousand women had been brought to Sweden on the White Buses in April 1945.

The entire mission extended over a period of two months, with a staff of 308: twenty medics, a group of nurses, thirty-six fully staffed hospital buses and nineteen trucks. According to the account of Jack G. Morrison, Ravensbruck German Commandant Suhren requested that the Red Cross accept fifteen thousand women. A subsequent order from Himmler on April 25 canceled the entire rescue. The evacuation order was reopened and on April 24, a train with four thousand women left Ravensbruck.

The Germans provided a sixty-eight-car freight train to be used at the disposal of the Red Cross. By April 29, more than eight thousand women, half the group Jewish, were brought to Malmo, Sweden, via Copenhagen.

The report to the World Jewish Congress by Norbert Masur lists the figure of ten thousand survivors from Ravensbruck who were rescued by the White Buses and brought to Sweden.

In his book, *Slutet* (*The Curtain Falls*), Folke Bernadotte vividly describes his rescue efforts. Of primary concern were the Scandinavian political prisoners. On February 19, four thousand were released from Neuengamne. On March 7, he met with Walter Schellenberg, head of SS Security, and realized there was a problem finding suitable personnel. On March 8, twelve trucks equipped with hospital gear and seventy-five other vehicles – including thirty-six buses and various cars, jeeps and vans – were located, and on March 16, two thousand one hundred sixty-one inmates were rescued from Sachsenhausen Concentration Camp.

Inga Goldfarb, of the American Joint Distribution Committee in Sweden and the Advisor on Immigrant Affairs of the Swedish Cabinet Ministers, wrote an eyewitness account of her participation in the reception of the White Buses in Malmo. According to her report, Niels Christian Dietleff, Ambassador in Sweden of the Norwegian government in exile in London, was anxious to rescue Norwegian political prisoners in concentration camps. The situation was discussed with Marcus Wallenberg, a financial tycoon related to Raoul Wallenberg.

Folke Bernadotte was approached on September 15, 1944 to meet with Himmler and negotiate to rescue the Norwegians in the camps. Subsequently, there were several meetings, the first one on February 19, 1945. The project was extended to include all Norwegian and Danish prisoners of war, including Danish Jews. Then Gilel Storch entered the scene to include Jewish women – from Ravensbruck, primarily. Norbert Masur completed these negotiations. For political purposes, the women were classified as Polish rather than Jewish, not to arouse Hitler's suspicion.

Inga Gottfarb's account states that three hundred eighty Swedish men and women were the participants in the rescue via the White Buses of twenty thousand inmates. This does not include the personnel of workers and volunteers in the one hundred fifty rehabilitation camps throughout Sweden and the one hundred doctors in Skane, the province where Malmo is located.

On April 16, four hundred twenty-three Danish Jews were rescued from Thereisenstadt. On the second of May, two thousand eight hundred seventy-three women from camps around Hamburg were brought to safety. Between June 25 and July 25, nine thousand two hundred seventy-three survivors were brought to Sweden.

The total figures of camp inmates that were rescued ranges from 19,000 to 30,000. Fifteen thousand were brought from concentration camps to Sweden. Seven thousand eight hundred Scandinavian prisoners were brought home, including inmates from Froslov and Horsens, German concentration camps located in Denmark.

The first group of survivors who came to Stockholm spoke of the White Buses with great reverence. They were filled with hope upon seeing the White Buses with the Red Cross, highly visible vehicles to protect them from enemy fire. I could not understand the importance of this project. The war was over in May of 1945. Why was it of such great import to be rescued a mere few weeks earlier? After all, the victims had suffered deprivation many months, even years.

Then I heard the horrendous descriptions about the Death March, the last desperate attempt to complete the Final Solution. The Nazis were uncivilized and depraved, yet appearances played an important role. Striving to cultivate a favorable world opinion, the Nazis decided it was necessary to dismantle gas chambers and crematoriums, and blow up camps to destroy all physical evidence. The SS evacuated the camps and forced malnourished, weak, starving, skeletal survivors to march countless miles, distances of forty, fifty, even sixty miles. Freezing, inadequately clothed, no shelter, starved, without food supplies, shoes held together with rags, paper wrapped around swollen, frost-bitten, unprotected feet, they stumbled, falling exhausted, often left by the roadside to die. The Nazis wanted no inmates to remain alive to testify about their bestiality. Tragically, with the smell of freedom in their nostrils, many succumbed just before the end.

I began to realize the crucial role that the White Buses had played, the thousands of fortunate survivors who were exempted and saved when they escaped the Death March.

Whatever negative rumors are wrongfully attributed to Count Folke Bernadotte, he should be remembered and recognized as a great humanitarian. His negotiations with Himmler to allow the release of concentration-camp inmates prior to the official declaration of the end, is fascinating. His heroic actions saved the lives of many Jewish women who subsequently built new families and raised new generations of our people.

In May 1948, Count Bernadotte was appointed by the UN to act as mediator in peace negotiations in the Middle East. He met his untimely demise in Israel.

CHAPTER 4

A Forgotten Hero – Gilel Storch

The audacity of a stateless Jew to arrange a meeting with Heinrich Himmler in Berlin during World War II defies imagination. Hardly the plot of an intriguing spy novel authored by a highly imaginative writer, but the actual life story of Gilel Storch, a dedicated, courageous, concerned and devoted hero during the Second World War. Unfortunately, he never received the recognition and rightfully deserved praise for his incredible rescue activity.

A successful Latvian businessman with Swedish connections, he was born in Dvinsk and later moved to Riga, where he established a thriving import/export business. Upon becoming aware of the impending danger for Latvian Jews, he relocated to Stockholm in 1940. At that time, Sweden's strict immigration policy prevented him from becoming a legal immigrant. Stateless, he had no foothold in Sweden, just his business connections, and it was difficult for him to establish residence. Employing great perseverance, almost superhuman effort, he was successful in bringing his wife and daughter to safety in Sweden. He feared for the lives of the relatives he had left behind and became obsessed with rescuing them. Failure to rescue the numerous relatives that had remained in Latvia distressed him deeply.

He may have been short in stature, but his personality was larger than life. Harnessing a boundless energy and determination, Storch used every waking moment to devise a solution to counteract the impending tragedy. Despite his active presence in the World Jewish Congress, at first his efforts proved fruitless. Yet, even after his relatives were slaughtered, Gilel Storch continued his activities on behalf of the other Jews whose lives were in jeopardy.

My sister Leya, employed by the HIAS in Stockholm, often saw him at the office. An impatient person, he appeared to be in a perpetual hurry. "His

failure to adhere to the unwritten laws of Swedish etiquette often antago-
nized bureaucrats," she told me. Leya thought him quite unconventional.
He insisted on meeting with people sans appointment, often barreling into
offices uninvited, and telephoning people late into the night. The Jewish
community in Sweden, accustomed to proper decorum, frowned at his blatant disregard for etiquette, but the urgency of the situation, according to
Storch, warranted breaking rules. Lena Einhorn's riveting documentary on
his life, appropriately titled *Stateless, Arrogant and Lunatic*, pays tribute to
his daring feats.

The successful negotiations of Folke Bernadotte in the release of prisoners of war encouraged Gilel Storch to seek the release of Jewish inmates.
With his insistence of rescuing inmates, his refusal to accept defeat – obsessed, restless, like a fever consuming his being – he forged ahead to fulfill
his mission. Inspired by the successful activities of the Swedish Red Cross in
supplying Scandinavian concentration-camp inmates with life-saving food
packages, Gilel Storch persuaded Folke Bernadotte to send 40,000 packages to Jewish inmates, the War Refugee Board contributing an additional
40,000.

As the war drew to an end, the virulent, vile activities accelerated. On
January 18, 1945, sixty-six thousand inmates were sent on a Death March.
Fifteen thousand died along the road. On March 21, Storch heard rumors
of plans to destroy Auschwitz. Sticks of dynamite had already been placed
under the barracks when his swift, immediate reaction prevented a tragedy,
saving the lives of sixty thousand inmates.

Episodes rarely occur in linear fashion and the disconnected events leading up to Storch's fait accompli are no different. Heinrich Himmler, Hitler's
henchman, was plagued with chronic, excruciating stomach pain that could
only be alleviated by invoking the skillful services of Finnish masseur Felix
Kersten. Gilel Storch was introduced to Felix Kersten at an intimate social
gathering toward the end of February 1945, the outcome nothing short of
miraculous. A close relationship developed between Gilel Storch and Felix;
Storch used this connection to arrange a meeting with Himmler to negotiate
the rescue of Jews.

On March 3, 1945, Gilel Storch begged Felix Kersten to arrange a
meeting with Himmler. Kersten told Himmler that it would be to his benefit
to negotiate with a member of the World Jewish Congress; Himmler was
receptive. At this point it was obvious that Germany's defeat was imminent;
Himmler must have realized that these negotiations would alleviate punishment for war crimes.

"A war can only be humanized by a country that is itself humane,"
quips Storch. Nevertheless, he invested a great deal of effort in planning this

historic meeting, scheduled to take place in Germany, the seat of insidious terror.

On April 13, 1945 two seats were reserved on a private plane, for Gilel Storch and Kersten, and on April 16, the special travel permits were received. On April 19, plans for the meeting were finalized. It was a moment of great triumph for Gilel Storch, the culmination of his dream to save his belea-guered, beloved Jewish brethren. Though he had failed to rescue his relatives in Riga, now he was about to save thousands of lives. Flying to Germany to meet with Himmler and persuade him to liberate the Jewish women from Ravensbruck had consumed Storch's every waking moment. He hoped to see the project to its conclusion, but it was not to be.

On April 19, two and a half hours before the scheduled departure, the plane ready to take off from Sweden's Bromma Airfield for the meeting with Himmler in Germany, Gilel Storch reluctantly contacted Norbert Masur, a colleague at the World Jewish Congress in Sweden to take his place. Masur departed from Stockholm in a plane marked with a swastika, a plane filled with Red Cross packages, he and Kersten the sole passengers. It was a strange situation, this being the first meeting of Kersten and Masur.

A Gestapo car brought them from the Berlin airport, Tempelhof, to Kersten's home, an estate called Hartzwalde, about seventy kilometers from Berlin. There was an unexpected delay of four hours until the Gestapo car arrived at the airport and it was night when they traveled in the vicinity of Oranienburg, Ravensbruck and Sachsenhausen, places that filled Norbert Masur's heart with deep terror. It was nighttime when they arrived and the darkness surrounding them increased the feeling of fright.

Gilel had invested several months in arranging the meeting, but an unexpected glitch impeded him from participating in the meeting. Lena Einhorn's documentary recreates this poignant moment. Gilel's wife, Anja, adamantly refused to allow him to go to Berlin to meet with the chief execu-tioner of European Jewry. Unhappy and displaced, she had never acclimated to Sweden. Adrift, without language or family, she felt lost and bewildered. "Should you leave to Germany," she declared, her voice riddled in despair, "search for me in the waters of Malaren." The effective use of Yiddish in this documentary enhances the emotion and heightens the authenticity.

Her hysterical threats of suicide made it impossible for Storch to follow through and attend the meeting with Himmler. A husband and father, he forfeited his active political role and remained behind to address his wife's fears. He behaved admirably and stood by his family, but he never recov-ered from his personal disappointment. The outcome was successful and the female survivors arrived on the White Buses just two weeks before the end of the war; but Storch did not experience the jubilation of a mission well executed.

On Friday, April 20, Brigade Commander Schellenberg arrived in the middle of the night. As it was Hitler's birthday, the meeting had to be postponed until after the festivities. *Inconceivable that this meeting actually occurred, that a Jew would meet face to face with the man responsible for the death of millions of Jews.*

Lena Einhorn describes this pivotal gathering: That afternoon, Masur and Schellenberg, a most unlikely pair, went for a walk in the surrounding woods. Mr. Masur emphasized that he planned to return to Stockholm on Monday. Himmler wanted to postpone the meeting due to heavy bombardment, but Schellenberg, his chief advisor, was aware of the urgency of the situation and insisted on finalizing the plans. This historic meeting took place at 2:30 at night and lasted for two and a half hours, resulting in the release of the women of Ravensbruck, in addition to some other concessions.

Himmler, in an attempt to appear civilized, justified the inhumane treatment of the Jews explaining that their presence was a constant irritant because they were a foreign element. Germany had urged the Jews to leave, to immigrate, but no country had wanted to accept them. Himmer rationalized the need for crematoriums because the Jews were infecting the German population with typhus. Anxious to make a good impression, Himmler scavenged to invent excuses for the vicious extermination of the Jewish people. He did not want to admit his nefarious callousness, not even to a Jew.

Gilel Storch died in 1983 at the age of eighty-one, never receiving recognition for his heroic efforts. Though the meeting with Himmler had been his original plan, Norbert Masur received the credit. A mere handful of people participated at the funeral at Mosaika Forsamlingens Begravningsplats at Haga Norra Cemetery outside Stockholm, en route to the Arlanda Airport. Olaf Palme, the Swedish Prime minister, attended the funeral.

The first time I brought a group to the cemetery to give recognition to this hero, I could not locate his grave. I expected a large, imposing headstone with salutary tribute. Near the Holocaust monument in the cemetery, we noted the numerous flat, rectangular stones on the ground, two feet by four feet, with the names of camp inmates who had died upon arriving in Stockholm or within the first two years. After conferring with staff at the chapel, I finally located Gilel Storch's final resting place. Gilel Storch, the great hero and successful businessman, is buried amongst those he rescued, a simple, small, flat stone marking the spot, identical to the ones for the Holocaust victims he had brought to Sweden. "He wanted to be in their midst, in death as in life," stated a member of the Swedish Jewish community.

Marcus Storch, his son, is a figure to be reckoned with in Sweden, in the Jewish and secular world, and the world at large. Chairman of the Board of AGA, Sweden's gas company, he is interested in health and welfare. Following the death of his beloved son Tobias, he developed a transplant registry to expedite and develop stem cell research. A member of the Nobel Prize Committee, he participates in selecting the winners.

One of the most impressive monuments in Raoul Wallenberg's honor, the Hope Monument, located in Manhattan, across the street from the United Nations, is a gift from Marcus Storch. It consists of five tall, black columns of Swedish bedrock. The tallest column, an impressive twenty-one feet, is topped by a blue glass ball symbolizing hope. The attaché case with the initials "R. W." gives the viewer a dramatic sense of urgency in his departure. The granite blocks on the ground are from the Jewish ghetto of Budapest. Gilel Storch was actively involved in the selection of Raoul Wallenberg as an envoy to Budapest. The monument is, indeed, an impressive reminder of a great hero and effectively displays the family legacy of dedication to humanitarian activities passed on to the next generation.

CHAPTER **5**

A Man with a Mission - Raoul Wallenberg

The Early Years

The wedding of Mai Wising and Raoul Wallenberg was an important social event in Sweden, the groom a member of the prestigious and illustrious Wallenberg family, and the beautiful, young bride, his perfect match. Within the first few months of marriage, the bride was delighted to discover that she was pregnant. Her happiness ended abruptly, however, and her glorious new fairy tale world fell apart, when just a few months after the marriage, her husband was diagnosed with cancer.

When Raoul entered the world on August 1912, his mother was a recent widow of three months. Eagerly sharing the joys of young motherhood with the parents of her departed husband, she described his development in letters that were later published in a book, *Raoul*. These letters were of great importance to the in-laws who, at that time, were living in Japan. The young mother, only twenty years old, showered her son with love and noted that he was "sensitive, passionate and attentive, never casual or superficial. He thinks so much about everything."

In 1918, his mother remarried, a man named Fredrik Von Dardell, and had two more children, Nina and Guy. The Wallenberg family concerned themselves with Raoul's upbringing. Already in his childhood years, it was apparent that he could one day become a great humanitarian. As a child he was a peacemaker, unwilling – even disdaining – to take part in physical brawls. Kind and gentle, he disliked schoolyard bullies. He would find injured birds and nurse them back to health. A dog with a broken bone, received his care and attention. Photographs reveal his kindness, his gentle nature.

He attended the University of Michigan, receiving a degree in architecture in 1935. The Wallenberg family played a prominent role in the banking business and Raoul obtained a position, through his family connections, with the Holland Bank of Haifa in 1936.

This was his first encounter with Jews and he was distressed to hear firsthand accounts of dangerous escapes to Holland to flee the persecution and the rise of Nazism in Germany. Raoul returned to Sweden and entered the import/export business of Kalomon Lauer, owner of the Central European Trading Company in Budapest, Hungary. The situation for Jewish businessmen was becoming increasingly complicated, so Mr. Lauer appointed Raoul as junior partner, for he could travel easily between the two countries. Raoul became familiar with the Hungarian language and the city of Budapest, and he met numerous Hungarian Jews, many of whom were relatives of the Lauers.

The Righteous Gentile

In Hungary, the Jewish situation had been relatively calm, at least in comparison with the surrounding countries. There were 750,000 Jews living just in Budapest then, and 437,000 had already been deported from the surrounding areas in the spring of 1944. In the latter half of April, an additional 335,000 were deported.

President Roosevelt established the War Refugee Board and the rescue of Hungarian Jews was made a top priority. On June 25, Pope Pius XII of the Vatican and King Gustav V of Sweden issued a plea to Miklos Horthy, the Hungarian head of state, to save the remaining Jews, yet an additional 440,000 were deported by July 6 and 230,000 were still in Budapest.

On July 18, Miklos Horthy permitted Jewish children under the age of ten to leave the country with visas. Switzerland offered to accept 13,000 of them, Sweden, 10,000 and the United States, a mere 5,000. Unfortunately, the plans were foiled because the negotiations took too long. The situation at this point had reached critical proportions.

Iver Olsen was sent by the United States to Stockholm as official representative of the WRB to search for a representative to be stationed in Hungary, somebody under the protection of the Swedish government. Raoul Wallenberg was contacted by Iver Olsen in June of 1944. Raoul's familiarity with Budapest and local people through his business experience, along with his basic knowledge of the Hungarian language, made him the perfect choice.

On July 9, 1944, at the age of thirty-one, he became the attaché of the Swedish legation, to assist Per Anger, the Swedish diplomat in Budapest.

Budapest was the last viable Jewish community left in Europe. Raoul lacked experience in the field of diplomacy and had been placed in the position, basically as an observer, to send reports of happenings in Hungary. The Swedish Foreign Ministry and WRB, well aware of the severity of the situation, wanted some degree of control.

Distraught at the plight of the Jews, Raoul took immediate action and worked tirelessly to alleviate the impending disaster. He organized a volunteer group of more than 250 people. He purchased a total of thirty-two buildings in the International Ghetto – housing that could accommodate a thousand people – to be used as safety houses. The Swedish flag was prominently displayed as protective cover and signs on the buildings identified them as Swedish Libraries, research institutes and the like, to camouflage the rescue activities. There were a number of Swedish staff brought from Sweden in addition to local helpers

He set up makeshift schools for eight thousand children and soup kitchens and hospitals to serve the needy. Fifty thousand Jews survived, 25,000 due to his direct intervention. He persuaded the Hungarian authorities that his staff members should not have to wear the yellow star; removal of that restriction provided them with more freedom of movement.

In April and May, the deportation of Jews in Hungary had become swift and cruel: 12,000 per day shipped on trains. When Raoul became aware of the death machine, he began producing the illegal Schutz-Pass, a document that became a passport to life and freedom. He placed billboards around the city to familiarize the Nazis with the "new" document. Schutz-Pass had existed previously, official documents that protected Swedish citizens living in Hungary; however, Raoul created his own version, distributing them randomly to rescue Jews.

He would stand on the platform at the station as a train was preparing for departure, with safety passes hidden on his body and behind his back, and call out common Jewish names, such as Schwartz, Cohen and Goldstein, announcing that he had their passes. Others would quickly catch on and from the inside of the train would ask, "Do you have a pass for Berger?" "How about Miller?"

With SS patrolling the platform, Raoul would surreptitiously scribble in the names, distributing more passes. The bravery of this man, brazen and ingenious, was phenomenal. He literally pulled people from the jaws of death to safety, to survival. He was described as an angel radiating life, the tall, young Swede who stood on the platform of death.

In the fall of 1944, ten thousand Jews were shot at the banks of the Danube River. Forty thousand went on a death march – by foot – to Austria.

Between fifteen and twenty percent perished from the cold during this inhumane march. Those unfit for labor were sent into the Hungarian woods to die.

Per Anger and Raoul Wallenberg knew of the excruciating 125-mile march, the week-long march to the Austrian-Hungarian border, and alleviated the horror by providing food, water and clothing. Their organized Red Cross trucks saved one thousand five hundred inmates from Auschwitz.

On October 15, the pro-Nazi Arrow Cross government was installed, displacing Admiral Horthy's legal Hungarian government. In November 1944, with the approach of the Russian Army, the situation became critical for Germany. In January 1945, Raoul Wallenberg received information that Adolf Eichman was planning a total massacre of the largest ghetto in Europe, He sent an ally, Szalay, to confront General Schmidthuber, commander of the German army in Hungary, to inform him that he would be held personally responsible for this action and hanged as a war criminal after the war. The threat resulted in the cancellation of the order and seventy thousand Jews were thus rescued.

Raoul's staff dispersed as the Russian army approached. He was told to go into hiding, and that his life was in danger. Raoul's response was that for him there was no choice. His activities had provoked the ire of the Arrow Cross, the Axis and Eichman. He had incurred their wrath. He hid in various homes, changing lodgings frequently to escape detection.

That winter, he celebrated the holidays with his staff, finding joy even in these bleak times. On January 13, he contacted the Russians, innocently sharing his activities regarding the rescue of the Jewish population of Hungary. He disclosed information about valuables that the Jews had placed in his trust for safekeeping, in secure areas of the safety houses. Trustingly, he welcomed the Russians and the defeat of Nazism.

Puzzled, the Russians could not comprehend his dedication, compassion and concern with the victimization of innocent people. On January 17, 1945, he left for Debrecen, the Russian Occupation Headquarters, unaware that this was the beginning of his disappearance.

His life had begun with great joy mingled with deep sadness and sorrow. During the final stages of his life, a mirror image presented itself. When the Russians entered Budapest in January 1945, he was relieved, perhaps even jubilant, because the frantic massacre and deportation of the Hungarian Jews had ended. Like a lamb entering a lion's den, he willingly reported to the Soviet Army Occupation Headquarters in East Hungary. He extended his hand in friendship, but encountered distrust and betrayal. On January 17, he was taken into 'protective custody' and mysteriously disappeared. Endless investigations and inquiries were fruitless. His fate to this day is unknown.

His attitude toward life is best summed up from his first report upon his arrival in Budapest on July 9, 1944, an excerpt on the situation of the Hungarian Jews: "…suffering beings, without limits. One must try to alleviate it." His final words from January 1945 complete the portrait. "For me there is no other choice. I have accepted this assignment and could never return to Stockholm without the knowledge that I had done everything in human power to save as many Jews as possible."

CHAPTER 6

Nina Lagergren - Raoul's Sister

Crossing the lawn, in front of her home, a tall, gaunt, elderly woman briskly approaches our taxi, her ski poles sans skis skillfully maneuvering the path. "Here," she says, thrusting the poles at me, "you will need these to cross the lawn."

"And what will you use?" I ask, rejecting the offer. "How will you get back into the house?"

"Don't worry," she responds. "I am accustomed to this weather. After all, I live here."

It was a chilly January morning in 2007 when we arrived at her home, a private, small house in the suburbs of Stockholm. The surface of the ground was covered with a thin layer of frost that glistened in the dim, gray winter morning light, barely visible, yet creating a slippery, hazardous terrain. Accompanied by Suzannah and Nachum, I was very enthusiastic to have been granted the opportunity to interview Nina Lagergren, half sister of Raoul Wallenberg.

An enthusiastic "member" of the Raoul Wallenberg fan club, I spoke about his exploits on all my tours, his having rescued twenty or thirty thousand – perhaps as many as fifty and sixty thousand Jews from deportation and eventual death. His activities expanded vertically as well as horizontally. He, influenced Swiss, Spanish and Portuguese legations and Red Cross chapters to become involved in the rescue activities; eleven to thirty thousand people were saved. In Switzerland, Carl Lutz issued safety passes and Girgio Perlasca, an Italian businessman, helped Jews in Spain. The Schutz-Pass that he produced was initially extended to individuals who had business dealings or personal connections with Sweden. But as thousands continued to be deported daily, he expanded his activities, allowing himself no rest, determined to rectify the urgent situation. He prepared passes using family, friends and acquaintances as guarantors and then simply chose random names from a telephone book.

"Raoul Wallenberg was the quintessential righteous gentile," I would remark, "defying retribution, overcoming obstacles, fearless, unconventional and unhesitating in his bold rescue missions. He is well known in the Jewish world, especially among the survivors." Several members on my tours had personally been rescued by him.

I was completely astounded by the reaction of my young Swedish Stockholm guide, Sophia. While attending our Shabbat afternoon gathering, the *Seudah Shlishit*, she expressed great surprise that she had never heard of Raoul Wallenberg. "His name was never mentioned in our history classes," she commented. "I cannot fathom why!"

For more than half a century, the activities of this great humanitarian went unrecognized in his own country. During his diplomatic mission in Budapest, his first and only venture in this field, he was merely supposed to be an observer, formulating reports. Sweden may have been displeased with his actions. The large and powerful neighboring Soviet Union had always intimidated Sweden. Since the Napoleonic Wars, there had been no altercation with Russia. Sweden had no wish to antagonize Russia. This was the era of the Cold War and neutrality was foremost on Sweden'sagenda.

Jan Lundvik, with a long, distinguished career in the United Nations, became the Ambassador of the Swedish Investigation Team, heading the search for Raoul Wallenberg. Nina Lagergren displayed an immense volume comprised of 769 pages of documents and letters, published in 1981 and titled *Diplomatisk misslycke* (An unfortunate diplomatic failure).

In 1981 Raoul Wallenberg became an honorary citizen of the United States, the second one to be honored after Winston Churchill. Congressman Tom Lantos of California was actively involved in this project, for he had been rescued by this great hero. In 1985 the Raoul Wallenberg Plaza in Washington DC was named in his honor. In 1986 he became an honorary citizen of Israel, and in 1997, a special stamp was issued in his honor in the United States. Twice he was nominated for the Nobel Peace Prize, once in 1948 and again the following year.

Wallenberg was honored in Yad Vashem in Jerusalem, and countless parks, streets and squares have been named in his honor, both in Israel and the United States. In 1998 the Hope Monument, created by Hungarian-born Swedish sculptor George Kraitz, was unveiled at Dag Hammarskjold

Plaza in Manhattan. A beloved hero, Wallenberg was admired by world Jewry, honored all around the world – yet, inexplicably, in Sweden it was different; there, the immensity of his efforts was virtually unknown.

Not until 2001 was a memorial finally dedicated in his honor in Stockholm, at Nybroplan in an area renamed Raoul Wallenberg Plaza. In April 2006, a statue was placed in a small park in Lidingo, a suburb of Stockholm, which was his place of residence. "This statue personifies Raoul Wallenberg," I explain to my groups. "A man of heart, with endless love for the downtrodden, his actions were guided by his heartfelt emotions."

His younger sister by a decade, Nina Lagergren spent most of her life, after his disappearance in 1945, assisting her mother in their fruitless quest. "My mother dedicated her life to locating him," she said sadly. "I accompanied my mother to Russia to see if a personal visit would be effective. During the first few years, the Swedish government desisted from confronting Russia. Those first years were crucial. That is when intervention would have mattered most."

Nina's living room is filled with family photographs, most of them of Raoul, and art objects, produced by her daughter Nane, a lawyer married to Kofi Annan, the former Secretary General of the United Nations. Nina showed me the book of documents and letters, pertaining to the search. "Look at all these attempts," she remarked, "hours of work with no concrete results, just endless rumors. My mother died in 1979, still not having resolved this chapter."

"May I see his room?" I politely inquired. Nina had mentioned that it was filled with memorabilia. Though Raoul had never lived in this house, she had dedicated a room for him.

"It's upstairs," Nina answered. "Usually only family or close friends are permitted." She hesitated for a moment and then a beautiful smile broke out, lighting up her face. "In your case," she said kindly, "I will make an exception. With your obvious admiration for my brother, I would be pleased to show you his room."

Upstairs, we entered a small room to the right of the staircase. It looked like the quarters of a busy young man, waiting for its occupant to return. The bookcase contained books of various sizes, colors and languages all featuring Raoul. Trophies, tributes, letters from around the globe, photographs, stamps that memorialized him and memorabilia from his student days and early adult years filled the room.

"It is amazing that in his thirty-two years he touched so many lives," I remarked. Nina nodded in agreement. "Isn't this beautiful," she exclaimed, showing me a Passover Haggadah printed in Jerusalem in 1965. Together we admired the artistically designed silver cover and the beautiful colored illustrations. Obviously every item in the room had been preserved with great love and admiration.

"Did you ever resent your mother's deep involvement with Raoul?" I queried, hesitantly. "This could have deteriorated into sibling rivalry."

"Absolutely not," Nina emphatically retorted. "He was my brother. I admired and respected him. I am proud to be an active participant in the organizations, committees, gatherings and special events in his honor."

Nina Lagergren presented me with a book from the Raoul Wallenberg Academy for Young Leaders, a school established in his memory. The school is dedicated to developing young leaders who will follow in Raoul's path to focus on building a future world filled with brotherhood, and free of racism and hatred. Nina is very active in the school, the administration and even with the student body in whom she takes a personal interest. More than sixty years have passed since his tragic disappearance; however, Nina's deep involvement in his legacy fosters continued growth and strength.

When I guide tours at the Museum of Jewish Heritage at Battery Park in NYC, I always pause in the small room dedicated to the Righteous Gentiles, to view the video of Raoul Wallenberg. He lived a meaningful life. His memory sustains us, imbuing us with hope, effectively demonstrating that one person *can* change the world.

The inscription on the back wall of this room aptly describes Raoul Wallenberg:

"Saving a single life is like saving an entire world" (Mishna Sanhedrin 4:5).

CHAPTER 7

Congressman Tom Lantos and Annette Lantos – Continuing Raoul's Legacy

Peering through the half-open door, I saw a lanky man seated at a large, rectangular desk, phone within easy reach and several stacks of paper perched precariously on a nearby table. A portrait of Raoul Wallenberg covered almost the entire left wall, his aura dominating the entire room. One could sense the effect of that portrait, the palpable connection between the two men. A small dog scampered happily through the room.

As soon as he entered the reception room in the Rayburn office building at the Capitol, I recognized him instantly from his photographs. Congressman Tom Lantos of California was, indeed, a magnetic presence; the six-foot-tall, self-assured politician exuded charm and effervescence. Offering a warm welcome, he ushered us into a room directly behind the reception area, the private office of his wife, Annette.

"Please share some of your experiences with Raoul Wallenberg," I urged. The congressman's admiration of and devotion toward Raoul Wallenberg was clearly evident in his sparkling eyes, his body language and every word he uttered. He owed his life to Wallenberg, who became his role model, inspiring him to dedicate his life to public service, to assuage the plight of the persecuted and downtrodden. Tom Lantos's experiences in Hungary during the Nazi era had developed his determination to combat evil.

As a teen, Tom Lantos had been captured twice by the Gestapo and placed in a labor camp. After his second escape, he found shelter in a Swedish safety house in Budapest and, due to his non-Jewish features, became a courier for Raoul Wallenberg.

With great emotion and deep conviction, he spoke about his love for the State of Israel. An outspoken advocate for Israel, all his legislative actions emphasized the need and necessity for a homeland for the Jewish people. Having witnessed firsthand the bewilderment of the Jews who, evicted from Germany, had nowhere to go, Lantos realized the importance of a Jewish homeland.

While waiting to interview his wife, Annette, I notice the extensive display of plaques and citations that have been presented to this unique couple in recognition of their humanitarian activities worldwide. The importance of family is evident in the photographs of their two daughters, each with offspring in two digit numbers. Tom and Annette had lost all their relatives in Hungary; now their daughters are rebuilding the future.

Annette's prominent family was socially connected with influential people. She and her mother had each received a Schutz-Pass from Raoul Wallenberg, which enabled them to flee Budapest and secure a hiding place.

Beautiful and regal, her gray hair stylishly coiffed, Annette made a dramatic entrance. Clad in an attractive business suit, her makeup flawless, she maintains her good looks. "You look amazing," I comment, "almost like Zsa Zsa Gabor."

"The Gabors are actually my cousins," Annette cheerfully answers. "Tom and I met initially at one of Magda's numerous weddings. We were so young."

The atmosphere in the room is wonderful – relaxed and comfortable. We had allotted half an hour for the interview, however, we become engrossed in a conversation that lasted more than an hour and a half, because of our mutual interest in Wallenberg.

I listened intently to a rendition of the heartwarming, romantic saga of the reunion of Annette and Tom. "I insisted on returning to Budapest after the war, to search for Tom," Annette told me. "We had been forcibly separated." They were dedicated to each other from the time they had met as youngsters. Her mother flatly refused to accompany her to a city filled with tragic memories. So Annette, a mere teenager, bravely made the trip alone.

She returned to her grandmother's deserted home, disclosing her whereabouts only to close acquaintances. The great changes that had occurred in Budapest were overwhelming. Alone, life felt strange. Tom had also returned to Budapest to search for Annette and they were miraculously reunited in that apartment.

Annette's eyes glowed with happiness as she reminisced about the reunion, describing his approach to the house. "He was whistling our private tune," she said wistfully. "Somehow Tom knew I would be waiting for him at my grandmother's home. I sat by the window, waiting impatiently. The first sign of his approach was the tune." I was mesmerized by this tale of true love related with great emotion.

Never parting again, they married and immigrated to the United States. After living in California for several decades, they moved to Washington DC. Their union, filled with mutual love and respect, was a glorious marriage of sixty years. Their involvement in humanitarian activities worldwide demonstrated their determination to create a better world.

The couple had been distressed by the lack of action in the Wallenberg case. Since they had been rescued by him, they felt compelled to dedicate themselves to spread his message of care and concern for all. After Tom's election to Congress, Annette initiated a campaign to grant United States citizenship to Raoul Wallenberg.

"Why was this important?" I queried. "He was no longer alive. Wasn't it pointless?"

"Legislative action was imperative," Annette replied, "and with Tom in political power, now I had the opportunity. Look," she continued, displaying a thick, oversized folder of newspaper articles, petitions, letters and notices about meetings all connected

with the project. "Sweden remained quite uninvolved," said Annette sadly, "and the situation was truly disastrous."

Once Wallenberg was granted American citizenship, the United States could become more actively involved and additional resources would be available. Her efforts proved successful and Wallenberg was awarded citizenship posthumously.

Annette developed a six-month internship program in Washington DC, Humanities in Action, for the study of American democracy and how it is implemented. She is involved in every aspect of the program, arranging yearly gatherings that are enthusiastically attended. They perpetuate the ideals of Wallenberg.

In the winter of 2008, Tom Lantos died. His legacy of humanitarian activities inspired by Raoul Wallenberg and his great love of and devotion to Israel will always be remembered.

In 2009, Annette initiated the Tom Lantos Foundation for Human Rights and Justice, where she serves as President.

CHAPTER **8**

Kate Wacz – Rescued by Raoul Wallenberg

An elegant woman, Kate exudes class. Her surroundings indicate her aesthetic sense: beautiful furnishings, tasteful decorations, a lovely home. Well dressed and stylish, she brought us to her table, set with fine porcelain, small, decorated spoons and artfully arranged cake and fruit platters. Warmly welcoming us into her home, she is eager to participate in the Scandinavian documentary, to share her memories of Raoul Wallenberg. We bring her a letter from Annette Lantos, her dear friend, who has connected us.

Katalin Kadelburger, her childhood name, came from an upper-middle-class family in Budapest. She recalls a happy, carefree, pleasant childhood with dear grandparents, who visited often. Her father, a well-known businessman in the steel industry, represented numerous steel companies; however, his Swedish contact with Fagersta, Hellefors and Udderholm became of major importance during the critical war years.

In 1939, following the Anschluss, he lost his German and Austrian business ventures. Within a short period of time, her father, together with other Jewish males, were placed in forced labor camps. He was among the first to be inducted.

He had been a highly decorated officer of the Hungarian Kingdom during the first World War, acquiring numerous medals for outstanding distinguished service. Being placed in a forced labor camp was a grave indignity that hurt him deeply. In October of 1940 he became very ill and was hospitalized in Budapest, where he eventually died of heart failure. "It was like his heart had been broken," I interjected.

Kate's mother became involved in the business, which required great courage and diligence, as she lacked prior experience. In 1942, when Jews were no longer permitted to conduct businesses, she appointed a Hungarian to act as a front. Her Swedish connections facilitated her contact with Per Anger, attaché of the Swedish Legation in Hungary since 1942.

The persecution of Jews intensified in 1944 and in March of that year, the Germans occupied Hungary. The Nazis immediately relocated the Jewish population, placing them in ghettos, and instituted the despicable yellow Jewish star. With great concern for Kate's older brother, Gustav, her mother contacted Per Anger for protection because she did not want her son sent to a labor camp like her husband was.

At this time, Raoul Wallenberg joined the staff at the Swedish Legation as a special envoy of the WRB, War Refugee Board, and the Swedish Foreign Ministry. Gustav became a messenger and Kate, with her mother, grand-mother and aunt, were placed in a "Jewish House," a safety house, on Ulloi Street, with 280 inhabitants. Eventually they were placed in a Swedish House of Wallenberg's staff at number one Jokai Street, together with important in-dustrialists and bankers.

On October 15, 1944, when the Arrow Cross came into power, the graveness of the situation intensified. They found refuge in a cellar where they remained in hiding until January 7. It was dangerous to venture outside because military personnel roamed the area constantly. The cellar was over-crowded, stifling, uncomfortable and rancid with fear.

"Inactivity and darkness, that is what I remember," Kate recalled. "There were about three hundred people crowded there, some lying on the floor, including mothers with children.

"On the night of January 7, the building was raided by the Hungarian Arrow Cross. The unfortunate ones who were caught were lined up on the banks of the Danube River and shot to death. The waters of the river became red from their blood. Children and women were encouraged to escape and were herded into ghettos.

"It was horrible," Kate recalled, "but far better than being killed instant-ly. We were brought to the headquarters of the Arrow Cross and placed in a large cellar on Varoshaz Street. Drunken Arrow Cross men beat us and de-manded our valuables. "Otherwise the fish in the Danube will have it," they said roughly. The next morning we were placed in an area three flights up in that building and strip-searched. We had to empty our pockets and I had to give them my carefully saved peanuts. Anything of value was confiscated.

"We were two hundred eighty people and the room was incredibly crowded. There was standing room only and we remained silent. Terrified, we dared not utter a sound of complaint." One hundred eighty of the two hundred and eighty from Jokai Street perished within that first week. Several committed suicide. There was constant shelling and every night, groups of

Jews were sent outside to remove rubble, dig ditches and do whatever else was essential. Afterward, they were executed. Conditions were frightening, but Raoul Wallenberg still refused to go into hiding.

"It was winter, freezing. We were forced to remove our shoes to prevent escapes. The room was filled with the stench of fear. Any minute, we thought we would be marched to the river. Our lives were in a tenuous balance. It was so overcrowded, there was hardly any room to sit.

"On January 8, at night, my brother Gustav and I ventured into the ghetto and were greeted by a shocking sight that I will never forget. There were piles of corpses everywhere, emaciated, covered by dazzlingly white snow. We did not see a single person alive. We slunk back to the shelter, defeated, broken-hearted, remaining there until January 16 when we were liberated by the Russians.

"We were unaware that seventy thousand Jews were in the Central Ghetto in Budapest awaiting execution on January fifteenth, while Raoul Wallenberg was being interrogated by the Russians. Rescuing these people became his final mission, stated in his own words, 'My life is one life but this is a matter of saving thousands'. Five hundred German soldiers, several hundred Arrow Cross men and two hundred police were ready to liquidate the ghetto. It was a dramatic, incredible rescue. Their operation was canceled at that last moment under the threat of postwar criminal trials.

"On January 16, 1945, the Soviet army liberated the International Ghetto of Budapest and on the seventeenth, in the evening, the group in the Central Ghetto. On January seventeenth, when Raoul Wallenberg was last seen, when he left for Debrecen, he left behind him the largest Jewish community to have survived the onslaught of the Nazis.

"We went to my grandmother's house, outside the ghetto, and stayed in the basement for three or four weeks," Kate continued.

"Why did you stay in the basement?" I asked, puzzled.

"We did not want to be noticed by the Russian soldiers." Kate replied. "They were known for their rough treatment of women."

Times were difficult and the situation worsened. Kate experienced a second totalitarian government when Hungary became a Communist country. She attempted to leave the country by joining the Youth Festival in Free Berlin, but the escape was unsuccessful.

In an interview on August 16, 1951, on Voice of America and Free Europe Radio Station, Katalin Kadelburger, stated that "people were deported to work on farms and in rice fields. They had no choices. They were forced to relocate. Businesses were confiscated. People had no boots and working in the wet rice fields was extremely difficult. We were forced to live in barns and stables, crowded, in horrible conditions. At night I would often just stay out on a balcony. It was nearly impossible to get any sleep. On Mondays, Wednesdays and Fridays, people were forced to go to the railroad stations where they were placed in cattle cars and just sent off to other locations. The Communists would just stand there, spitting on us and hurling insults. It was not very different from the Hitler era."

Kate relates, "In 1947 my brother went to Sweden and eventually became an engineer, specializing in steel production. In 1948 my mother brought me to Sweden but I insisted on returning to Budapest to attend Music gymnasium, a decision I later regretted. Being young, I had no idea of the possible consequences. My mother stayed in Sweden and was unable to return to Budapest, which was under Communist rule, and I was unable to leave Hungary. Our family business was confiscated by the Communists. My mother became ill but used all her energy to release me from Hungary in exchange for a shipment of Swedish steel. On the sixteenth of August 1951, I was finally reunited with my mother and brother with the intervention of the Swedish UD, Utrikes Department, which deals with immigration. It was like a dream and I just wanted to be near my mother, to touch her, to be in her presence.

"There was great dearth of food in Budapest. Butter, for example, was given once every two months, and then only for those under ten years of age, one tenth of a kilo. The first day of my freedom, I ate cheese, bananas and oranges; I gorged myself with food," concluded Kate. In the first five weeks, she gained four kilo.

"My first job was in an office, but it was difficult since I had no skills and the language was new, so that did not last long. I was excited to procure a position in a health treatment center, hoping to learn some valuable skills. However, I was required to engage in menial tasks, basically housekeeping, so I left. The owner stated that immigrants should be grateful to find a job, and do whatever was required. I earned spending money by giving private piano lessons. Freedom was wonderful and though life had many challenges, the opportunity to live with my mother and brother in peace is all that mattered."

Those early years were difficult, but gradually, step by step, life normalized. Eventually Kate became a well-known makeup artist, mixing with the rich and famous. Kate was familiar with the important cosmetic firms like Revlon and Max Factor. She introduced Estee Lauder to the Swedish industry, which was of great importance. Kate also introduced Yves St. Laurent to Sweden and owns a branch of that company. Yearly she presents the well-known Honorary Kate Wacz Makeup Prize at the Cidesco International Congress.

Kate is deeply involved with projects pertaining to Raoul Wallenberg, for she personally owes him a great debt of gratitude. Kate is also grateful to the other righteous diplomats to whom she felt particularly indebted – Per Anger, Valdemar Langlet and Carl Lutz – and wants their memory to be kept alive. She is involved in numerous humanitarian activities around the world and devotes her time and energy to help create a better world.

Raoul Wallenberg will forever exemplify for her the best mankind has to offer. He will always be the shining beam of light, of humanity, in the midst of a world gone mad with depravity.

CHAPTER 9

An Unrecognized Hero - Valdemar Langlet

W e arrived at the home of Bjorn Runberg and his wife in Jarfalla, a suburb of Stockholm, where we were graciously received. The couple had
apparently been anxiously awaiting our arrival because as soon as we rang the
bell, they both appeared at the door. In their small, immaculate home, the
table was set with coffee and refreshments.

Bjorn Runberg, an archivist and librarian of the Swedish Red Cross,
with his quiet demeanor and gentle ways, personifies the image of a librarian. His book, titled *Valdemar Langlet*, focuses on the life of another
forgotten hero of World War II. In the subtitle, *The Rescuer in the Face
of Danger*, the author implies that Raoul Wallenberg was not the only
hero. Bjorn Runberg was visibly moved by the life of Valdemar Langlet,
an unrecognized hero who dedicated his life to save the defenseless Jews
of Budapest from the brutality of the Nazis and Arrow Cross. He was very
excited to have the opportunity to share his enthusiasm with us, an ap-
preciative audience.

Valdemar Langlet was born in December, 1872, and was already seven-
ty-two years old when the Germans occupied Hungary on March 19, 1944.
He arrived in Budapest in 1931 after extensive travels through Russia, Asia,
the Far East and Hungary. From 1932 until 1944, he was an instructor of
Swedish at the University in Budapest. He was a volunteer for the Swedish
Consulate, engaged in cultural activities, arranging programs with music and
art. He translated several Hungarian literary masterpieces into Swedish. He
also volunteered at the Swedish Red Cross because he was the ultimate humanitarian, with a kind, warm heart.

When anti-Semitism reared its ugly head, Valdemar Langlet protected his Jewish students from unpleasant acts of classmates. In May of 1944, he began to issue safety letters for them with text in Hungarian, Swedish and German, complete with photo identification and Red Cross Stamp, with his signature, to complete the official look. About 20,000 to 25,000 of these letters were issued, saving countless lives from the grave danger. He was non-salaried and received no funding for his work. He received financial help from wealthy Hungarian Jews. With great dedication he was able to make apartments, houses, castles and church property available for his rescue activities. These safety letters were the precursors to the Safety Passes of Raoul Wallenberg.

Mr. Langlet assisted Marton Voros in one of the largest and most successful rescues in the Hungarian countryside, in Pecs. In the spring of 1944, he received information from two Slovakian Jews who had escaped from Auschwitz regarding the conditions in that concentration camp. Langlet contacted the Hungarian Red Cross and that subsequently led to the involvement of the Swedish Red Cross. Valdemar Langlet suggested Count Bernadotte to become involved; however, the Hungarian Red Cross suggested Langlet as the director.

Langlet was a low-key, humble person, non-political and not a bureaucrat. He initiated, organized and financed humanitarian activities and was self-directed. He was an unselfish idealist and reacted with total love and dedication to fight the brutality of the Nazi regime. At his age, most people already are longing for a life of leisure, yet he preferred to face the enemy and participated in the dangerous rescue missions with courage and bravery. Not a team player, he was overlooked by the Swedish rescuers who had worked with Per Anger and Raoul Wallenberg and he pretty much carried out his activities on his own, basically a one-man operation.

After fourteen years in Hungary, he returned to Sweden in September of 1945 because when all the others left, he was too ill to travel. Upon his arrival to a small village near Katrineholm, he was quite destitute. He was at first unrecognized for his achievements and received no compensation.

Loyal friends were aware of the situation and with their prevailing support, he received a silver medal from the Swedish Red Cross on January 2, 1946. He was honored as Knight of Nordstjarneorden for his selfless humanitarian activities of the Red Cross in Hungary a few years later, on June 4, 1949. In the *VRK*, the Journal of the Swedish Red Cross, in volume number 2/45, he received a meager mention of eight lines and in *The 100-Year Book of the Swedish Red Cross of 1865 to 1965*, he is not mentioned at all. He spent the final years of his life in Stockholm, where he lived a very ordinary, simple life, undistinguished and quite unknown. He died on October 16, 1960.

Bjorn Runberg thoroughly researched the life of this hero prior to writing his book of tribute. The author is concerned with the lack of notoriety, appreciation and recognition for the heroic life of Valdemar Langlet. We offer our thanks to this selfless humanitarian intellectual who bravely fought for the dignity of the Jews of Hungary.

This dramatic, six-foot-tall statue of a Chassid, entitled "Teka Beshofar Gadol," was dedicated in May, 1997. About two thousand Jews were rescued from Gilleleje, a small fishing village in Denmark. Gilleleje, 2005: Photo Dr. Ivan Nelson.

One of the fishing boats that were used in the rescue of Danish Jews. This boat is located in the grounds of Pyramiden, the Museum in Gilleleje with displays of the rescue. Gilleleje, 2005 . Photo: Dr. Ivan Nelson.

In Gilleleje, Denmark, with a fisherman and his wife. In his youth, he participated in the rescue of Danish Jews; 2006.

Marcus Storch, son of the forgotten hero Gilel Storch, well known in the world at large, and a member of the Nobel Prize Committee. Stockholm, 2007.

Viewing a magnificent silver haggadah, a gift from admirers of Raoul Wallenberg in Israel, with Nina Lagergren, sister of Raoul Wallenberg. Suburbs of Stockholm, 2007.

Annette Lantos at the office of the Congressman of California in Washington DC 2008. Both Mr. and Mrs. Lantos were rescued by Raoul Wallenberg.

Kate Wacz was rescued by Raoul Wallenberg. Today she is actively involved in humanitarian activities. Stockholm, 2007.

In the home of Bjorn Runberg and his wife; Stockholm vicinity, 2007. Bjorn dedicated himself to memorialize the unrecognized hero Valdemar Langlet.

Section 4

SCANDINAVIA TODAY

CHAPTER 1

The Fiftieth Yahrtzeit - Our Family Trip

"I hear that you are planning a trip to Stockholm," said Yenti, gazing at me in shocked disbelief. "Is that true?" An uncomfortable laugh escaped her pursed lips and she waited.

"Yes. Are you interested in participating?"

Another chuckle escaped Yenti. "Absolutely not. What a ridiculous idea. Who would ever want to go to Stockholm?"

"Your son Izzy," I calmly replied. "He is my biggest supporter. In fact, he plans on bringing his entire family."

Completely speechless, Yenti was at a loss for words. Surprised by what she deemed a betrayal, for Izzy had never told her anything, she muttered, "I don't understand this at all."

I had expressed my dream of organizing a family trip to Stockholm to commemorate the fiftieth anniversary since the passing of my father, Rabbi Yacov Yisroel Zuber. Few grandchildren had actually known him, and now there were great-grandchildren, even fourth generation individuals lacking knowledge of our family history. Henie in California and Izzy from Boston were my most enthusiastic followers, encouraging me and promising to include their spouses and children. Gradually, more family members signed up and by November 2002, forty-two people had joined the group.

Relying on my experience as a tour director, I addressed the numerous picayune details, thus ensuring the success of this event. Group tickets were purchased directly from SAS, the Scandinavian airline. The bus company with which I was familiar was contacted for transfers and sightseeing; my faithful guide Birgit was notified and the itinerary was carefully planned.

Locating a suitable hotel for the occasion proved a considerable challenge. My customary five-star choices, the SAS Radisson, Royal Viking or Continental, proved financially prohibitive. A less costly establishment was necessary for this particular group, causing me to venture down paths previously unexplored.

Pensionat Oden, on Hornsgatan, a mere seven-minute walk from the Adas Yisroel synagogue on St. Paulsgatan, was selected, both for price and location. The hotel boasted a total of twenty-three rooms, eighteen of which were booked by us for the tour – eighteen, the numerical value for the Hebrew word *chai*, life; a perfect selection.

The lobby became the family living room, with nightly conversations, sometimes until the wee hours of the morning, two or even three o'clock; this was a scene out of a storybook. Yenti kept the group spellbound, sharing her precious memories, details of her childhood, the ghetto, the harrowing concentration camp experience, her life in Stockholm. She was glowing: eyes sparkling, voice strong and animated, with several interruptions of chuckles as she recalled details of life after the war. The room was overcrowded.

There weren't enough seating places, but the younger generation managed to join the group by bringing in additional chairs from nearby rooms. Family members were seated or sprawled out on the floor, and a few remained standing. These late-evening sessions were an invaluable part of the family tour experience. "Many of these happenings, we had never heard before," remarked her granddaughter Shayna. Living in Boston, she frequently visits her Bubby and has heard countless stories of her life. "This was fascinating," Shayna continued, "to hear about her courtship with Zeidy and their early years of marriage." Avigail, another granddaughter, nodded in agreement.

Catering meals was also financially prohibitive and there was a dearth of kosher restaurants. Henie became food/menu manager – quite a change from her usual occupation as Dr. Fialkoff, the pediatrician. Individuals were assigned, aka drafted, with tasks of shopping and meal preparations to create makeshift, yet delectable, dinners. Kitchen quarters in the Pensionat were kashered and used exclusively by the group, who squeezed together for meals during breakfast and evening, resulting in closeness and bonding, fostering memorable togetherness. There was even turkey to commemorate Thanksgiving.

My underlying purpose in planning the trip was to facilitate an understanding for the new generation, to elucidate the immense sacrifice of my father, Rabbi Zuber, in choosing to replant our family in the United States. He had reached the half-century mark when he opted to relocate. He could have continued his life in comfortable, familiar surroundings; after having moved often during his youth, he had certainly earned the right to a life of tranquility. Yet he deliberately chose to uproot himself for only one reason: to ensure that future generations would be given the maximum opportunity to develop and maintain our Jewish heritage.

Emigrating was very difficult; it was soon after World War II and large numbers of survivors who were Torah scholars were arriving in the United States en masse. The move was a steep step down economically, but spiritually it proved highly enriching.

The carefully planned itinerary maximized the time spent in Stockholm. Our group landed early Wednesday morning, pleasantly surprised to discover a deluxe coach bus waiting to transfer us to our hotel. After settling in briefly and arranging the food, we departed for a neighborhood walk, an informal orientation session.

Our first stop was Sodra Latin, the prestigious boys' gymnasium that Mendel and Shalom had attended; now it is co-ed. Leya and I shared our vivid recollections of Shalom's graduation with the relatives. Studentexamen! That was an important step.

"Our father was very proud of his accomplishments," Leya related wistfully.

"We had a huge party at the house," I added. "Shalom looked so debonair with his fancy cane that he twirled so elegantly, and the special white cap with a black rim."

"That hat was very important to him," Yenti interjected. "After graduation, in the spring, the appropriate season for wearing that cap, he would wear it with great pride."

"You better believe it," I remarked. "It was a mark of prestige."

"When he wore it in Boston that first spring, it was a disaster," Yenti sadly remembered. "People asked if he was a baker. Totally humiliated, he never wore that cap again."

My brother Shalom never really adjusted emotionally to American life. Despite his financial success, and his generous charitable contributions, he never could overcome the initial immigrant status, with the Jews in Roxbury disparagingly referring to him as *ah greener*, a greenhorn.

"Telemarketers would phone him," his son, Izzy, added. "Even after living in Boston for fifty years he would tell them, 'I am just an immigrant – leave me alone.'"

In moving to Boston, he had forfeited his important position in Sweden, a validation of his intellectual achievements. And then, to be referred to as a "greenhorn" by blue-collar, working-class immigrants – that, he found demeaning.

"Each spring he would take the hat out of the plastic bag, wear it for a few moments, and then replace it with a sigh." Yenti brushed a tear out of her eye, a weak attempt to wash away memories of disappointment.

An aura of melancholy momentarily permeated the atmosphere. We continued our walk to the school we girls had attended – Sodermalms Kommunala Flickskola on Timmermansgatan – a co-ed school today. The grandchildren were amazed that the school their bubbies had attended was still in good condition. They marveled at the rotunda, the open center of the building, the circular hallways – an architectural style indigenous to many Swedish schools.

We stopped at Bjorns Tradgard, a favorite spot from my childhood. In the spring and fall, I had swung on the swings, climbed the monkey bars, bounced balls and jumped rope. In the winter, I had skated on the ice. I pointed out Medborgarplatsen across the street, the House of the Citizens, which had a large swimming pool that was frequented by me and my friends.

We continued past the public library, another favorite place in my memory. An avid reader, I was forever borrowing armfuls of books for the long, dark winter nights. Gotgatan boasted an array of stores, the same stores that had been in existence during our childhood, some still with the same name. Neutral during the war, the country had remained undamaged and intact. Jet lag eventually caught up with us and we returned to the hotel for supper and an early night.

The following morning, Thursday, we visited Adas Yisroel, the shul where my father, Rabbi Zuber, had presided. The group members received specific directions, in the event that they would not wake up on time. "Punctuality is of utmost importance in Scandinavia," I warned the relatives, some of whom were frustratingly casual regarding time.

The short walk was fairly uncomplicated. "Cross Hornsgatan, walk across Mariatorget and then you will reach St. Paulsgatan. Turn left and on the right side of the street, about two or three blocks away, you will reach number thirteen. A simple white door marks the entrance to the shul. Nondescript, ordinary, no different from any other door on that particular block of apartment buildings," I described. "In no way does this door reveal the presence of a shul," I added.

Upon entering the edifice, the group was astounded. "This looks like a real shul. There even is an upstairs balcony for the women," remarked my daughter Raizel. Her husband Yanki was likewise surprised and commented about the charm of this building.

The shul has remained unchanged, appearing the same as in my childhood, except that all the benches had been replaced with furniture transplanted from Kibbutz Lavi.

"The first time I returned to Stockholm, I cried tears of joy when I saw the shul," I tearfully recalled. "The beautiful blue canopy with the white pillars surrounding the Aron Kodesh, the Bimah in the center, everything was unchanged. I loved the delicate little flowers dancing around the circumference of the huge window frames, but when the shul was repainted, the flowers disappeared."

I dramatically described my father standing at the pulpit, adjusting his Tallit prior to delivering his sermon. A hush would descend on the congregation as they listened, spellbound, to his speech. In the women's balcony, I pointed out my mother's seat: first row on the right, near the door that led to the outdoor balcony where the Sukkah stood. Laughingly, I demonstrated how my gloves and hats would fall down in the men's section. And my scarf would be used as an imaginary fishing rod, hanging down the side of the balcony.

That Thursday morning prayer service was undoubtedly the highlight of the trip. The shul was filled with the Zuber family joining the small group of daily regulars. Witnessing the grandchildren and great grandchildren davening, participating in the service, was truly meaningful. My nephews were actively engaged in the service: David had the honor of reading the Torah portion and Izzy had the honor of wrapping the *vimpel* or scarf around the Torah. Cameras were clicking and videos were rolling. Everyone was in agreement that the visit on Thursday morning was very memorable, with the entire group of relatives attending the synagogue of my father, Rabbi Yacov Yisroel Zuber.

"This, I shall never forget," I said to my family members around me. "The service was word-for-word identical to that of my childhood. I could feel the presence of my father. I could see him standing at his pulpit. My heart sang with happiness that my children and grandchildren could experience this extraordinary event.

"Here, at this place, at this moment, I feel that my father's spirit lives on," I said, my emotion-laden voice trembling. "When I visit the cemetery in Boston, I just feel sad, suffocated by the tragedy. Being here is the affirmation that his courageous move to unfamiliar shores proved to be of indescribable value." After the conclusion of the prayer service, everyone gathered downstairs to examine Rabbi Zuber's plaque. The Swedish text, prepared by Mendel, my oldest brother, stated that "Rabbi Yacov Yisroel Zuber faithfully served the community during the 1930s and 1940s, when Nazism was sweeping across Europe. A spiritual guide and mentor, he advised and inspired the indigent community, the immigrants and the visitors. His presence during this tumultuous era was of crucial importance to World Jewry."

"It was as a very moving experience, Tante Annie, when you translated the plaque that honors our Zeidy," commented my nieces, Seema, Cyrel and Sterna.

The tour bus arrived by mid-morning and transported us to City Hall, Riksdagshuset. The group was guided by Birgit Blideman, an enthusiastic Swedish Jewess.

"City Hall in the United States hardly looks like this," remarked Yaakov in astonishment. Everyone was impressed with the magnificent building, with the steeple holding the Three Crowns, the symbol of Sweden.

We walked through the long, rectangular room, filled with murals by Crown Prince Eugene, depicting scenes from Stockholm. In the Golden Hall, where the walls are covered with thousands of gold-leaf mosaics surrounding the incredible artwork portraying the history of Sweden, the group was breathless. Scientists – like Linneaus and Berzelius – important kings and historic events were depicted. Birgit dramatically described the celebration dinner hosted here for the proud Nobel Prize winners with the King and Queen in attendance among all the dignitaries. The group marveled at the portraits and the splendor of the artistically decorated rooms.

Chavie giggled at Birgit's presentation of the map of Stockholm, tossing her silk scarf to point out various islands comprising the city. Everyone enjoyed the lighthearted spectacle.

We continued on to Skarpo, the island where the Zubers had enjoyed countless summers.

"How strange, to drive to the island," I noted. "Years ago, you could only come here by boat, and there was no electricity, only gas lanterns." Then I added laughingly, "Who needed artificial light anyway with twenty-hour-long summer days?"

"And no running water," added Leya. "Remember how we used to walk with large pails to the local pump or well?"

"I had to stop often to rest my hands, especially when the pail was full," I recalled. Everyone was amused by our running commentary, and they found it quite interesting to note the great difference between the modern facilities in Stockholm and the primitive life on the island.

The island was largely deserted during this time of year, but everyone could easily imagine what a wonderful vacation spot this had been. We peered through the windows of the yellow house, which had been painted white during our childhood, and noted the summer furniture and sports equipment packed into the large rooms.

"If only the walls could talk," Michal said. "We could hear lots of great stories."

Leya and I pointed out the cherry and apple trees, the currant bushes and some of the other foliage that surrounded the property.

"Every summer we had a pet chicken in the yard," I said. "And the last Shabbat before we returned to the city, we had a feast – a huge, fat chicken. I never ate that Shabbat. I cried to see my pet on the table."

The stop at the cemetery at Haga Norra was a very moving experience. We visited the grave of Baby Chaim, who departed on July 4, 1941. We read the inscription stating that he was the son of Rabbi Yacov Yisroel Zuber. We visited the left section of the cemetery dedicated to the Holocaust group who died within the first two years of arrival. Small, flat, rectangular stones on the ground mark their final resting place. Yenti was very visibly moved when she carefully read the inscription for her cousin Frayda Ganz, who died at age sixteen.

Birgit acted as private detective and assisted me in locating the present owner of our childhood home on Katarina Vastra Kyrkogatan. The apartments had been converted to condominiums and I had contacted the owner while still in New York.

"Kerstin," I explained, "I used to live in the apartment you now own. Would I be able to visit on my forthcoming trip to Stockholm?"

Highly receptive, and somewhat intrigued, Kerstin answered in the affirmative.

I am bringing some family members," I confessed. "This is a special nostalgic family tour. Could they accompany me?"

Kerstin hesitated a moment and then agreed. Then I had to tell the whole truth, that the visit would include forty-two family members.

"That is quite a crowd," said Kerstin hesitantly. "You know the area is not that large. It will be quite crowded."

"I understand," I said comfortingly. I explained the agenda to Kerstin and surprisingly, though this was an imposition on a total stranger, Kerstin amazingly agreed. She provided me with the entrance code and her cell number to reconfirm the time for the visit.

We arrived punctually at six o'clock in the evening, to the ornate oak door, with the trademark cut diamond shapes.

"That door was really heavy," I remarked as I patted the door lovingly. "I could barely open it as a child."

"You're right," said my great-nephew Dani, holding the door and panting while everyone entered.

"There is the same little elevator," I said excitedly.

"Bubby, this is unbelievable," said Dassy. "You had elevators when you were little!"

Kerstin had thoughtfully placed a coat rack in the hallway on the second floor outside the apartment. "Welcome," she cheerily remarked, her smile never fading as she invited the oversize group into her home. Cameras clicked constantly as the crowd listened, spellbound by my detailed description of the furnishings.

Leya added details sporadically and Kerstin and her sister shared in the enthusiasm of the group's interest in the family history.

"Repeat what you just said," requested Asher Chaim, as he adjusted the settings on his video camera and surveyed the scene. His great interest in family history was contagious. He had recently become a doctor and was uncomfortable taking time off from his new position. However, his interest was strong and so, within the last few days before our departure, he joined the group.

"Isn't this incredible," I remarked excitedly. "The pocket doors are still here." And I slid the white, shiny, wooden doors, with the brass handles, out of their pockets, to demonstrate how the bedroom and study had been divided.

"This is where Father's desk stood, and there was the couch," Leya added.

"Remember when Mendel and Sara were married?" I said. "This is where the chuppah was placed, right near the bookcases. And there was the alcove area where the large radio dominated the scene. Hitler's loud strident voice really scared me, and that was before the world realized what a totally evil person he was."

Kerstin and her sister listened intently and afterward, thanked us for coming. "This has been an unforgettable experience. I feel so important, like a celebrity, all these visitors from America." She had thoughtfully prepared refreshments – drinks, nuts and fruit – a wonderful hostess; we appreciated the precious opportunity to visit this home.

On Friday morning we traveled by subway from Mariagatan to Ostermalmstorg and then walked down Nybrogatan toward the Royal Dramatic Theater.

Walking down Nybrogatan, I pointed out the apartment building that had once housed the Adas Yeshurun synagogue. Across the street was the Jewish Center, with a kosher kitchen, which offered catering services, and offices of Jewish organizations.

When I brought groups in the summer, this was where the kosher meals were served. We walked through the connecting yards and walkway to Riddargatan, where the Hillel school was located.

The Adas Yeshurun synagogue was located on the top floor of the school building. My husband, Mottel, read the plaque about the history of this Carlebach shul, brought from Germany by the Lehman family. The shul furnishings – the benches, the Bimah, the Aron Kodesh – had been separated into planks and transported to Sweden during the Nazi era. The Hillel school, the Jewish day school of 350 students, had been established by Joseph Ettlinger, a student of Rabbi Zuber.

Overcome with emotion, Yenti's eyes glistened as she watched students with kipot, some even sporting tzitzit, walking down the hallways.

"Who would have ever imagined, who ever would have thought this would be possible," she said, in an emotionally charged voice.

"When we first arrived, we couldn't believe the difference between Stockholm and our home in Romania." This scene was of particular interest to her as the majority of the students, eighty or even ninety percent, were offspring of survivors. This was immediately evident by the tinge of heavily accented speech of family members arriving to pick up their children earlier than usual on this "short" Friday.

"That first summer, soon after we came in 1945, there was an article in the Swedish newspaper, with a photograph on page one, of a group of twenty-five Hungarian girls, some whose names were familiar to me, who had converted. I was heartbroken." Yenti was near tears as she continued. "To see the reawakening of Yiddishkeit here, in this far-flung location, in the cold North, it is a most heartwarming sight."

"How sad, how unnecessary," I commented. "The Swedes are totally disinterested in religion, so their conversion had no great significance."

The group meandered down to Nybroplan and viewed the unusual statue of "The Man in the Manhole," holding up the cover to view the world. We crossed Berzelius Park and viewed the Great Synagogue, with the statue, "Flight of Torah" and the Memorial Wall inscribed with the names of victims of the Holocaust.

"The administrative office contains the book of the Forty-fivers, the refugees who arrived from the camps," I said. "Your name is listed, Yenti, and Sara's is there also."

We read names on the Holocaust memorial wall, some known to Yenti, and touched the small stones left on the ledge by visitors.

During this time of year, at the end of November, candle lighting is early, about three thirty in the afternoon, so we had to return to prepare for Shabbat. Both the dining room and breakfast room were filled with tables and chairs to accommodate the family. Folding chairs and extra tables were brought out of storage with the kind help of the hotel staff. Everyone assisted in preparing salads, setting the table and arranging the meal.

I had invited guests: Yngve from Oslo, Dr. Abe from Stockholm and my "adopted" Swedish Jewish daughter, Mirjam. I was hoping there would be a match, but they all subsequently married happily and remained friends. The atmosphere was splendid, with singing and words of Torah, punctuated with laughter and conversation. It was remarkable, the celebration of a traditional Shabbat, in far-away Stockholm, the regular reenactment – week after week – celebrating Shabbat the same traditional way.

On Shabbat we hosted a lavish Kiddush at Adas Yisroel. The regular attendees joined in the homecoming, in meeting members of the Zuber family and sharing memories of that era. They enjoyed the cold cuts and pastries from New York, while the family members enjoyed drinking Swedish Absolut and Swedish delectables, particularly the different types of Swedish herring. It was, indeed, a feast.

Shabbat, the oasis, an opportunity for family bonding, for reminiscing, for forging new memories, is always welcome. At the end of November, it ends early, 4:10 PM. The stars were glistening when I suggested a walking tour of the city. "Stockholm at night is an unforgettable experience."

It was a cold, dark night with a star-studded sky. We walked from Hornsgatan to Gotgatan and then across Slussen to Gamla Stan. We paused at Kornhamstorg.

"This is where I went with my mother on Thursdays, to the open market, to buy fish, fruit and vegetables. Look," I continued, pointing toward Sodermalm. "That outside elevator stops at the bridge that connects with the heights of the island. Katarinahissen is part of the public transportation. Look carefully behind the elevator, slightly to the right."

It was difficult to see the wooden stairs amidst the rocky granite area surrounding that section of Sodermalm. "We used to walk down the stairs and go back up on the elevator," I said. "That's what we did for fun many times."

"And here," I continued in an excited voice. "This is my special sign!" High up, on the side of a building, was a huge advertisement for Stomatol toothpaste, splendidly lit in neon colors. "The toothpaste is squirted onto the toothbrush. Watch. Isn't it fantastic? And just imagine. That sign was here when I was your age." I pointed to the grandchildren.

The grandchildren seemed enthralled by my words. "Bubby," said Dassy, "this is fantastic. This is the first time I really had an opportunity to think of you as a child. Bubby, thanks for sharing!" And she gave me a wonderful, warm hug. "Bubby, that was really long ago!" said Menachem in his newly emerged manly voice. "Stockholm really is an unbelievably modern, beautiful city," added Shira.

We entered Gamla Stan and proceeded along Vasterlanggatan. "This is so exciting," Avigail remarked. "It's like being in an old, medieval town." With her degree in Fine Arts, Avigail found this of particular interest.

"Yes," I nodded. "This section of Stockholm dates back to 1250 when Birger Jarl established the city. That's why there are such narrow cobblestone streets suited for traveling with horses. Also note that the side streets branching off this main thoroughfare all lead to the harbor. Stockholm developed into a major metropolis because of its location as a port city."

At Morton Trotzig Grand, I laughingly extended my arms and touched the buildings on both sides. The group detoured for a photo stop, posing, arms stretched out, to touch both walls simultaneously. Eli Meier, my tall grandson, did not even have to fully extend his arms with his long, lanky limbs. "You must read the book *The Prize* by Irving Wallace, a mystery novel about Nobel Prize winners," I said. "There is a great scene that takes place here at Morton Trotzig Grand."

"Bubby," a Feder girl exclaimed, her eyes shining with joy, "we never saw something like this before." Shira and Dassy had seen window displays on Central Avenue in Cedarhurst, but this was special. They paused, staring in wonder at the large picture window displaying an incredible assortment of candy: gigantic lollipops; long, striped candy canes; jars of candy and nuts; chocolate bars of all kinds – white and dark, with nuts or raisins or both – and a large assortment of boxes of fancy candy. Passers by smiled at the enthusiasm of the group.

"Coocosbollar," I said, my mouth salivating. "Rolled in coconut, or chocolate or toasted coconut. I remember that from my childhood. That is a special Swedish confectionery."

"Can we buy something?" begged my grandson Menachem and the Bostonians, Shayna, Rifka and Avi.

"Sorry," I said. "I didn't bring my Kashrus list to check the items."

"Oh well," said Chavie, laughing. "That is really unfortunate. Everything looks so fresh and delicious, so bright and colorful." They left reluctantly.

Zlata Meyer, a great-granddaughter, a journalist in Detroit, contacted Dagens Nyheter, a widely circulated Swedish newspaper, to inform them of the family trip. It resulted in an article and family photo in the "Family Home" section of this reputable paper. After I returned to the United States, I received emails from my classmates Alice and Margareta. They had read the article and contacted the newspaper to obtain my email address.

"We were so excited to find you," the message stated. "We often spoke about you and pondered your whereabouts." I was surprised to see a note addressed to my "Swedish" name, one I had not used for many years.

After graduating from college, I decided to reinvent myself, and made a decision to use my Hebrew name, Chana, exclusively. No longer did I want to feel fragmented, like two separate individuals, divided into a secular and Jewish role.

When my family had an audience in Stockholm at the Grand Hotel with the Rebbe Rayatz, the *Frierdige Rebbe*, on the first leg of his journey to the United States, he inquired, in Yiddish, what my name was. His response had been that the name Chana was beautiful, and that I should always value it. *My life surely has changed*, I thought. *Now I am always Chana*. After I received my citizenship papers and graduated college, I changed my name on all official documents to state Chana.

Initially, upon returning to Stockholm I had attempted to locate my classmates but they had grown up, married, moved and changed names. Plans were now formulated for a reunion and the following summer I spent a memorable evening with my childhood friends. Several reunions took place after that.

"Would you have saved me if the Germans had invaded?" I wondered out loud. No doubt, I would have been uncomfortable verbalizing that query during my youth.

"We knew you were Jewish," they echoed. "We knew where your father's synagogue was. But to us, you were one of the group, a friend."

"We were just children," stated Karin, one of my old classmates. "Surely we would have helped, but we would have sought our parents' permission."

My friends expressed their concerns regarding our departure from Sweden. "Why did you leave?" they asked. "Weren't you happy in Sweden? We were your friends. We all liked you."

Heartbroken, I attempted to explain how I had felt as a child, but couldn't find the words to explain the importance of living among one's own, of being in Jewish surroundings, of feeling the sense of belonging. These were feelings that could be experienced only by an outsider and not readily understood by native Swedes.

My grandchildren were thrilled to be in Stockholm. "This was a trip to remember," they stated. Rivka Zuber, my great-niece, remarked enthusiastically, "We heard about Stockholm our entire lives. This is incredible. We can hardly believe our good fortune to be here."

"The trip to Sweden was expensive for us," stated the Brooklyn teenagers, Rochel and Raizel. "We emptied out our entire savings, but it was worth it. This was a lifetime experience."

"Money was no deterrent to me," said Asher Chaim. "It was of great importance, a type of pilgrimage, a journey of following the footsteps of our family, of finding roots. Tante Annie, the memories of this trip I will cherish forever." Tante Annie became my special family name when my first niece was unable to pronounce Chana clearly.

After our return, I was delighted to receive thank-you notes from satisfied "tour members." Yenti's note was very special. "Chana," she wrote, "words are inadequate to describe the fantastic tour to Stockholm. It was a highlight of my life. I am so happy to have been a participant. I would not have missed it for anything. Thank you for arranging the tour. It was a truly meaningful experience."

Of special importance to Yenti and to her children, Izzy and Rifka, and their children, was the visit of Bjorn Afzelius, Shalom's classmate and dear friend. He spent several hours reminiscing about their childhood years, and spoke with great admiration about Shalom, a young boy not yet a teenager, who, all alone, arranged for his own admission into a gymnasium. Bjorn discussed Shalom's great accomplishments in school, his strong feelings of patriotism for Sweden, and his constant, strong, unwavering faith in Yiddishkeit. Though Shalom was the only Jewish student in his class – just like the rest of us siblings, we all knew that we were Jews.

Henie's note of praise was also much appreciated by me. "I am thrilled that we made your dream come to fruition. Passing on the legacy to the next generation is of great importance. We have all been talking about the trip since our return. Tack, Tack!" This means "thank you" in Swedish, the word everyone learned.

Zlatie wrote, "Thank you for a wonderful and truly unforgettable trip to Stockholm. It is obvious that you devoted much time and energy in your planning and execution. Everything went off without a hitch, from the flight down to the food."

The participants witnessed the unfolding of family history and were now more able to fully understand and appreciate their roots. Visiting Stockholm was a wonderful experience, without the tragic overtones of the Holocaust.

CHAPTER 2

The Ice Menorah

C haos reigned in our *Pensionat*, the tension increasing in direct proportion to our departure time. Sunday, the last day of our tour, was the first night of Chanukah and we would be attending the public lighting of the menorah. The morning had been free to explore Stockholm, see another museum, take more photographs or do last-minute shopping. I had scheduled our departure for three o'clock, to allow for a leisurely walk to Nybroviken in Norrmalm. Last-minute stragglers were arriving breathless, hungry, cold and tired.

"I am sorry," I insisted, "but I am not waiting for anyone. If you are not ready, you will have to figure out the way yourself."

Strident voices were growing louder and tenser. "I can't find my other glove." "Has anyone seen my earmuffs?" "Who has an extra scarf?" I felt the excitement rising within me. "It is now two thirty," I said. "In thirty minutes I am leaving."

Promptly at three o'clock, we began our walk, down Hornsgatan to Slussen, and then the scenic route around Gamla Stan. On a warm summer day, this is a delightful promenade along Skeppsbrokajen with the breezes from the harbor, but now, the area was deserted. The harbor, with numerous docked ships and boats of varying sizes, was on our right, and across the water, the beautiful city of Stockholm was spread out. The narrow streets leading into the Old Town were on our left and we passed the Royal Palace prior to crossing Strombron, the small bridge connecting Gamla Stan and Norrmalm, the business center of Stockholm.

As we exited the bridge, we viewed some of the most fascinating places in the city. Facing us was Kungstradgarden, the Royal Garden open to all visitors. On our left, across the garden, was Operan, the Royal Opera House, and on our immediate right, the massive structure of Handelsbanken, built in 1905. Off to our right, down on the peninsula of Blasieholmen, we noted the stately Grand Hotel with its green roof, and further down on the right, Nationalmuseum. Viewing all these historic buildings, we were reminded of the blessing of visiting a European country unharmed by the devastation of World War II.

We turned right on Kungstradgardsgatan and continued up the quiet, narrow Stallgatan. When we reached the top of the hill, Blasieholmstorget, Avi and Menachem exclaimed, "Those bronze statues of horses are quite interesting, but why are they here?"

"The Royal Stables once were located here," I said. We walked down the hill, noting the Strand hotel, turned toward the left, and within moments, toward the right, to our final destination. As we passed the Aaron Isaac Walkway and the Wallenberg Memorial, I became keenly aware of the deeper connection of these monuments with Chanukah, far beyond the physical sight. The slogan "Never Again" emblazoned on the globe by the walkway was a vivid reminder of the survivors of the Shoah who refused to be spiritually destroyed, courageous like the small band of Maccabees. And the Wallenberg memorial, the tribute to the man who spread light and hope in the midst of bitter darkness, like the flames in the menorah, reinforced our appreciation of the Festival of Lights with renewed strength and faith in a brighter future.

And then we reached our destination, Raoul Wallenberg Plaza, a superbly fashionable area, where Birger Jarlsgatan, Hamngatan, Nybrogatan and Strandvagen converge. Though it was not yet four o'clock in the afternoon, darkness was already blanketing the city. At the end of November, the time nearing the shortest day of the year, the winter solstice, the nights are deeply dark, a heavy, thick, rich, charcoal dark. Here at Nybroplan, on a tall, wooden platform, proudly stood a huge, beautiful ice menorah, a masterpiece of art. Decoratively carved, solid and strong, this symbol of Chanukah in ice, resembling glass, was at home in Sweden, renowned for its crystal.

I experience a strange feeling of unreality as I view this familiar scene from my childhood, today imbued with Jewish tradition. *This is indeed miraculous*, I thought. *This huge ice menorah publicly displayed in Stockholm.* When I was growing up here, I would never have envisioned such a sight. I never discussed our Jewish holidays with my classmates. It would have simply accentuated our differences; in any case, it was really difficult to be the only Jew.

This was a sight to behold, to store in one's memory. Behind the menorah was Berzelius Park and across the park, on the left, the classic old Berns nightclub. Behind that, above the rooftops, we could see the twirling circle enclosing the letters "N. K." – the insignia of the largest department store in Scandinavia. I turned toward the harbor, and now on my left was the Royal Dramatic Theater in all its glory, an Art Nouveau building with embedded gold designs, and the harbor filled with boats. We could see the water tower on Mosebacketorg, my old neighborhood, straight across the water. This is one of the most scenic spots in the city, and I always appreciate these beautiful surroundings.

I turned back toward the menorah and darkness had descended upon the city. Now the ice menorah looked like a crystal monument as it reflected the lights of the street. I felt immensely proud, a moment of victory, of celebration. In no way could I share my deep emotions with other family members; they could not begin to understand. Growing up in America, they had never experienced the feeling of alienation, set apart from everyone. A public menorah lighting in the heart of Stockholm was an experience I never would have imagined during my childhood. It was a special moment to cherish forever.

"I have never seen so many stars in the sky," Dassy remarked excitedly.

"So scintillatingly dazzling," Shira shrieked. "Look, there's the North Star!" Everyone agreed that the star-studded night in this open area was quite spectacular.

The crowd density was increasing rapidly, an eclectic mélange of humanity. There were the Jews of Sweden, a large percentage of whom were Holocaust survivors and their offspring, "Viking" Jews, a scattering of politicians and dignitaries and a group of smiling, interested Swedes. "Viking Jews" is a term used to represent Jews of more than two generations in Sweden.

"Stay next to me, Menachem," admonished my daughter Seema, worriedly. "I'm terrified that we might get separated." Her sister Sterna shook her head, smiling broadly. She would have uttered that remark whether they were in Brooklyn, Los Angeles or just about anywhere, for Seema always worried about her offspring.

The crowd was in a festive mood, eagerly anticipating the lighting of the menorah on the first night of Chanukah. For us, the Zuber family, this nostalgic evening marked the climax of the family tour.

"You all look wonderful," I commented exuberantly, "warm and comfortable in your winter gear. And Eli, I like your Viking hat! It really is unique!" The cap with the two Viking horns on the sides was quite noticeable. His mother, Rifka, Yenti's daughter, looked rather disapproving. After the trip that hat would probably be placed in a drawer for safekeeping. Definitely not an article of clothing suited for proper Bostonians, except for Purim. The California crew sported the newest clothing, woolen socks, gloves and scarves, purchased specifically for the trip.

Since almost all Swedes are fluent in English, the family group was interacting with the friendly, welcoming crowd. "They are so secure and comfortable in their Jewishness," I mused as I listened to them answer questions about Chanukah with self-confidence and ease. Filled with thankfulness and pride, I thought, *How vastly different from my childhood days.*

There was complete silence as Rabbi Greisman addressed the crowd, speaking in a mixture of Swedish and English. I was visibly impressed with his knowledge of this new, somewhat unfamiliar tongue, but not totally surprised because Chabad Rabbis, in their desire to influence their Jewish brethren, unhesitatingly set about to learn the language of their adopted country as a tool to enhance their ability to communicate with the local population.

Rabbi Greisman spoke of the importance of removing the darkness in the world, racism, unkindness, insensitivity. *A truly appropriate topic,* I thought, *for Raoul Wallenberg Plaza, because Raoul was the quintessential example of the power of good.*

The crowd applauded enthusiastically and waited. The dramatic moment arrived. A long taper in his hand, Rabbi Greisman kindled the first light, the flame dispelling the darkness. It was a sight to behold.

"Let's sing with the band," my grandson Yaakov called excitedly. Jubilant voices chanted a rendition of "*Maoz Tzur,*" the traditional Chanukah song. Then the Swedish Jews sang the Swedish version, "Skydd ock stod i storm ock strid."

"I am so happy we are here to witness this," I exclaimed emotionally. "In my childhood, in my wildest imagination, I would never have conceived of a public menorah lighting." I quickly wiped away a tear of joy.

Chavie and Eli Meir joyfully responded, "We are happy, too, Bubby. Thanks for bringing us."

Everyone indulged in the plentiful supply of soft, sugar-coated jelly donuts. The Zuber family invited all the spectators to join in the Israeli dancing to the joyful music.

"Initially, when I presented the idea of a public menorah lighting," Rabbi Greisman told a small, intimate group, "the idea was met with immense criticism and negative vibes."

"By the Swedes?" asked my brother-in-law from Springfield, Rabbi David Edelman.

"No," Rabbi Greisman laughed. "By the Jews, especially the longtime settlers."

"The Ghetto mentality," I interjected. "Swedish Jews are, and always have been, a very small minority. They have always been scrupulously careful about not being noticed. To maintain acceptance in mainstream Swedish society, they refrain from accentuating differences. Judaism is in danger in Scandinavia because of the increasing assimilation that threatens Jewish identity. When a country does not discriminate against us, adhering to our heritage becomes of critical importance."

"That is why this is so unbelievably wonderful," Rifka Zuber commented. "This event is truly important in strengthening Jewish unity and awareness."

"Yes," I continued. "that is the power of Chabad. Just imagine that all around the world, on every continent, in the most remote communities, this same menorah lighting is happening. It makes one pause in pride and awe at the strong bonds that unify our people."

It was an emotional evening. My nieces, the three Edelman sisters, Seema, Cyrel and Sterna, had left their families in Brooklyn to participate in this event. "It has truly been wonderful to reflect on our family history," said Cyrel, "to have this opportunity to foster and strengthen family ties."

"Tante Annie," exclaimed Seema, "your experience in arranging tours was very evident in this trip." I appreciated her comment, for Seema is a professional party planner and well aware of the myriad of details involved.

"My daughter Goldie really wanted to join and I am very sorry that I did not encourage her to come," said Sterna wistfully. Upon our return I heard that comment repeated time upon time by those who remained at home.

My dream had been fulfilled. The Zuber family had rediscovered and rekindled roots. "I finally understand the quest of my father," I declared. "A thirst for Torah that began in the treacherous Stalin era of Russia was transported to the cold North, where he was confronted with the dangers of assimilation. To ensure a safe Jewish future for his family, he took the great step to immigrate, at the age of fifty. My parents' Chassidic warmth and vitality, their selflessness and devotion to the community during the turbulent war years, paved the way for the miraculous merging of fire and ice represented in the kindling of the flames of the ice menorah. Now here we are, strong, proud Jews returning to Sweden to participate in a public Chanukah celebration."

My voice, tremulous, tears welled up in my eyes. "What an appropriate ending!" I sighed. The family group chanted happily in unison, "Hip, hip, hurrah! Hurrah, hurrah, hurrah," a typical Swedish cheer.

The small, flickering, warm flame embedded in the cold structure of the ice menorah was a fitting symbol for Jewish identity in the North. The light of Torah and Mitzvot was dispelling the darkness. The vital Jewish identity in a cold, foreign environment was powerfully evident in this remote part of the world on that first night of Chanukah.

In 2002 I arranged a family trip to commemorate the fiftieth Yahrzeit of my father, Rabbi Y. Y. Zuber. Dagens Nyheter, the largest daily newspaper in Sweden, interviewed us and photographed our group of forty-two members. We still vividly remember the experience. Hotel Oden, Sodermalm, Stockholm.

After forty-five years, we had a class reunion in Stockholm. My classmates read about our family trip in the newspaper and we then were reunited. It was an exciting gathering; Alice on left, me and Margareta, Stockholm, 2003.

Participating in the lighting of the menorah on that first night of Chanukah was awesome. The public display of a menorah in the center of Stockholm was a scene I never would have envisioned in my childhood. Chanukah, 2002. Photo: Sterna Maline.

Glossary

***Aguna* (pl. *agunot*)** – Lit. "anchored" or "chained," refers to a woman whose husband refuses to grant her a get. In the case of a missing husband or one presumed dead, a halachic authority must make the decision whether to grant a get. Without a get, a Jewish woman cannot remarry according to Jewish law.

Aliyah – Defined as "ascent" in Hebrew; refers to immigration of Jews to Israel.

Aron Kodesh – Holy Ark, ornamental closet which contains Torah scrolls.

Appel – The daily roll call that took place at the *Appleplatz*, the main square in a concentration camp.

Bar/Bat Mitzvah – According to Jewish law, at thirteen years of age for boys and twelve for girls, Jewish children become responsible for their actions, and this transition in called becoming Bar or Bat Mitzvah.

Bimah – The elevated platform in a synagogue, on which the person reading aloud from the Torah stands during the Torah reading.

Bnei Akiva – See Hashomer Hadati.

Brit – "Covenant [of circumcision]." In Yiddish, "bris." A religious ceremony within Judaism to welcome infant Jewish boys into a covenant between God and the Children of Israel through ritual circumcision performed by a *mohel*. This normally takes place on the eighth day of the child's life.

Chabad House – A center for disseminating Orthodox Judaism by the Chabad movement. Chabad Houses are controlled by the local shliach, or emissary, of a certain city, town or remote location.

Chanukah – The Festival of Lights; an eight-day Jewish holiday commemorating the rededication of the Holy Temple in Jerusalem at

264

the time of the Maccabean Revolt, which took place in the second century BCE. Chanukah is observed for eight nights, starting on the twenty-fifth day of the month of Kislev according to the Hebrew calendar. On the Gregorian calendar, it may occur anywhere from late November to late December.

Chassidism – The movement within Judaism founded by Rabbi Israel Ba'al Shem Tov (1698–1760), which stresses service of God through the mystical, in addition to the legalistic dimension of Judaism.

Chumash – From the Hebrew word meaning five, it refers to the five books of the Torah.

Chuppah – A chuppah literally means a canopy or a covering, and refers to those traditionally used in Jewish weddings. A makeshift chuppah is sometimes a cloth, sheet or Tallit, stretched or supported over four poles, or sometimes carried by attendants to the ceremony. The chuppah symbolizes the home the couple will build together.

Daven – Pray (in Yiddish).

Dvar Torah – A talk on topics relating to a section (*parashah*) of the Torah, typically the weekly Torah portion.

Galut – The exile and subsequent dispersal of the Jewish people; also refers to their continued dwelling outside the land of Israel.

Get – An official bill of divorce according to Jewish law.

Hashomer Hadati – The youth organization that eventually evolved into Bnei Akiva (lit. "Akiva's children"). The largest international religious Zionist youth movement, with over 125,000 members in thirty-seven countries. It was established in Mandate Palestine in 1929.

Havdalah – A Jewish religious ceremony that marks the symbolic end of Shabbat and holidays and ushers in the new week, separating the sanctity of Shabbat from the rest of the week (lit. "separation")

Judenrat – A council of Jewish leaders who served as liaison between the German Nazi authority and the Jewish ghetto or community under occupation in WWII. Their responsibility was to govern the day-to-day activities.

Kipa (pl. *Kipot*) – Yarmulke or skullcap worn by Orthodox male Jews at all times, to remind them that there is a God above.

Kosher – Suitable, usu. referring to food products that are permitted according to Jewish dietary laws.

Lager – The barracks in a concentration camp.

Lager Schwester – A term of endearment used among inmates in the concentration camp; schwester means "sister" in German and Yiddish.

Lubavitch – A town in Belarus that was the center of the Chabad movement for a brief period during the nineteenth century. Today it is a large

265

Chassidic movement known for its hospitality, technological expertise, optimism and emphasis on religious study.

Lubavitcher Rebbe – Known as simply, "the Rebbe" among his Chassidim, Rabbi Menachem Mendel Schneerson was a prominent Chassidic Rabbi, the seventh Rebbe of the Chabad Lubavitch movement.

Matzoh – A brittle, flat piece of unleavened bread, associated with Passover.

Mikvah – A ritual bath with specifications according to Jewish law. Adhering to the laws of Family Purity (*Taharat HaMishpacha*), married women immerse in a Mikvah during the childbearing years.

Mitzvah – One of the 613 commandments in the Torah. The term has also come to refer to any act of human kindness. According to the teachings of Judaism, all moral laws are derived from Divine commandments.

Mohel – A person qualified to perform the brit milah or rite of circumcision.

Moshiach – Literally, "anointed [one]," this term has come to refer almost exclusively to a future Jewish King from the Davidic line, who will be anointed with holy oil and rule the Jewish people during the Messianic Age.

Ner Tamid – Lit. "Eternal flame"; a light that is placed in front of the ark in every Jewish synagogue. It is meant to represent the menorah of the Beit Hamikdash, the Temple in Jerusalem, as well as the continuously burning fire on the altar of burnt offerings in front of the Temple. It also symbolizes God's eternal presence, and is therefore never extinguished.

Pesach – A Jewish festival of eight days beginning on the fifteenth of Nissan, celebrating the Exodus of the Israelites from Egypt. From Hebrew root "to pass over."

Pogrom – An organized and often officially encouraged massacre of or attack on Jews. The word is derived from two Russian words that mean thunder.

Pushka Tzedaka – Charity box. Literally, "palm" in Aramaic, equivalent to the Hebrew word "ama" (אמה). This is the source for the term, since tzedaka boxes are like an outstretched hand asking for charity.

Rav – A person trained in Jewish law and tradition and ordained for leadership of a Jewish congregation, especially one serving as chief religious official of a synagogue; a scholar qualified to interpret Jewish law.

Rebbe – Master, teacher or mentor (in Yiddish). Derived from the Hebrew word "Rabbi," it often refers to the leader of a Chassidic Jewish movement.

Rebbetzin – The title used for the wife of a Rabbi, typically from the Orthodox, Charedi and Chassidic movements.

Rebbe Rayatz – Acronym for Rabbi Yoseif Yitzchak Schneerson, the father-in-law of Rabbi Menachem Mendel Schneerson. The Rebbe Rayatz